D0364009

...wn Stock

THE 8.55 TO BAGHDAD

Also by Andrew Eames

CROSSING THE SHADOW LINE
FOUR SCOTTISH JOURNEYS

ANDREW EAMES

THE 8.55 to Baghdad

BANTAM PRESS

LONDON • TORONTO • SYDNEY • AUCKLAND • JOHANNESBURG

TRANSWORLD PUBLISHERS
61–63 Uxbridge Road, London W5 5SA
a division of The Random House Group Ltd

RANDOM HOUSE AUSTRALIA (PTY) LTD
20 Alfred Street, Milsons Point, Sydney,
New South Wales 2061, Australia

RANDOM HOUSE NEW ZEALAND LTD
18 Poland Road, Glenfield, Auckland 10, New Zealand

RANDOM HOUSE SOUTH AFRICA (PTY) LTD
Endulini, 5a Jubilee Road, Parktown 2193, South Africa

Published 2004 by Bantam Press
a division of Transworld Publishers

Copyright © Andrew Eames 2004

The right of Andrew Eames to be identified as the author of this work has been asserted in
accordance with sections 77 and 78 of the Copyright, Designs and Patents Act 1988.

A catalogue record for this book is available from the British Library.
ISBN 0593 051696

The author and publishers are grateful for permission to quote from the following: *Come Tell Me
How You Live* (1946) – Copyright © Agatha Christie Mallowan, reproduced with permission of
Hughes Massie Ltd, London; *Murder on the Orient Express* – Copyright © 1934 Agatha Christie Ltd,
a Chorion company. All rights reserved; *They Came to Baghdad* – Copyright © 1951 Agatha
Christie Ltd, a Chorion company. All rights reserved; *An Autobiography* – Copyright © 1977 Agatha
Christie Ltd, a Chorion company. All rights reserved.

All rights reserved. No part of this publication may be reproduced, stored in a retrieval system,
or transmitted in any form or by any means, electronic, mechanical, photocopying, recording, or
otherwise, without the prior permission of the publishers.

Typeset in 11/14pt Sabon by
Falcon Oast Graphic Art Ltd.

Printed in Great Britain by
Clays Ltd, St Ives plc

1 3 5 7 9 10 8 6 4 2

Papers used by Transworld Publishers are natural, recyclable products made from wood
grown in sustainable forests. The manufacturing processes conform to the environmental
regulations of the country of origin.

For my father, who would have loved this journey

ACKNOWLEDGEMENTS

This book is not all my own work. Besides the considerable contribution of one Agatha Christie, several key people helped it out of the authorial sidings. In the UK I am grateful to Flora Turner at the Croatian embassy, Julia Berg of Charisma PR, the Slovenian tourist board and Agatha's grandson Mathew Prichard, for his green light. Henrietta McCall at the British Museum generously shared her knowledge of Max Mallowan and Mesopotamian archaeology. For railway expertise I am indebted to the trusting team at Orient Express, to George Behrend, and to the Man in Seat Sixty-One. Julian Alexander deserves credit for waving the agent's flag with such conviction, as does Doug Young of Transworld for taking heed. John Quick and Mark Perrow tightened up crucial nuts and bolts to make sure the text didn't get derailed.

Particular thanks are due to Ivan and Darya in Zagreb and Boyan and Marinko in Belgrade for opening up to a stranger and telling it like it is. I am grateful to Armen and Sally Masloumian at the Baron Hotel in Aleppo for unwittingly setting me on my way, and to Geoff Hann at Hinterland Travel for shepherding me into Iraq – and out again.

And finally particular thanks go to Susanne, stationmaster and controller of my network, in the knowledge that sometimes the hardest part is staying home.

CONTENTS

PROLOGUE: ENCOUNTER IN ALEPPO

The souq in the northern Syrian city of Aleppo meanders for a couple of miles under a ceiling of vaulting brick and mortared domes. It's a dusty, ochre place, a sinuous set of cathedral naves lanced by shafts of daylight and lit by lanterns of dulled brass on plunging iron chains. Some of those chains are wrapped with trailing limbs of greenery, uninvited ambassadors from a world of photosynthesis above.

The souq dates from the days when Aleppo – aka Alep or Halab depending on which direction you approach it from – was a crossroads of trade strategically placed on the spice routes from east to west. These days the spices have jumped ship from camel-trains to deep-sea containers, but the souq appears not to have noticed. The traders are, as they always have been, effectively barricaded into their niches in the walls by their piles of coloured yarn, mountains of pomegranates and Taiwanese plastic toys. In this self-imposed prison they are kept well supplied by a constant stream of chai-sellers and handcarts bearing fresh bread, grapes, and pistachio-based sweetmeats.

Entering into their labyrinth is like walking into the mouth of a French horn, into a warren of dim, odoriferous tunnels where heavily laden donkeys are still the main form of transport. The cobbled floor is soft with centuries of dust and the air is heavy with cardamom-scented coffee and roasting pumpkin seeds. At intervals side passages lead off into khans, or merchants' quarters, where men with clipboards load sacks of liquorice root and dissect giant bales of plastic flipflops in a courtyard behind huge metal-studded doors. The souq's arteries are so intricately threaded that you need a ball of string or a good nose for fresh air to find the way through to the Citadel, a giant knuckle of granite around which flocks of speckled brown pigeons fly in tight formations, practising their bombing runs on the speckled brown battlements.

It was the souq that had lured me to Aleppo, in the last year of the last millennium. I'd heard that the longest roofed market in the world was still a scene straight out of *Aladdin* or *Indiana Jones*, and I wanted to see it for myself. In my experience such time-warped exoticism needs tourism to keep it going; no doubt, I'd thought, it'd be mainly souvenir stalls and the traders would be making their living from passing foreigners, while all the locals did their shopping in the new mall just down the road.

Quite the contrary. There were practically no western tourists – fear of Islamic fundamentalism was seeing to that – and to a wide-eyed visitor like me the souq was just as I imagined it would have looked 100, 200 or even 500 years ago.

I had booked myself into a well-known Armenian-run hotel, to which I was directed by a courteous shopkeeper who left his merchandise completely unattended to walk me across to the more modern part of town. The Baron is cited as one of the Middle East's classic colonial establishments, but unlike Singapore's Raffles or Zimbabwe's Victoria Falls, it has not been refitted or reconstructed to bring it up to date. Inside, the fixtures and fittings belonged to a British prep-school common room from the 1930s, but without any of the eccentric geography teachers. Most of the furniture was upholstered in a pea-green leather which had long since lost its sheen, and the gents' toilet had an antiquated hand drier with foot-pedals to pump the bellows. The staff behind the reception desk had been working there for so long that they could no longer summon up much enthusiasm for new visitors and nor did they have much left to say to each other; loyalty to long-serving employees was at least as important in the Baron as the concept of service with a smile.

I took a room which had en suite facilities, but began to doubt the wisdom of my choice when I saw the plumbing. The tap in my bathroom growled furiously when I turned it on and gave me a salutary squirt every time I tried to shut it off. I had my own hatstand – but no hat – and when reception called up on my bakelite phone it sounded as if they were speaking from another planet, though at least I got the gist of what they were saying: Mr Masloumian was happy to talk to me.

Armen Masloumian, owner and manager, was heavy, moustachioed and sententious, with a touch of the Homer Simpsons, albeit with a British accent. He was the third generation of Masloumians at the Baron, and he prowled through its tall corridors wreathed in pipe-smoke, his overweight golden retriever padding loyally after him, puffing away too.

'The hotel was the brainchild of my grandfather, an Armenian farmer and a very devout Christian,' he explained, tamping down a new bowl of tobacco once we'd sat down in his office. 'Back in 1909 he undertook a pilgrimage from Armenia to Jerusalem. I take it you are familiar with the traditional Arabic obligation of offering hospitality to travellers?'

It didn't matter whether I was or I wasn't, because Mr Armen was already explaining how that obligation had effectively rendered hotel accommodation unnecessary, at least in Aleppo, for locals. In Jerusalem, however, it was a different story, thanks to the demands of all the pilgrims from overseas. It was there that his grandfather had first come across the concept of a hotel as a purpose-built mansion of dignity and style, somewhere more sophisticated than just a place to unroll your sleeping mat. On his way home he'd passed through Aleppo, and realized – with a true Armenian eye for a business opportunity – that this great city didn't have one of these hotel thingys yet, so he'd seized the opportunity, securing a piece of duck-rich marshland on the edge of the city.

It was a very auspicious location. At the time Syria was a French protectorate, and the hotel's public areas – the terrace, grand dining-room and bar – quickly became the centre of Aleppine expatriate life. The hotel prospered and Mr Masloumian's grandfather soon became known locally as 'Monsieur le Baron', a term of great distinction in those days.

By this time Mr Masloumian had got his pipe going, and his retriever relaxed over his feet as the fog of smoke began to spread, and groaned loudly. It'd heard it all before.

'When the railway link through to Turkey was completed,' his master continued, more slowly now, as he chugged away at the stem, 'I forget when, a handful of years later, the Wagons-Lits company,' puff, 'created a new luxury service,' puff, 'all the way from Istanbul to Damascus.' Puff puff puff.

That train had been called the Taurus Express, and its schedule linked in with the timings of the hugely successful Orient Express, which by that time was running four times a week from Paris to Istanbul. Together, the two trains brought a new class of European traveller to Aleppo. They were aristocrats, wealthy industrialists, high-ranking army officers, government servants and government messengers, travelling both for business and for pleasure, and they needed somewhere to stay that was in line with their expectations. The Baron had been the only possible choice.

As he once again investigated the inner workings of his pipe, Mr Armen ran through a list of people who'd stayed at the Baron over the years, among them Lawrence of Arabia, Theodore Roosevelt, Kemal Ataturk, Charles Lindberg – and Agatha Christie. At the time I didn't pay much attention, being more interested in Aleppo and in Mr Armen himself; now that I'd met him, I could understand where the hotel's style emanated from, and yes, he had attended private school in England.

We talked for a while of London, and afterwards, given that I was a passing journalist, he invited me to join him and his mother for tea. She, he said, was also from the Old Country. I agreed that that would be delightful.

The following morning I swept out of Aleppo in a 1955 Studebaker in search of an eccentric saint. In the driver's seat was Mr Walid, an Armenian with the demeanour of an undertaker who'd been commended to me by Mr Armen. As a guide he was stolid and unforthcoming, but his car was perfectly behaved despite its vintage. We had to stop only once to re-inflate one of the back tyres with a footpump.

Northern Syria is strewn with ancient settlements. Some of these so-called Dead Cities are just rubble with atmosphere, and others are distinctive ruined villages in a remarkable state of preservation thanks to a dry climate and a static local economy. The ochre earth is no good for crops, and there'd been no surge in local population that justified lifting the stones from the ruins to build anything new. So the Dead Cities just stayed, refusing to deteriorate, and refusing to come back to life.

The Studebaker eventually ground to a halt by the most famous ruin of them all, the remains of the basilica at Deir as Sama'an. It was on the hill called Jebel Sama'an that the ascetic Simeon Stylites chained himself to the top of a sixty-four-foot pillar, with no shade or even – supposedly – any food or water, for thirty years. These days you'd not get many disciples who really gave a toss for such a futile feat of endurance, but in his day Stylites became something of a phenomenon. A whole community of buildings was constructed around the foot of his hill to cater for all the pilgrims who flocked to see him.

Simeon had been born in 390 AD to a shepherd's family, and at the age of sixteen he was already wearing a spiked girdle, walling himself into his monk's cell and spending his summers buried up to his chin in the ground. As word of his ferocious ascetism spread, so the numbers of curious onlookers increased, and eventually he had to resort to his pillar to escape the crowds. He never came down again.

After his death, squatting on pillars became all the rage. The Deir as Sama'an basilica was built around the original pillar, and today is a well-preserved ruin with a commanding view over rolling plateaux patched with struggling olive and pistachio fields, and with the purpled hills of Turkey in the distance. The pillar itself has been reduced to a sad, shapeless rock by centuries of souvenir hunters, and when I arrived it was draped in a hiking party of Syrian students, singing, drumming and clapping. Half an hour later it was just me, Stylites' stump and the soughing of the wind in the casuarina trees.

Left to my own devices, I tried to emulate the saint by climbing to the top and sitting there, but I was scratchy after half an hour. Our generation is not good at contemplative inactivity, and besides, I could see the Studebaker in the distance with its boot up, reminding me that Mr Walid had said something about lunch.

Simple, fresh food benefits from a sense of place, and the *déjeuner sur l'herbe* that followed couldn't have been in better surroundings, among 1,500-year-old ruins on a crest of salt'n'pepper rocks occasionally bandaged by green. Mr Walid had laid out a tablecloth with olives, tomatoes, oranges, apricot jam, a wodge of flat round breads and woven ropes of white stringy sheep's cheese. Then he pumped up the primus and proceeded to brew up a jasmine tea swiftly followed by a thick, sweet Turkish coffee. When it was done, he suggested that it was time we went back to Halab; he was getting anxious about the Studebaker's back tyre, and I had to prepare myself for tea.

Lapsang with the Masloumians was taken in the Baron's dark, wood-panelled dining-room, where we three sat alone, eating white-bread sandwiches off mono-grammed crockery brought from behind a screen by one of the hotel's more sprightly old retainers.

Armen's mother Sally turned out to be a cool septuagenarian with an unwavering gaze. I suspect that she didn't relish being wheeled out for passing journalists, something which Armen obviously appreciated too. He became more discursive and enthusiastic than was natural to him, more so than he'd been when I'd talked to him the previous evening, as if he still felt the need to impress his mother after all those years. We talked of the Syrian regime, of the potential for tourism, and of the problems of running a hotel. In the end the conversation turned to those celebrity guests.

'My mother remembers several of them, don't you, Mama?' said Armen. 'Agatha Christie in particular. She stayed here regularly.'

This was the prod in the ribs that finally woke me up. What was the crime writer doing in such an out of the way place? Researching a book? Now that I came to think about it, a couple of her titles suggested overseas voyages in this general direction.

'She was probably getting material for *Murder on the Orient Express*,' I hazarded.

Mrs Masloumian quickly set me right. 'No,' she said, 'she used to come here to do her shopping. And to get her hair done. From Nineveh. With Max.'

I don't know whether I looked confused, but I certainly felt it. Surely Nineveh was some get-thee-behind-me reference from the Bible? If it had survived the pages of the Good Book into the modern era, where was it, why didn't I know about it – and what had Agatha Christie been doing there? Did modern Nineveh not have any shops? Or hairdressers? And what had any of it to do with her normal milieu, the vicarages and village greens of the Home Counties, the mysteriously dying aristocrats, et al? And who – or what – was Max? A husband, a faithful dog, a local toyboy or perhaps a vintage car? It was one of those names that could have been any of the above.

All were questions I would have liked to ask there and then, but Mrs Masloumian was not a particularly willing interviewee. Besides, I felt an expectation on the Masloumians' behalf that it was the business of writers, especially those working for newspapers, to already know everything about everything, and for me to have confessed ignorance would have been a shameful admission that I wasn't up to the job. So in the end I merely asked whether she had liked the author.

'I didn't speak to her very much, she was more a friend of my late husband's,' was her response, and with that the tea was determined to be at an end.

I left Aleppo later that night, via the railway station. Normally I'm a sucker for a bargain, and the one-hour flight to Damascus must be one of the world's best deals at the equivalent of just £8. But I wanted to see the land – and I hadn't been best impressed by the bus journey which had originally brought me north: roads attract ugliness, and for a foreigner the eternal reiteration of the Koran on the bus's PA was a bit like constant exposure to the Shopping Channel. So instead I opted to take Chemins de Fer Syriens' Damascus sleeper, at half the fare of the flight, which left at midnight. I was pleasantly surprised to be allotted a cabin of my own with fresh linen, a cup of tea on departure and a simple bar of soap by the sink.

The thing I particularly like about sleeper trains is that breathless moment when they start, almost imperceptibly, to move. One minute you are lying silently in darkness, with the only sound the murmur of the cabin attendants and the cough of a fellow-passenger. Then comes the click of a spoon on a tea-glass, like the conductor calling his orchestra to attention, followed by a timorous creak, a metallic scrape, and then an answering chorus of scrapes, creaks and groans which eventually sorts itself out into a rhythmic clippety-clop as the train gets under way.

But you don't get much of a view, travelling like this, and I knew as I lay there at the epicentre of that sleeper symphonietta that the train was passing through an army of olive trees drawn up in readiness for the coming of another day. By the time I woke at first light, however, we were in mid-desert, and the locomotive's dawn shadow was flickering over a biblical scene of sleepy bedouin emerging from their tents. Was Nineveh somewhere nearby, I wondered, and what on earth had the author of *Lord Edgware Dies* been up to out there? Giving Lord Edgware a decent burial?

In that early dawn, lying on that train, I realized that the Masloumians were quite right: I was shamefully ignorant about the life of a woman who was still, thirty years after her death, Britain's best-selling author by far. If pushed, I would probably have characterized Mrs Christie as someone who belonged in the heart of English village life, among her cast list of vicars, retired majors, spinster aunts, exotic governesses and dashing young gardeners.

I wasn't aware, for example, that she interrupted her output of crisp detective fiction with altogether more profound titles published under the pen-name Mary Westmacott. Nor was I aware that she inspired fan websites in Slovenia, her books were set texts in Bulgaria, and you could buy Arabic editions by the shelf-full in Damascus.

Most of all I had no idea that this doyenne of the drawing-room mystery had first travelled out to Iraq, alone, by train, as a thirty-something single mother. And that thereafter she'd spent thirty winter seasons living in testing conditions 3,000 miles from home, in a land of Kurds, Armenians and Palestinians, doling out laxatives to help the sheikh's wives with their constipation.

It took an uncanny coincidence, a week after stepping off that Syrian sleeper, to finally get me engaged in the project that fills the next 300 pages. Flicking through a box of old books at home, I picked up a copy of *Murder on the Orient Express*, and stalled on the very first sentence: 'It was five o'clock on a winter's morning in Syria. Alongside the platform at Aleppo stood the train grandly designated in railway guides as the Taurus Express . . .'

For me that was the beginning, not of a whodunit, but a whydunit, and how.

THE 8.55 TO BAGHDAD

You can't judge a journey by its starting point – or so I was telling myself as I loitered on the street corners of Sunningdale on a bright and blowsy autumn morning. Even before I'd set foot in this place I'd found its ersatz name disconcerting. Surely 'Sunningdale' was what you'd christen an old people's home in a spirit of unrealistic optimism? And now that I was actually here, on pavements between super-high walls and extra-dense hedges, it was more than just the name that was disconcerting; everything around me was more than lifesize, too. Either all the cars, houses, fences and gardens were twice as big as usual, or my early morning cup of coffee had shrunk me, as the potion had shrunk Alice before she entered Wonderland.

I would have liked to peer into a few living-rooms to see whether the sofas were more than lifesize too, but this real estate Wonderland had no intention of letting the likes of me get that close. Security has vastly increased since Alice first followed the white rabbit down the hole, and every other Sunningdale lamppost was the bearer of the digital equivalent of Cheshire Cats (CCTV) so trying to squeeze through the keyholes of garden gates was quite out of the question. I contented myself, as Alice had, with glimpses of what lay within.

Around me, between stands of beech and larch, well-oiled electric gates were purring apart to emit shiny, Wonderland-sized four wheel drives setting off on the school run, with tiny nannies peering dormouse-like over the wheel. In the back were Tweedles Dum and Dee, identical in blazers and school caps. The local MILTs – Mothers In Leather Trousers – in sleek little soft-tops were going hunter-gathering down to the neo-baronial Waitrose to replenish the household supply of tarts, pausing at their front doors to shout Off With Their Heads (or similar – it was hard to tell from that distance) over their shoulders. Staff were jumping to it, laundry was being shuffled into vans, wine racks replenished by the neighbourhood vintner, and somewhere in the distance a mower was busily laying candy stripes across an unseasonably green front lawn, no doubt for the playing of croquet, although probably not with flamingos.

In truth it was probably just a normal morning in a particularly upmarket suburbia, but it made a surreal starting point for a train journey to Baghdad.

Sunningdale is the sort of development which puts blisters on an estate agent's adjectives. A golfer's nirvana twenty miles west of London, it is as upscale and leafy as commuter towns can ever be, with virtually every generously proportioned house sitting within its own mini estate surrounded by lawns as soft as putting greens. The occasional opening of those gates, like the drawing apart of steel curtains, reveals gravel driveways up to some of the most expensively columned, marbled and mock-Tudored properties in England. Behind every pseudo-historical façade lurks the latest in underfloor heating, plasma screens and whirlpool baths. You need serious lucre and several housekeepers to live here – albeit for just five months and thirty days of every year, so as to avoid the scrutiny of tax inspectors.

It is not my kind of place, but then maybe that's the travel writers' fate – to feel happier anywhere other than on home turf. I am as British as they come, but among traditional-sounding residences called Hillside Lodge, Tanglewood and Bearsden Grange I felt like an outsider, and being a diminutive pedestrian downgraded my status by a country mile. In those super-expensive residential streets only the children of domestic staff travel on foot, so just wandering along the pavement was enough to make me appear suspicious, and I could feel, more than see, the Cheshire Cat TV scanning the back of my neck. I must have cut a rather incongruous figure, clearly prepared for an overseas getaway with my suit-carrier and battered, roll-along suitcase, and equally clearly showing an unhealthy interest in peering through hedges at the MILTs and the extra flourish on those mock-Doric porticos. An unemployed gigolo touting for work, perhaps.

Anyone bearing a suit-carrier on those pavements should by rights have been hailing a taxi for a boardroom breakfast in Basle or lawyery lunch in Lucerne, but I had time to kill before the 8.55, and I was loitering, plain loitering. Essentially, I wanted to get a good feel for the place where the inspiration of my imminent journey – my very own white rabbit – had also begun hers. So what would my story have been to the police, when they'd stopped me as the suspected knave of hearts behind the great Sunningdale *pain au chocolat* heist?

'Honestly, officer, I was on my way to Baghdad.'

'From Sunningdale station? With a dinner jacket? A likely

story. What's it to be, then, a Mad Hatter's Tea Party with Saddam?'

'No, you don't understand, I'm following in the footsteps of Agatha Christie . . .'

'I see, sir. That nice Mr Poirot coming along too, is he?'

'Very clever, officer. And you're right, it is a sort of investigation. A literary one, if you want to look at it like that. I wanted to start here because this is where everything started to go wrong for Agatha . . .'

'It'll go wrong for you too if you don't get on that train and get out of town.'

And the squad car moves away. Its occupants disappointed. I sounded far too posh to be a burglar, and only a nutter would come up with all that guff about Agatha Christie.

In fact Agatha had lived in this idyll of suburbia for the last four years of her fourteen-year marriage to Archie Christie. It had been a torrid time in her life, and at one point she was reported as saying, 'If I do not leave Sunningdale, Sunningdale will be the end of me.'

I sympathized. To me, on the cusp of a long and uncertain journey emulating hers, Sunningdale felt artificial, parochial and insulated from the real world behind its long drives and high fences. You could become deeply unhappy here, as she had, and nobody would notice. The locations closest to the residential streets, where most normal neighbourhoods have essential services such as a newsagent, laundrette and chip shop – good and necessary places for good and necessary human interaction – were occupied by a huge BMW dealership, an accountancy firm with the blinds drawn down suggesting untold secrets offshore, and a traditional gentlemen's outfitters for those who didn't have the time to go all the way up to Savile Row for the sake of the inside leg.

There was no feeling of community; how could there be, with none of the normal meeting places? The only time you'd ever bump into your neighbour was if they happened to emerge from their electric gates at the same time as you. Of course you might see them at the celebrated golf clubs of Sunningdale or Wentworth, but it was those very golf clubs which had been the undoing of Agatha's marriage, as no doubt they have been for many other marriages since. Golf widowhood comes with the territory in these parts, although these days there are plenty of spas and health clubs where the niblickly-bereaved can meet each other for mutual support, massage, bottles of Bollinger and the attentions of a muscular personal trainer. It is not so tough being a golf widow as it used to be.

As for Sunningdale station, that was a real non-performer in the start-of-the-big-journey department. As I drew near, with all the enthusiasm of a reluctant boy hauled to school by the climbing long hand on the Waitrose clocktower, I could see no Victoriana, hanging baskets or weskited platform attendants with shiny watches. In their stead was a nondescript pair of platforms parked in a glistening sea of cars, their wing mirrors winking in the sun.

A mother and her teenage daughter were ahead of me in the queue for tickets. The mother was fashionable and well-presented, courtesy of a judicious nip and tuck, and the daughter was just entering the age of artless, sulky, perfect-skinned beauty.

'*How* much?' the mother repeated, recoiling from the ticket window as if she'd been shot. '*Surely* not.' I was expecting her to add, 'I thought only poor people travelled by public transport.' She half-turned towards me as if to seek a second opinion, then decided against it; what would an unemployed gigolo know about train fares? Her daughter looked appalled, too, but in her case the cause was not the price but her mother's over-reaction – she'd escaped up to town often enough to know the costs that were involved. When I passed the pair of them on the platform a few minutes later they were separated by a large amount of daylight, suggesting that strong words had been exchanged.

No, thankfully, you can't judge a journey by its starting point, but a voyage of a thousand miles, runs the Chinese proverb, must begin with a single step. Sunningdale station didn't feel like a natural launch pad to anywhere other than the cosmetic surgeons of Harley Street or a nice little number in the City. If there'd been any staff in evidence I'd have been tempted to ask whether I'd got the right platform for Baghdad, but I'd only have got a 'yer what?' and I'd have deserved a clip round the ear for trying to be too clever by half.

When the 8.55 finally arrived (seven minutes late, in a vain attempt to retitle this book) it turned out to be the ropey old slam-door variety which had already done thirty years of service and reeked of that traditional railway smell of metal nappies. We passengers settled back, each in our own cocoon of silence like a monastic order sleepwalking its way to London, and I breathed a sigh of relief as the guard ring-dinged us on our way. I'd seen enough of my journey's beginning to understand a bit more why Agatha needed to leave, and now I was off on the trail of what she herself described as her Second Spring.

We were an odd assortment of passengers on the 8.55. It was too late for the phalanxes of *FT* readers, who'd have been on the seven o'clock anxiously reading reports of a further plunge in the stock market and wondering about the impact of menacing world events on the sanctity of their year-end bonuses. There were a couple of shoppers, a teenager or two drastically late for school and trying to look unconcerned, a sales assistant on her way to a job interview frowning over her notes, and a pin-striped director using his phone mike to ensure that his staff were all installed at their desks and that the whole enterprise was surging purposefully forward even though its helmsman was just emerging from the no man's land between Winnersh Triangle and Martin's Heron.

On the seat opposite mine someone had already discarded that day's newspaper, as if to reinforce the message that, in this fast-moving modern world, media consumed at 8.15 is old hat by 8.45. Not that this edition said anything different to those of the last few days, whose headlines were focused on whether or not the UN weapons inspectors were going to return to Iraq for one last rummage around. On one of the inside pages I came across a little ditty which the editors had lifted from the Internet, to be sung to the tune of 'If you're happy and you know it', by someone called John Robbins. It ran thus:

> If you cannot find Osama, bomb Iraq
> If the markets are a drama, bomb Iraq
> If the terrorists are frisky
> Pakistan is looking shifty
> North Korea is too risky, bomb Iraq.

I carefully copied the lyrics down into the first notebook of my journey. If everything went horribly pear-shaped, I would at least have something relevant to sing.

Those few minutes of busy-ness served a purpose in another, more emotionally significant, way. They didn't exactly carry me beyond the point of no return, but they did get me past Staines and the magnetic pull of home. A change of train and a different rattle of points, and I would have been twenty minutes away from resuming those discussions about which kitchen worktops to choose, which school was right for the children, and what to cook for friends on Saturday night. Not that there was anything wrong with those topics, but there comes a stage in the middle period of life when they begin to get top billing, to the exclusion of any more fundamental impulse to realize one's own destiny. When you're young, you tend also to be centred – some would say self-centred – with a firm idea, however unrealistic, of where it is you want to go. As you get older, other priorities fight for the helm, and what lies at the centre becomes less clear. You've probably got less selfish, but life-control has been handed over to fate.

At that early stage, passing Staines, I couldn't say with any certainty that the pursuit of a thirty-eight-year-old author, seventy-five years too late, was a fulfilment of my destiny, but I certainly felt the need to strike out of the world of the hatchback and the semi-detached. Life in my forties had become a series of departures and arrivals, a scramble of deadlines and a chasing of invoices, and some sort of re-assessment from a distance was overdue. I was hoping that the process of travel itself would clear the palate, like a Calvados between courses. That it would set the personal compass free and see if it found any new magnetic poles. Some people go on monastic retreats for spiritual refreshment and a sense of self-affirmation; I was intending to catch a few trains for the same effect. As Agatha had done, back in 1928.

But there was another, equally compelling, reason to be embarking on her 1928 itinerary in late 2002. In the modern world there are few journeys which are far more complex and difficult than they were seventy-five years ago, but to travel from London to Baghdad, by train, is one of them. Her trip had been made in considerable style at a time of peace and using just two famous expresses; mine was going to be constructed from a series of all-but-forgotten trains operating in a world dominated by that unfortunate trinity, 9/11, religious fundamentalism and weapons of mass destruction. Moreover, following my white rabbit's route on the map was to trace one's finger-nail through the troubled Balkans, where history was so fresh and raw that it had yet to make it into the museums, and thence down the hallway of Islam and into the reception room of what President Bush was calling the Axis of Evil, the lair of Saddam Hussein, where Off With Their Heads could definitely apply. Her adventure had been undertaken at a moment of major personal change; mine was beginning at a moment that could change the world.

THE LONGEST TRAIN IN EUROPE

I'd caught the 8.55 from Sunningdale not because I knew for sure that Agatha had travelled on it back in 1928, but because it got me to Victoria in plenty of time for a train I knew for sure she had.

Today it is hard to imagine Victoria station as it used to be in the golden age of railway travel. This was once the gateway to the world, and stylish luxury trains like the Bournemouth Belle and the Golden Arrow used to depart for parts of England and the Continent with much banging, whistling, and uniformed scurrying. Sure, there are lots of different complexions in the station concourse, but yesterday's exotic foreigners are today's Londoners, a hurried crowd of urbanites whose every movement suggests they know exactly what they are doing, why they are doing it, and how they won't brook any delay in getting it done. In this new environment the dirty business of trains is all but invisible, hidden away behind advertising hoardings, shops and sandwich bars, as if it was something to be ashamed of. The departure board titled 'Channel Trains' is uncompromisingly blank, and the echo of the living, hissing beast of a steam engine is no more.

In fact it is not instantly obvious that Victoria is a railway station at all. There's no feeling of the excitement or trepidation of travel in the air, and the only suggestion of the Continent is Bonaparte's café, the destination of a man pushing a trolley bearing chicken tikka, of which I am not sure Bonaparte would have approved. Were it not for the giant cantilevered roof, this could have been a shopping centre. Even the free copy of *Station News* is all about new boutiques, not trains, presumably on the basis that train travel is a chore, while more shopping is always good news.

A century ago there were two railway stations and two railway companies here, side by side and bursting with pride. The South Eastern & Chatham Railway Company and the London, Brighton & South Coast Railway merged to become the Southern Railway in 1923, and the station was so grand and important that it even had a newsreel cinema to keep waiting passengers entertained. The station would have been filled with the reek of coal, the hiss of steam and the gunfire of slamming doors, and the surrounding streets were fashionable and sophisticated places to live – until the bombs of World War II reduced them to rubble. They have since been reborn as canyons of glass and steel.

The original two stations have themselves been knocked about drastically since the early 1900s, although you can still just about see the join, with the western section used for suburban lines and the eastern side for more distant departures. If you search hard, you can also find two original tiled LB&SC Ry route maps in the entrance arches. These maps emphasize Motor Halts, Golf Links and Race Courses, suggesting that the trains of the past were in the business of taking the privileged to their choice of recreation, rather than delivering the multitudes to their place of occupation.

It is easy to forget how revolutionary train travel was in its time, bringing distant destinations magically within the grasp of people who until a generation earlier had never travelled faster or further than they could walk. Seaside resorts like Eastbourne, which had previously been small, exclusive domains of the upper middle class who had the money and leisure to travel by horse and carriage, were now accessible for the masses, who could easily get there and back with a cheap day return. The arrival of the great unwashed on the promenade may have turned a few gouty-complexioned old gents apoplectic in their glass-walled sun lounges, but on the whole the upper classes benefited too, using the railways to push further afield. While the masses swarmed over the likes of Eastbourne, their betters would take the glamorous international trains for shopping in Paris and summer holidays on the French Riviera.

The most glamorous of all those trains was the Orient Express, the Magic Carpet to the East. It was the brainchild of Belgian engineer Georges Nagelmackers, who'd admired the pioneering work of George Pullman in the United States and returned to Europe determined to design a new generation of long-distance luxury train with proper sleeping-cars. Nagelmackers' Wagons-Lits service was first announced in the pages of *The Times* in 1883, with the ambition of running a bi-weekly service all the way to Constantinople, as Istanbul was then called. The train was to have, said the announcement, three saloon carriages, forty-two beds, a refreshment saloon, 'and a sufficient number of luggage vans in which the luggage will be so arranged that it can be examined in the vans by Customs officers at the frontier stations, thus avoiding the delay and annoyance unavoidable when the luggage has to be removed from the train. There will be no change of carriages . . . it is expected that the entire journey between Paris and Constantinople will be completed in about 75 hours.'

In fact the announcement was a tad premature, given that not all the rail networks supposedly involved were actually completed. But the alternative sea journey was so much slower that after a shaky initial period the new train rapidly became a major success, reducing journey times to the Middle East and India by weeks. Indeed, within a few short years it became the fashionable way to travel, and between 1890 and 1914 every royal, aristocrat and adventurer wanted to experience the route. Many of the crowned heads of Europe would travel incognito with their mistresses – Leopold II of Belgium with a famous dancer called Cleo de Merode, Carol II of Romania with Madame Magda Lupescu – and if the mistress wasn't available then they'd sometimes ask the cabin staff to procure a companion somewhere along the way.

By the 1920s the Express was running four times weekly in each direction and at the height of its popularity. It was interrupted, and re-routed, by war, in which it also played a walk-on part; it was in a Wagons-Lits car at Compiègne that the Allies accepted Germany's surrender at the end of World War I. In June 1940 Hitler ordered the same car back to the same spot, and had the French surrender in it to him. Thereafter it was put on show in Berlin, but when the war started to go badly for Germany in 1944, Hitler had it blown up. He didn't want to be humiliated.

Today, however, the train no longer registers on any timetables or departure boards. It officially ceased to exist back in the 1970s after a long decline, unable to compete any more with the increasing convenience of air travel and struggling to cope with the uncompromising bureaucracies of the Iron Curtain countries it travelled through. It had sunk a long way from the prestige express it used to be, and in 1975 French police recorded over 2,000 complaints from passengers who'd been drugged with chloroform aerosols and robbed somewhere between Paris and Yugoslavia. It ended its days ignominiously, as little more than a sleeping-car attached to a succession of local expresses, and the very last departure from Paris in May 1977 consisted of one shabby sleeper with three scruffy day coaches and no restaurant car. The passengers had to complete the 1,872-mile journey carrying their own supplies of food and drink.

The fact that the Orient Express didn't die for good is partly thanks to Agatha Christie. The working train may have had no passengers, but such was its legendary reputation that its last ever departure attracted a lot of media attention. That was swiftly followed in October 1977 by Sotheby's auction, in Monte Carlo, of five original coaches which had been restored for use in the classic 1974 film of *Murder on the Orient Express*, a huge box office success which starred Albert Finney, Lauren Bacall, Sean Connery and others. The Sotheby's auction was attended by James Sherwood, a millionaire who'd made his money out of shipping, who had with him a couple of friends who were railway enthusiasts. Sherwood didn't have a firm plan of action, but he was impressed by the amount of media interest generated by the Orient Express, and once the King of Morocco had had the satisfaction of snapping up the first two coaches for his royal train, Sherwood was able to pick up two of the others. With these two as his nucleus he set off in search of more, and the idea of resuscitating the Orient Express as a privately run land cruise was born.

It is fair to say, therefore, that if it hadn't been for Agatha's book, prompting the film and thereby the Monte Carlo sale, there wouldn't still be that moment of glamour around Victoria's platform 2 at shortly before 11 a.m., once a week.

The new journey of the restored Venice-Simplon Orient Express may be travel for travel's sake and its price tag may be artificially high, but the rake of British Pullman coaches drawn up by platform 2 is far more authentic than much of the station. Many of them were once part of trains like the Golden Arrow and the Brighton Belle, and as such they would have drawn up alongside these platforms many thousands of times.

I was early, but the Pullman was already there, its umber and cream dripping gently from a last-minute hose-down. It is charged with the task that was once performed at precisely 11 a.m. every day by the Golden Arrow – that of getting its passengers as far as the English Channel in suitable style. In its heyday the passengers would then have boarded their very own boat, the *Canterbury*, at Dover, for the crossing to Calais Maritime, where the *Flèche d'Or* would have been waiting, with handsome navy-blue Orient Express coaches attached. We, however, would be using the modern route through the Channel Tunnel, but not by train: the British Pullman coaches are wood-framed and therefore don't meet the modern safety requirements for undersea crossings, so that bit of our journey was to be made far more prosaically. By bus.

There was little ceremony in the business of departure from Victoria. The VSOE check-in lounge is a brave attempt, with potted palms and mirrors, but too much daylight did it no favours, and chairs around the walls made it feel like the anteroom for a casino which hadn't yet opened. The passengers, too, were largely past their prime, with a disappointing shortage of loud, unsuitably dressed Americans and of the dowager duchesses who would have taken such pleasure in disapproving of them. There was very little in the way of period clothing, not many hats, a fair bit of corpulence and a fur stole or two. A couple of handsome women were evidently mother and daughter, the mother a touch too heavily made up for the hours of daylight and the daughter more demure in the knowledge that she still had time on her side.

I looked in vain for a celebrity face, but the closest I could see was a celebrity hairdresser (or so I assumed), a man in black shiny shoes, black polo-neck and black trousers with a crease like a knife which were over-tight around the bum. His face was tanned almost orange, his Stringfellow haircut was ash blonde with highlights, and his eyes were distressingly cold and grey.

'How embarrassing,' I heard him say in a stage whisper to the bent bundle in white fur and gold-rimmed glasses sitting next to him. 'Will you just look at that. My suitcase is the largest of the lot!'

He had nothing to be ashamed of. When Noël Coward set off to travel by train to Asia in 1929, he took with him twenty-seven pieces of luggage and a gramophone.

As far as I could see I was the only passenger travelling alone. So when we were eventually seated, in properly upholstered chairs at tables set with monogrammed silverware and crystal, I was pleased to find myself within talking distance, across the aisle, of Terence and Audrey – the camp hairdresser and his mother. I was in no hurry to make allegiances, but a pairing like that, travelling together, were far more likely to communicate with a single stranger than a couple on their anniversary or their honeymoon who only had eyes for each other. Apart from the sidelong glances at the mother and daughter, that is.

The first sign we were under way was the gentle tinkling of touching glassware, and as we broached the Thames the first pouring of Bouvet-Ladubay Saumur was already frosting our glasses. The lunch menu took a bit of deliberation, and I plumped for Warm Vichysoisse with a Smoked Haddock Timbale as a starter, followed by Roast Breast of Kentish Guinea Fowl wrapped in Mature Cumbrian Ham and Fresh Sage with a Tarragon and Riesling Reduction. As we rumbled through Brixton I instinctively prevented myself looking out of the window; in other circumstances the contrast of delicate ovals of interior marquetry with deprived exteriors of inner city life would have been something to contemplate, but it wasn't the time or the place.

I was seated in a coach called Phoenix, with brass window frames that must have been a Sisyphean task to polish, and marquetry floral motifs delicately crafted from polished veneers of boxwood, sycamore, walnut and a sort of Burmese rosewood called padouk. Phoenix was over seventy years old and like most of the other coaches it had a septuagenarian's chequered career. In its first manifestation as Rainbow it had been built specifically for the Golden Arrow in 1927 but had also been regularly selected for the Royal Train at the request of the Queen Mother. In 1952 it had been gutted by fire and rebuilt, and under its new name became the parlour car occupied by General de Gaulle on his state visit in 1960. It had been one of the coaches that formed the very last Golden Arrow departure in 1972, after which it was sold to a French entrepreneur who turned it into a static restaurant in Lyons. There it stayed until Sherwood's team of Wagons-Lits sleuths tracked it down, negotiated its purchase and brought it back. In the UK it joined the increasing collection of recovered coaches, many of which had been found on the national rail networks of Spain and Portugal, where their finer details had been boarded over with plywood so they could make up the numbers on the local expresses.

The British Pullman coaches were reunited in a giant shed in Carnforth in Lancashire. There they were worked on by up to seventy disciples, who'd abandoned their figurative fishing nets when they'd heard the call. Many of them had simply materialized out of the surrounding post-industrial countryside, having heard on the grapevine that the skills they thought they'd never use again were required for one last glorious project which was to take three years, 23,000 man hours per car and £11 million to complete. The epic story of this detailed restoration has become part of the legend of the train.

Phoenix/Rainbow's original build date of 1927 meant that the coach could very easily have been part of the Golden Arrow which took Agatha to Dover in 1928, still smelling faintly of wood varnish and walnut oil from its Birmingham makers. She too had been travelling alone, which was no light undertaking either in that day or in this; how many single mothers in their late thirties would set off to travel across Europe by train these days, let alone all the way to Iraq? Admittedly she'd had the where-withal to park her daughter Rosalind in boarding school, and admittedly the Orient Express wasn't exactly roughing it, but it was still a brave and unusual thing to do.

Her decision to travel to Baghdad had been taken quite on the spur of the moment after a conversation at a London dinner party with a couple who'd just returned from Iraq. The most painful chapter of her life – the end of her marriage to Archie Christie – had finally come to a close, and she felt the need to mark it with a holiday. She'd been planning on going to the Caribbean, but that dinner party conversation had changed her mind, and five days later she was off on a completely different trajectory.

The choice of Iraq for a holiday seems highly unlikely these days, but at the time the country was a British protectorate and very much in the news thanks to archaeologist Leonard Woolley's discoveries, which were being talked up as a second Tutankhamun. It was also one of the new destinations being offered by Thomas Cook, who'd gone into partnership with Wagons-Lits and were offering a one-way ticket to Syria and Palestine for £87. For Agatha, a good part of the attraction was the method of transport. 'All my life I had wanted to go on the Orient Express,' she wrote in her autobiography. 'What can beat a train? Trains are wonderful . . . To travel by train is to see nature and human beings, towns and churches and rivers – in fact, to see life.' But Iraq, too, must have had an intrinsic appeal for her, given that the whole concept of going on holiday is based on setting out for one's own personal idea of paradise. Although she doesn't attempt to analyse the choice herself, the fact that she elected for a train to Iraq rather than a boat to the Caribbean says something about the sort of person that she was. Not particularly Sunningdale-esque.

From this distance it is hard to judge her mental state in 1928. The prospect of the journey itself undoubtedly filled her with excitement, but she'd just been through a period of great personal difficulty, and in a rare moment of self-revelation in her autobiography she shows how well aware she was of the imminent journey as a deeper personal test. Her life had reached a crossroads where she could either cling to the familiar, or else choose to strike out on her own. And she chose the latter. 'Now I was going by myself,' she wrote. 'I should find out what sort of person I was – whether I had become entirely dependent on other people as I had feared.'

This is an acute and honest perception, because solo journeys can do that; they can strip away all the edifice of a created life and open the traveller to new possibilities. Within the structures of the home environment your self-image is built on the foundations of accent, friends, family, education, clothing, profession, size of house, brand of car, etc. When you are on the road, however, the relationships you make with others no longer rely on all those perceived signals, but come down to your personality alone. It's an unfettering, liberating experience for those who can cope with it.

For Agatha it was the right moment to undertake such a travel-based exercise in self-examination. Up to that point her whole life had been based on the supposition that one day Mr Right would come along; she had thought that Archie had been that Mr Right, and that everything was just as it should be, until suddenly it had all fallen apart. Life had gone horribly wrong for her at Sunningdale and the relationship which she had assumed would last her all her days had turned to dust, so now she needed to re-examine and re-assemble the pieces of what remained. Crucially she also needed to prove to herself that she could exist on her own. Plan A had failed, so now it was time to try Plan B.

To understand how wrong her life had gone, and what crisis it was that prompted a thirty-eight-year-old writer – by then already a celebrity – to pen that adolescent and anguish-ridden sentence about 'finding out what sort of person I was', it is necessary to go right back to the beginning.

Mary Clarissa Agatha Miller was born in the year 1890, as a 'much-loved afterthought' into a relatively well-to-do and happy family in a large house called Ashfield on the outskirts of Torquay, in south Devon. Her father, Fred Miller, described as a 'gentleman' on her birth certificate, was a lazy but agreeable American with an inheritance large enough to ensure that he didn't need to work. Her mother, Clara, was a romantic, imaginative English girl who'd been brought up in rather sad and lonely circumstances by her childless aunt and uncle, after her own mother had decided she couldn't cope with all four of her children following the sudden death of her husband.

Although her parents were always to hand, and were very fond of each other and of their little girl, Agatha's childhood was also essentially fairly solitary. Ashfield was on the edge of town, in a world unto itself with a large kitchen garden full of vegetables, a main garden with lawns and exotic trees, and a small woodland of ash. Beyond lay Devon lanes. Her brother and sister were respectively ten and eleven years older than she and spent most of their time away at boarding-schools Harrow and Roedean, so the young Agatha's main companions were the family dog, Jane the cook and Nursie in the nursery. Although she didn't actually play with the child very much, Nursie's presence filled the girl with a sense of security and she'd set up her own games around her.

Agatha's mother, Clara, ruled this household with a sure enough touch, although she could at times be poetically distracted and had a leaning towards bizarre philosophies, believing, for instance, that no child should be allowed to read until it was eight years old, in order to let the eyes and the brain mature. It was Clara's decision that Agatha would have no formal education whatever, but the girl had a great curiosity for what lay on the inside of books and effectively taught herself to read at the age of five, consuming anything she could lay her hands on, even if she didn't really understand it. Arithmetic didn't have the same bad connotations for her mother, and was introduced to her by her father, who'd sit down to do sums with her after breakfast before disappearing off to spend the middle of the day in his club. There he'd read the newspapers and have agreeable conversations over a long lunch.

The fact that Agatha didn't go to school and therefore met few other children of her own age didn't stop her having friends. An imagination kindled by her mother and fuelled by all that Dickens, Trollope, Byron, Kipling and George Eliot had no difficulty in inventing classmates to share her nursery, furnishing them with backgrounds and relationships just like characters in a novel.

Nor was she completely isolated. She was taken out to dancing lessons by Nursie, a music teacher called regularly to introduce her to the piano, and other girls she met at the dancing lessons sometimes came to tea. But home life and the family were inevitably her focus, and there was no talk of any potential future career other than her own eventual marriage and children.

This secure, closed-in world was dealt a savage blow when Agatha was eleven. Her father had been suffering from ill health for a couple of years, but its seriousness had been kept from the children. Therefore his sudden death, from double pneumonia, came as a major shock. It left her mother deeply saddened and the family finances in an unexpectedly parlous state. Although he'd done no work, Fred Miller had been the much-admired head of the family and the emotional anchor of the household, and he and his wife had always enjoyed each other's company. His very presence in the house had emanated a sense of stability. Unfortunately, however, he'd also paid his financial affairs little or no heed, and bad management by his representatives in the United States had frittered it all away.

The impact on the family was instant. To make ends meet, the contingent of Ashfield staff – a housemaid, parlourmaid, cook and gardeners – was drastically cut. Even so it was still too expensive, and Clara was forced to rent the house out during the summer months, while she and Agatha headed overseas to live in a modest hotel in the resort town of Pau, on France's less fashionable Atlantic coast. These unforeseen changes to what had seemed such a secure environment, and what had once been Agatha's whole world, filled the over-imaginative girl with new emotions and she started to be afraid that her mother, too, would die and that she'd be left all alone. So great did this anxiety become that she'd sometimes creep along the corridor at night to listen to Clara's breathing from outside her bedroom door, to establish that all was well.

With the older children now effectively launched into their own lives – sister Madge had already married well before Fred died, and brother Monty had joined the army and disappeared off to India – mother and daughter now spent most of their time together. As she grew older Agatha became more integrated into local society, attending garden parties and going roller-skating and sea-bathing with other teenage girls from good Torquay families, but her mother increasingly depended on her for companionship and entertainment, and they would sit together and read to each other in the evenings like characters in a Jane Austen novel.

Clara's philosophy that life's path was dictated by whomsoever one married was naturally adopted by Agatha, particularly with the example provided by her sister Madge, who'd now produced a son whom Agatha adored. Looking after this young nephew while Madge and her husband went off skating in St Moritz became a highlight of her year. In those days there was little talk of women's careers.

To guarantee a good match, her mother set about making sure that Agatha acquired the correct accomplishments to go with a certain amount of natural beauty. She had already learned to play the piano well, and when she was fifteen her mother once again rented out Ashfield and decamped to France, so that she could attend a Parisian finishing school run by a certain Mademoiselle T. After a miserably homesick first few days, Agatha settled happily enough into a diet of learning how to dance and paint watercolours and going out to visit dressmakers and the opera. But her mother wasn't impressed by the results and after a couple of months removed her to an English school in Paris, which Agatha found boring. From there she was moved again to a Miss Dryden's, which was more to her liking and where she stayed for over a year. Miss Dryden had much more of a work ethic than Mademoiselle T, and her girls had to study the likes of Racine, Molière and Corneille. More emphasis was placed on piano and singing lessons, and Agatha made such progress that she even began to think in terms of becoming a concert pianist, until she was asked to perform for a visiting dignitary and in her nervousness made an embarrassing quantity of mistakes. Miss Dryden was also realistic enough to realize that young women needed to know how to talk to young men, and the male of the species was occasionally introduced to her girls in a very controlled way at social evenings.

When Agatha was seventeen her mother adjudged her ready to meet men in quantities, and the pair spent the three months of that year's Ashfield rental doing a society season in Cairo, because a London season would have been way beyond their means. Egypt was a fashionable place at the time, and was administered by the British, which meant plenty of young army officers and civil servants to choose from. Mother and daughter took rooms in the Gezirah Palace Hotel, and during the day they would play croquet and attend the races and the various ceremonial occasions staged by the military. In the evenings Agatha slipped into her first ever evening dresses and sallied out to no fewer than fifty dances, taking to the floor with thirty different dance partners.

There was no doubt that, after a slow start, the young author-to-be was growing in social confidence. She was clearly attractive and was never short of invitations to dance. But all those protected childhood years meant that she was still shy, and in her autobiography she recalls a cruel moment when one of her male escorts delivered her back home to her mother with the cutting words, 'Here is your daughter. She dances beautifully. Now you'd better teach her how to talk.'

Outside my window, Brixton had been replaced by Penge East and Bromley South, and the barbed wire and builder's yards of central London had been supplanted by the conservatories and herbaceous borders of the suburbs. One garden was fence-to-fence concrete with a small swimming-pool at its centre, in which a large man was ploughing from side to side in short and absurd flurries of machismo.

Despite its vintage, the Pullman didn't seem to perform any differently to the slam-door Sunningdale commuter train, although by now the Saumur had had its effect and I was feeling suitably mellow and generous towards the hoi-polloi who stared at us from the platform as we dawdled through Swanley. The guinea fowl appeared at much the same time as the countryside, with the train embarking along the route of the Pilgrim's Way, the medieval path taken by pilgrims travelling from Winchester to the shrine of St Thomas à Becket at Canterbury. Across the aisle, the hairdresser was admitting to his mother, with a giggle, that he was feeling a bit squiffy. Behind me an Indian gentleman was using his mobile for a series of the ultimate 'I'm on the train' telephone calls, reviewing the journey-thus-far. Then the train rocked momentarily and one set of windows was filled with the flickering stripes of an overtaking Eurostar, the old-fashioned umber and cream of the Pullmans reflected back at us from its windows. Both trainloads were effectively making the same journey through the same scenery, but while our experience was labelled 'holiday', theirs was labelled 'transport'. The essential difference was not the speed or the plate of guinea fowl, but the fact that, for us, the process of getting there was at least as important as the destination.

For a while the Phoenix fought a running battle with flickering embankments. There were momentary flashes of urbanization and momentary flashes of agriculture, glimpses of fly-tipping and paddocks with ponies and jumps. Then, with the lunch service tidied away, the train came to a halt, creaking and ticking gently, and refused to move for at least twenty minutes. Among the passengers the initial excitement of the journey had quietened into a gentle murmur, so now a sleepy post-prandial silence descended and I could hear the click of someone unlocking the distant toilet door. In normal circumstances the instinctive reaction to any train delay would have been an automatic tut-tutting, but in this case there was little point, as nothing was going to go anywhere without us. Terence, though, was a worrier. 'I don't like all this sitting around,' he confided to his mother. 'They could have parked somewhere with a better view.'

Folkestone, when we finally drew in, was worse. Cheriton Industrial Estate and Shearway Business Park were deeply unglamorous bits of scenery, and the jazz band on the platform couldn't disguise the town's essentially drab, down-at-heel feel. The passengers were decanted out on to the platform and sorted into buses. I stuck with Audrey and Terence. By now we'd exchanged a few pleasantries and I'd gathered that the trip was a surprise present from son to mother.

'I'm not expecting to get any sleep,' Audrey said.

'Course you will, dear,' said Terence. 'A couple of G&Ts and a nice bottle of wine and we'll be out like a light.'

'You may be. Never mind how luxurious it is, I've never been good at sleeping when I'm not in my own bed. Besides, you never know what might go on during the night on the Orient Express, do you?'

'It does have a certain reputation,' I said, not sure whether she was referring to pyjamaed shenanigans at midnight, or whether the ghost of Agatha Christie had just passed overhead.

'Nobody's going to do away with you,' said her son, giving her a squeeze. 'You've never had a nasty thought in your life.'

From Folkestone a luxury bus took us through the slow wringer of the Eurotunnel process and a smooth-voiced woman in uniform offered us a drink from the bar. 'No thank you,' Terence responded waspishly. 'It's too early for tea and I certainly don't want any more wine.'

Audrey started to tell me how she'd come down on the train, first class, from Sheffield the previous day and how Terence had organized tickets for *An Audience with Dawn French* for that evening.

'It's an acquired taste, that sort of entertainment,' she

said, doubtfully, from which I gathered it had not been a great success. Nor, for a while, was the journey; passing through the Channel Tunnel is transport, not travel.

Two hours later our equilibrium was restored. We were rattling across northern France, tugging open the top of a long zip of a journey that extended all the way down across the Alps to Venice. The rake of seventeen navy-blue Wagons-Lits coaches, each with their crest and polished metal lettering, had looked majestic at Calais station, and now it was unwinding its length – the longest passenger train in Europe – across unfenced fields, bisecting rows of willows planted in straight lines as if they were part of a grand plan for something that had never quite materialized. If the British landscape is a jumbled mosaic of homes and farms, fields and gardens, the French equivalent comes in great, sweeping swathes, painted with a far thicker brush. Giant carpets of colour are broken only by the speck of a tractor, the smear of a war cemetery and the smudge of a red brick town. It is a landscape which draws clear lines between agriculture and domesticity; this is where we live, it seems to say, and beyond that line is farming.

My berth was in sleeping-car 3425, which had had as chequered a history as the Phoenix. It was built in 1929, spent its early career on the Rome Express, its later years travelling across Turkey and finished up in the sidings in Portugal, where it was hunted down and rescued for restoration. The wood-panelled cabin had a luggage rack of polished brass and a shiny lever which raised and lowered the window. There was a sink in the corner covered with a lid; lift that lid, and the sound of wheels invaded the room. A levered ventilation panel in the door meant I could watch the slippered feet of other passengers pad by on the carpeted corridor outside, just as Hercule Poirot might have done.

In the old days Wagons-Lits used to hire staff on a strict quota basis according to the mileage travelled through their country. French staff were the most numerous because they had 467 miles, then came Italians, with 259 miles, and lastly the Swiss, 148 miles. And they all had to speak each other's language.

I don't know whether that rule still applied, but the sallow-faced pianist playing in the bar car before dinner had to be French. He reminded me of a character in a detective story, but one by Simenon, not Christie. He looked every inch the under-cover detective from the Sûreté, his fingers flickering expertly around the keyboard while his inquiring eyes lingered on the unlikelier notes in the room. For a moment they lit on me, standing alone and dinner-jacketed at the bar, but there were more interesting tableaux to take in. In particular, a Belgian gentleman built like a bullfrog with a bouffant hairstyle and the granular complexion of someone who had lived too well – and was unlikely to do so for much longer – who had ordered champagne and caviar. He had appeared to be alone when we'd boarded at Calais, but now he was sitting with a tall, immensely striking African princess with hair braids, high cheekbones and legs of dark mahogany. She was perfectly made and well prepared to show it, in a crepe miniskirt and a silk top which etched out her nipples. He was talking hard, and she was in-clining her head graciously at regular intervals to indicate that she was listening. A politician, I reckoned, spilling out state secrets to an African Mata Hari.

Closer to hand was a group of very British sixty-somethings. The men were talking about sailing holidays and how they always slept on deck in the Virgin Islands, and the women were quietly comparing notes about how many of their friends' husbands had already died, and what a liberating experience bereavement could sometimes turn out to be. One of them raised her voice. 'Peter,' she shrilled, interrupting herself to cut into the male conversation. 'You're not allowed to talk about cars.'

A familiar pair made their entrance through the distant door and began working their way up towards the bar. It was the mother and daughter I'd noticed before, the former now rather impressively décolleté and heavy with jewellery in all the right places, and the latter nicely, coolly, understated in a sheath of cream silk. They both wore the slightly knowing smiles of people who realized their arrival was making the required impact, and I guessed from the way their eyes swept across the other passengers that both would have been interested in encounters on the train. By travelling together, however, each was a handbrake on the other; who would have had the better time if they'd travelled alone, mother or daughter, older or younger? I looked towards the pianist, to see if he was showing an interest. He raised his left eyebrow a fraction of an inch, as if to say, 'You can have the inexperience of youth, mine's the fruity one on the left.'

The summons for 8.45 dinner came through as the train was bumping around Paris' Ceinture, a lurching, pothole-prone belt of track which links the Gare du Nord with Gare de l'Est and all stations south. The restaurant car was looking fabulous; the walls were decorated with opalescent Lalique glass panels of sculpted small-breasted nymphs tra-la-la-ing with bunches of grapes, the chairs were upholstered in cut moquette velvet and the tables were glittering with Limoges china and specially designed heavy-based wine glasses by Cristallerie. Outside it was dusk, drawing on to darkness, and a full harvest moon was rising above the Parisian rooftops, puffy, swollen, the colour of mature Cheddar and covered in lunar acne.

Guided by the Maître d', I took my seat next to Rachel and Steven from Northampton. He was in event management, she brought up the kids, and they were on the train as a celebration of their fortieth birthdays. Both looked ten years older; he prematurely florid and tubby with a red bow tie, and she dowdy and pale in a dress of a colour which couldn't make up its mind whether to be purple or mauve, speckled or mottled.

'You're by yourself?' Rachel asked with a note of surprise – and just a hint of suspicion.

I shrugged. 'It's exciting this way. Single travel is a bit like setting off on a fishing trip, you never know what you're going to catch.'

'And are you trying to catch something – or someone?'

'I didn't mean it quite like that . . .'

'Personally, I don't think I would enjoy all this unless I had someone to share it with,' said Steven.

'Someone like your wife, for example,' added Rachel, pointedly. 'Unless of course you prefer the company of others.'

Now I felt defensive. Agatha had travelled alone, but I didn't want to get involved in explaining the whole Agatha thing. So instead I merely said, rather lamely, 'I generally get the sympathy vote. I look needy, so people talk to me. People like you talk to me.'

'But isn't it lonely?' Rachel was like a dog worrying a bone.

'Sometimes. When it works, it's wonderful, but when it's bad, it's dismal. You can feel very exposed eating alone in smart restaurants, so I tend not to do so. Very few people travel alone these days, so those of us that do are regarded as weirdos or axe-murderers.'

The pan-fried scallops provided an opportunity to change the subject, and we embarked on more typical, how-many-children type conversation. I wanted to know what the social life was like in Northampton, and Steven started to say 'Good', when his wife interrupted.

'We don't get out much. He is always at work and I am always with the kids. We don't do dinner parties. They don't seem worth the effort any more.' She put undue emphasis on that 'any more'.

'Rachel had kidney failure a couple of years ago,' Steven explained, quietly. 'We didn't think you were going to make it, did we, Rache? When something like that happens, and there are young children involved, it rather changes one's priorities in life.'

I agreed that it rather would, and felt ashamed at being rattled by her directness.

After dinner I returned for a last look in the bar car. The bouffant old goat and his African princess hadn't bothered with a sit-down meal and were still picking at their caviar. The décolleté mother was sitting with the two men who had been talking about sailing in the Virgin Islands, and laughing too loudly to be sober. Of her daughter and their wives there was no sign. And as for the pianist, his eyes were still flickering around the room, irrespective of what his fingers were up to. If he'd come to any conclusion about who might be about to do away with whom during the night, he was giving nothing away.

Breakfast was served in the cabin, with a silver teapot, croissants and pastries wrapped in napkins, a purple orchid in a vase and Sir Nigel's Vintage Marmalade from those nice people at Fortnum and Mason.

'No murders last night?' I asked the cabin attendant.

'No, sir.' From the way he said it, I suspect it was a question he had been asked many times before.

Audrey was certainly very much alive. I'd been awake for a while, lying in bed watching the Alps rolling around in my window frame, and I could hear her bumping around in the cabin next door. The arrival of breakfast was her cue to begin a shouted conversation with her son, who must have been in the cabin beyond. I couldn't help but overhear her, although most of his replies were lost.

'Have you got a nice orchid?' Distant mumble.

'Did you order tea or coffee?' Again, answer indistinct.

'You were snoring like a trooper.' There was a pause, filled by the sound effects of old lady getting stuck into her breakfast pastries.

'I had to call the steward to come and turn my light off,' she continued eventually, through a mouthful of croissant.

This time I could hear him. 'Why didn't you call me?'

'You were on your mobile. For hours. You're a pair of gossips, you two. I don't know what you find to talk about.'

Terence's voice became suddenly clearer. Perhaps they had an inter-connecting door.

'Ghastly night. I had to sleep sitting virtually upright, you know, for the sake of the hair,' he complained. 'Could have done with another pair of sheets. I didn't want to go messing it up, you see. Takes hours to get it like this. You want to look your best on the Orient Express.'

I picked up the *Herald Tribune* which came with the breakfast, and the next time I tuned in on them they'd moved on to discuss our whereabouts.

'Austria,' said Terence, decisively.

'How can you tell?'

'Because we keep changing direction. You find that

with Austria. You don't know whether you're coming or going.'

Personally, I suspected we were in Switzerland. The train was moving between sheets of light and dark, ploughing across valley bottoms like a slicer, drawing its handsome blue blade across rivers, orchards, sports grounds, and whipping its tail across the backsides of generous, well-organized villages with generous, well-organized houses. It was so long that the bright red locomotive would be exiting a valley which the last coaches hadn't yet entered, with the resulting paradox that passengers on the same transport, moving at the same speed, were having totally different visual experiences, simultaneously. The mother and daughter, up at the head, could be deep in a town, while Rachel and Steven, bringing up the rear, could be clattering through a farmyard full of Milka cows. I'd have liked to be in a helicopter somewhere way up overhead, watching the red needle and its navy thread sew stitches through Switzerland.

We stopped inexplicably in a couple of overwhelmingly neat and subdued small stations. The train stood quite silently, unmolested by any shouting, whistling or slamming of doors. The only visible human beings were train- and track-men, who walked the length of the rake muttering into walkie-talkies, keeping their eyes firmly fixed on the wheels. To raise their gaze to window level would have risked invading the privacy of a camp hairdresser touching up his highlights or a bouffant old goat touching up his African princess.

Inside the coaches there was a definite morning-after feeling, and nobody really moved from their cabins until lunchtime. It was a strange, unaccustomed luxury to lie back in starched sheets in a rhythmically rocking bed to watch some of Europe's finest scenery put on a matinée performance outside the window. In the foreground a rushing stream, in the middle-ground a house with floral window-boxes in meadows surrounded by woodland, and in the background a mountain with a snow-capped peak against a deep blue sky.

Gradually, though, as the morning progressed and the train climbed, those rightful places looked less assured. The stream became more violent, elbowing everything out of its way, and the land it tumbled through became more brutal, jagged and raw. Houses, where they existed, were parked on ledges out of harm's way. Outcrops of rock appeared out of nowhere, throwing punches which fell just short of the train window, and the peaks were no longer a distant piece of scenery, but a lurking, threatening, invisible force.

There was a fierce brightness in the air. Concrete roofs protected the track at vulnerable spots and metal barriers were strung across the mountainsides like rusty suspender belts, preventing the tree line from sliding embarrassingly downwards and revealing the shiny excrescences of naked rock. Whereas before it would have been a pleasure for the passengers if the train had stopped and we'd had to walk a bit, now it would have provoked anxiety as we stumbled over boulders and tripped on the roots of trees. Moreover the train itself sounded alarmed. The tracks were slapping it this way and that and it screamed and squealed like a stuck pig.

Lunch was served as we punched through the last of the long alpine tunnels, hit the daylight on the other side and started to descend through the vineyards and fruit orchards of the Trento Valley with the relief of a swimmer hitting the surface after too long under water.

As the day progressed the atmosphere inside the train became much more relaxed. Elaborate over-dressing was no longer *de rigueur*. Terence, who'd appeared the previous evening in a grey velvet suit with rock star stripes, was now in a satin paisley shirt and spotless cream trousers.

'So go on, tell, mystery man,' he said, buttonholing me in the corridor outside his cabin.

'Tell?'

'Audrey reckons you're either the Inland Revenue or the man from *Holiday Which*.'

'Nothing so exciting, I'm afraid.' Briefly I outlined my Agatha interest.

'But that *is* exciting! Audrey will be thrilled, she's read all her books. My friend and I, we've watched all the Poirot programmes on the telly. Not so much for the mystery as for the detail. The clothes. I've always liked a nice bit of costume drama. You know, glass of chardonnay, sofa, Sunday night.'

Now he peered at me more closely. 'But you don't seem to me the Agatha Christie type. Blue rinse and all that.'

So I explained how I'd stumbled across Agatha's tracks in the Middle East and first became aware of her little-known second life.

'Did she just!' Terence's eyes widened. 'I never knew.'

'So this is a sort of investigation,' he continued, thoughtfully. 'A quest, even? A personal one? Are there any personal connections? You and her? You're not a love-child or something deliciously messy like that?'

'I'm afraid not.'

In fact I had discovered a few personal connections, and although each individual one didn't amount to much more than a hill o'beans, when put together they served to encourage me on my way. Agatha had been brought up in Devon, as was I. By coincidence we both quoted Lewis Carroll's White Knight's Song on the frontispiece of books. We both considered ourselves inarticulate; she once said her lack of confidence in speaking was what made her a writer. We both liked trains, loved travel and had no pretensions to creating great literature. We even had an Isle of Skye connection; my grandfather was born there, she retreated there to avoid the publicity prior to her second wedding . . . Terence interrupted my train of thought.

'So do you think you would have liked her? You know, if you'd actually met?'

'I think I'd describe it as empathy. Perhaps admiration . . .' It was a good question, and one I hadn't really considered before. 'No, maybe I would have really liked her, odd though it might seem. Otherwise I don't think I'd be dragging my backside all the way to Baghdad.'

'Oohh, all that way by train.' Terence winced. 'All that way without a proper bath. I already feel dirty,' he confided as the cabin attendant sashayed down our corridor with Earl Grey and macaroons. 'I need a bath, I need hot water, I need to do my hair. They call this a luxury train and they don't even provide a bath, I mean to say!'

I tried to nod sympathetically, but secretly I disagreed, because that lack of bathrooms is one of the things that had impressed me about the VSOE. In truth, I hadn't expected to like the train as much as I had. I'd been ready to mark it down on the basis that it wasn't a real working train and its passengers weren't making a real journey as my fellow-travellers henceforth would be. In the event, though, I had been impressed by how un-tarted up the VSOE was, at how little it had felt the need to change to cater to the appetite of its public. I was impressed by the smell of burning coal at the end of the carriages where the water for the sinks was still heated by old-fashioned stoves. I was impressed by the authenticity of the fixtures and fittings, by the back-story of every bit of hardware, by the passion and the dedication devoted to ensuring that every detail was correct.

I was also impressed by how the train had got on with its journey, covering its 1,071 miles between London and Venice in thirty-one hours. This was no leisurely cruise, and indeed proved to be a far more impressive performance than any other train managed to put in on the 1,500 miles that lay ahead of me. We rolled into Venice pretty much on time, having exchanged the Alps for mountains of scrap metal in the industrial lowlands, until those too fell away to reveal the Venetian lagoon. A helicopter escort with a TV crew on board accompanied us across the last causeway into the mirage of a city, but that was the last bit of VIP treatment of the journey.

Any Orient Express glamour we might have borrowed for the duration evaporated instantly with the last hiss of the brakes in Venice Sta Lucia. The heads which turned to watch the arrival of such a handsome train must have been disappointed with the ordinary-looking bunch of ordinary-looking people who stumbled out, fussing over their luggage.

Disembarking with the same suit-carrier and battered roll-along suitcase that had featured so suspiciously on Sunningdale's Cheshire Cat TV, thirty-six-odd hours before, I was, quickly, just another face in the crowd.

INTERMEZZO TRIESTINO

By early afternoon the next day I was on another train, sitting opposite two large, voluble Italian ladies on a functional, crowded regional express to Trieste which reeked of sweat and hot plastic. The curtains were closed to keep out the sun, so for me the Venetian plain was just a flickering shadowplay with a soundtrack provided by a young man who spent the whole two-hour journey on his mobile phone. A feat which I, as a comparatively inarticulate person, couldn't help but admire.

I couldn't help but admire my two no-nonsense ladies, too. They'd climbed aboard at the station after mine, by which time the surrounding seats were filled with a party of Koreans who'd somehow all managed to go to sleep with their feet up on the seats even though the train had only been under way for a matter of minutes. Skilful deployment of copious luggage and large rear ends had scattered the diminutive Koreans like skittles, and now they'd got out the family photographs and were rapidly getting to know the bad habits of each other's daughters-in-law.

I'd decided not to linger in Venice. There's something decadent about the Painted Lady at the end of the season, its colours as bruised and rich as a pile of rotten apples in a cornfield. The vaporettos looked rustier than ever, the pavements were sticky with melted ice cream, the foot-bridges were flowing with young Europeans excessively rouged by the sun, and the smell from the canals was so strong you could have taken it away and coloured it in. I'd secured a room in a budget hotel near the station which cost too much, had damp stains on the ceiling and a couple of flies circling lazily in the foyer. I personally find this sense of decay rather intoxicating, but on this occasion it wasn't enough to encourage me to stay.

In any case, Venice is already too well known. It doesn't need me to add to the pile of words already written about it, and nothing I can dream up will dent the image of culture and serenity it projects to the world. Coming to a place as famous as this is a bit like going to see a long-running play on the basis of a lengthy review; you know what you're going to get, and almost what you are supposed to think about it, before you even set off.

Personally, I feel that travel writers have too much of a responsibility towards the unfamiliar to waste their time endorsing what is already very well-trodden. People can, and do, find out what Venice is like for themselves; it is those other parts of the world which are far less well known, and often unnecessarily feared or unjustly mis-understood, that need someone to lift their lid.

Travel writing is practically the only mainstream media left which presents places in anything approaching an objective light. I don't mean the sort of travel writing which extols the best beaches and the designer hotels, or even the sort which describes a lone voyage across the Atlantic in a barrel, but the type which can be loosely defined as soft adventure, venturing into those destinations which we would otherwise see or read nothing about unless they were to host a small war, an earthquake or a passing hurricane. Normally it is only under the shadow of disaster that such destinations get paraded in front of the eyes of the world, and the images of people trapped under buildings is how they will be remembered until the next disaster comes along. In this way whole swathes of the planet are effectively labelled as anything from highly dangerous to hugely repressive, whereas the reality on the street is often of a peaceable country with a great tradition of hospitality, a culture far more ancient than the stuff which we get excited about from Greece and Rome, and with far greater personal security than any of us enjoy at home.

The middle-aged, middle-sized port city of Trieste is a case in point. Banged up against the Slovenian border, it may be more overlooked than misunderstood, but for me on my journey it marked the beginning of the under-publicized, and from here on my route lay through lands that are increasingly misrepresented almost to a point that justifies war.

Shoehorned into the armpit of the Adriatic for shelter from the Bora, the cold and fierce 'Slav wind' from Dante's *Inferno* which comes sweeping down from the north-east, Trieste has long since been dismissed as little deserving of any tourist attention. 'The average traveller,' wrote Thomas Cook back in 1925, 'would not make a point of staying long.' But a great many people have grazed the city, many of them – including Agatha – travelling in style on the Simplon-Orient Express, Wagons-Lits' southerly route which was created after World War I specifically to circumnavigate German-speaking lands.

There may have been few obvious reasons for Cook to encourage his customers to linger, but Trieste was already a household name when Agatha's train passed through. Back in 1844 the Trieste-based shipping company Lloyd-Austriaco had won the contract for postal traffic between England and India, and the stamp 'Via Trieste' was common currency in the post offices of the shires, as fond mothers sent completely inappropriate hand-knitted socks out to their sweltering sons in the Empire.

In those days the city was the major port on the Adriatic and the northernmost port in the whole Mediterranean region. Lloyd-Austriaco had launched the first steamship built completely of iron back in 1865, so when the Suez Canal opened in 1869 it was perfectly positioned for all its Christmases to come at once. In the 1880s and 1890s the city was described by Jules Verne as 'a colossal emporium and a prodigious trading centre', and in 1886 Lloyd-Austriaco peaked with eighty-six ships, many of them deployed on the most successful routes across to Alexandria, Port Said and on to Bombay. At the turn of the century, with new trans-alpine rail links bringing heavily populated northern Europe within easy reach, the company decided to diversify further into passenger and tourist traffic, even launching a route to Shanghai. In fact Trieste's access to those European rail connections even helped populate the emerging United States with middle Europeans. In 1912–14 some 87,000 emigrants left from here for the USA, Canada and South America, most of them from German-speaking territory. For a while the influx was so dramatic that there was strong support domestically within the US for a campaign to have new laws printed in German as well as in English.

Even the radical post-war restructuring after 1918, when Lloyd-Austriaco was forcibly dissolved because of its Austrian heritage, didn't halt the shipping line's momentum. The company was reborn as Lloyd Triestino, under the control of the Italian government, and for some years between the wars Lloyd-Austriaco/Triestino cultivated a very smart liner market as an extension of the Orient Express across to Egypt and North Africa. The steamers emulated the style of Nagelmackers' Wagons-Lits, with dancing, musical entertainment, and fine dining on Triestine specialities such as *jota*, a soup made from sauerkraut and pork, and *scampi in busara*, prawns with tomato and herbs. These steamers also competed head to head with the new train-created market to oriental destinations like Constantinople and Beirut.

For a while that mixture of luxury rail to Trieste and onwards by ship was as popular as the train, particularly among government officials. Four years before Agatha's train journey, Gertrude Bell, Britain's special envoy to the Middle East and the first member of the establishment who vigorously promoted the idea of self-rule for Iraq, embarked on a ship headed for Alexandria, where she was to transfer to another ship to Beirut before travelling cross-country to Baghdad. In letters home she describes arriving at Trieste station late at night and being taken directly to her cabin at the quayside, although the actual departure wasn't until late the following day. The ship was very full, but Captain Secco was sufficiently gallant as to welcome two young English ladies (Gertrude was travelling with a friend) on to the bridge, to show them the stars viewed through a sextant. There was plenty of time for deckchair socializing, albeit not with everyone. 'I have succeeded in avoiding a pestilential American missionary called Zwemer whose political activities in the Persian Gulf have been a bye word,' wrote Gertrude to her mother. 'Col. Fell told me he had been hunting for me since we started, but concealed in the long grass I have evaded notice.'

Trieste's Golden Age through the nineteenth to the beginning of the twentieth centuries is clearly reflected in its downtown architecture, with huge, ornate palazzos built to accommodate local government and shipping companies. Their style, however, is not Italian. The city's anomaly is that, despite its location in the corner of the Adriatic where Italy and Slovenia meet, its guiding hand was neither Italian nor Slovenian. Until the early years of the twentieth century it was part of the Austro-Hungarian Empire, a huge imperial power which dominated much of central and eastern Europe for decades, but which disappeared almost overnight after making the fatal mistake of initiating a war which it went on to lose. Trieste had been, in fact, the third largest city within that empire after Vienna and Prague, and for many decades it was Austria's solitary, much-cherished sea port, on the end of a carpet of land which was the empire's corridor to the sea. It is those imperial origins (i.e. Austrian, not Italian) which colour the way the city looks – and the way it has effectively been overlooked – in the years since.

In the carve-up of Europe at the end of World War I Trieste was handed over to Italy, but it was always an unnatural union, and the city struggled economically as soon as it was deprived of its Teutonic hinterland. Besides, Italy had plenty of ports of its own, and it didn't need another one perched out on its eastern corner. Being welded to what turned out to be the losing side in World War II provided an opportunity for the city to cut loose again, and this time it was granted the status of an Independent Free Territory by the Allies. But that didn't work either, and in 1954 the city fathers gave up the attempt to stand alone, and Trieste became Italian once more.

Fifty years on, after an epoch of energy-sapping negation and subtraction, it is a wistful place with a high suicide rate and a low-threshold university to which rich Italian families dispatch their least academic children to be sure of a degree. It may have been part of Italy for fifty years, but a poll conducted in 1999 discovered that 70 per cent of Italians did not know that it was in their country at all. Its glorious era has long gone and is unlikely ever to return, and it doesn't know whether to look west, north or east for a knight on a white charger. Economically and politically it is part of Italy, but spiritually it stands alone, the last full stop in western Europe before the alphabets begin to change.

I arrived in the city armed with Jan Morris's *Trieste and the Meaning of Nowhere*, a salutory lesson in how a good travel writer can create a whole discursive volume out of a little-known destination. Thomas Cook's tourists may have found nothing to linger for here, but Morris is one of a line of authors who'd been intrigued by Trieste's messed-up childhood. Rilke, Kafka, Stendhal and James Joyce all spent periods in the city, and arabist and explorer Richard Burton was the British consul for a while, finding the time to translate *1001 Arabian Nights* into English. And now here was I, primed by Morris's depiction of a *triste* Trieste with nowhere to go. To be honest, they made me a little anxious, her acute observations; what if I was too much of a plank of wood to identify any of those undercurrents?

The last part of the journey from Venice had proved to be easily the most scenic. With the power of the sun beginning to wane, I drew back the curtains and was thus able to witness the giant shoulder of limestone karst known as the Carso emerge from the distance and charge like a bull across the Venetian plain, forcing the railway to crowd fearfully to the edge of the land. Meanwhile the view out of the other window pretended nothing was happening, persisting with a slide show of peaceful blue images of the flat Adriatic, littered with becalmed yachts, and the distant Croatian shore.

Trieste station had all the presentation, dimensions and acoustics of a cathedral, rising from floors of polished marble through giant limestone pillars to a neo-classical dome. From the outside it looked imposing, serious and very important. On the inside, though, it was a sombre place, a pale, under-tenanted shadow of what it used to be. Distant voices sounded like monks practising vespers in the cloisters, and on the wall was a timetable of Mass in the city's seventeen churches. I noted that nine of the seventeen had services in Slovenian, one in German, and the number in Italian went unrecorded. And yet virtually every train listed on the official departure board was for Venice, back the way I had come. Only two were indicated as heading east, the way I wanted to go. Trieste definitely had its back to the wall.

In the old days this was one of two terminus stations. It was responsible for the westward journeys into Italy, while the Südbahnhof, over on the other horn of the port, was for trains to Vienna, Budapest and points east. The latter would have welcomed all those German-speaking immigrants *en route* for America, but its career had effectively been ended when Trieste was amputated from Austria, and although it still stands, across the water, it serves only as a parking place for old trains with nowhere to go. Among the dinosaurs corralled within its walls are several steam engines from the turn of the century, a Red Cross hospital coach from World War I, an armoured truck from World War II, and a lot of oak-encased switching equipment with instructions in German. The old waiting-rooms have become a sleepy museum, the main roof has long since been removed, for safety's sake, and nothing arrives or departs except for the pigeons. The few trains that do still head east out of Trieste for destinations which were formerly served by the Südbahnhof have to emerge from the other station and describe a giant circle up on to the Carso to end up facing in the right direction.

Downtown, Trieste is laid out in blocks of rather pompous nineteenth-century buildings of great weight and stature, behind whose walls smug insurers and shipowner's agents once thumbed through bills of lading, totting up their percentages, and then sent the office boy out for a celebratory cigar. The shops, like the buildings that host them, are overwhelmingly matter-of-fact, selling the likes of letterboxes, medical equipment and Chinese wine, with very little attempt at presentation. Tarnished brass plaques announce the presence of several consulates, including one for Colombia, suggesting that this is a place where people get into all sorts of trouble that requires adept diplomatic manoeuvring to get them out of it again.

Between the pompous blocks the streets run in rifle-straight canyons, and at certain times of day the sun barrels down them to smash into the façades at the end, façades which are handsomely if conservatively presented for just such moments of glory. For a pedestrian, emerging from a darkened side street into the full glare of this late sun is like suddenly finding yourself spotlit and on stage, but not quite sure which play it is you are to perform, or which language you are meant to speak.

The biggest stage of all is where the canyons come to a sudden stop, and the lugubrious blocks stand to attention in a respectful semi-circle. Emerge from their shadows and you find yourself on the quayside, in a wide panorama of stone and sea. This was once the epicentre of Triestine life, smelling of salt, steam, oil and hawsers. Giant steel hulls loomed over scurrying stevedores, freight trains rumbled to and fro along the seafront, and ships' horns and whistles echoed off the amphitheatre of watching buildings. Today, though, it is a blank space where lone men linger, contemplating what next to do with their lives. It's a quayside without boats, and there's no trace of the sacks of spices, coffee, cotton and coal that were once piled high by the water's edge. The passenger terminal used by Gertrude Bell *en route* to her cabin is still there, and it has retained its art deco marble staircase. But there are no liners any longer, and the interior has been converted into a conference centre.

Trieste is still a port, but most of the port activity has long since been relocated to a new set of wharfs on the southern side of the city. So walking out here, into this open and somnolent space, is like emerging into a giant auditorium where the audience is waiting for a performance which has already happened, long ago, and will never happen again. The only bums on seats are the lovers on the rusty bollards.

The pivotal point of the empty waterfront is the Molo Audace, a broad and bosomy mother of a wharf which drives straight out at the heart of the setting sun. Behind it stands the Piazza dell'Unita d'Italia, the grand cobbled ceremonial city square, flanked on three sides by three Viennese-designed neo-classical palazzos, with bare-breasted ladies playing in their fountains and Atlas figures supporting the lintels of their giant wooden doors. The Palazzo Communale, a clocktowered *rathaus* straight out of central Europe, takes pride of place at one end, behind the Fountain of the Four Continents. It is flanked on one side by the Governor's Palace and on the other by the flamboyant former headquarters of Lloyd Triestino, which is now the office of the President of the Giunta. Lloyd Triestino still exists, but these days it is owned by a Taiwanese shipping company which deals solely in containerized cargo, and its offices have been relocated to a functional glass headquarters near the new port.

My first priority, after finding a room in a modest *pensione* opposite a bra shop on a street ringing with Vespas, was to package up my tuxedo and send it home. It was only going to get trashed if I tried to haul it all the way to Iraq, where there was little chance of a dinner-dance with Saddam. So I set out for the post office, dodging Albanian lorry-drivers map-reading their way to the port and passing through a distinct Chinatown, complete with red paper lanterns and bow-legged grannies haranguing their grandchildren in Hokkien. A pizzeria with the striking name of Luigi Dick testified to the Mittel European mix. In the backstreets men in tracksuits leaned against Croatian-registered cars, talking quietly, and two drunks, one Italian and one Hungarian, wove through the traffic arm-in-arm, singing loudly. None of these individuals met the eye of a new arrival in town, giving the impression of a place where you could go to ground, change your name and adopt a new nationality without anyone taking a blind bit of notice.

The post office turned out to be almost as grand as the railway station and just as empty, in a theatrical turn-of-the-century glass-roofed hall up an imposing flight of marble steps framed with wrought iron lamps. This was a temple to the postal service, erected at a time when the post was still a holy and wholly wonderful thing, and an eminently suitable place for a dinner jacket to be tied up with string and left to wend its own way north. The days of sending parcels via Trieste may have long gone, but it still felt like a moment of historical re-enactment, sending a parcel from Trieste to home. Even if it wasn't hand-knitted socks.

Afterwards I headed across to the Piazza dell'Unità d'Italia to have a creative cappucino in the Caffè delli Specchi, under a sky which was somewhere between turquoise and navy blue at the last leavings of the day. The Caffè, supposedly where Rainer Maria Rilke and James Joyce hung out, was very highly polished and smart, with a large outside enclosure of linen-covered tables and dapper, multi-lingual waiters. Its menu listed goulash and strudel, its prices were steep, and I didn't see anyone who looked like a writer. The only other customers were men in suits and mature women with expensive tans who preferred the evening light because it treated them like a lady.

It was hard to imagine Joyce spending much time here. He lived in the city from 1904 to 1915 and again in 1919 to 1920 with his wife Nora Barnacle, tutoring the children of wealthy Triestine families (and then sleeping with them when they were old enough), drinking, whoring and writing. His two children were born here, as was *Portrait of a Young Man*, most of *Dubliners* and much of *Ulysses*. But all of those words were completely uninfluenced by anything Triestine.

The Joyces were always desperately short of money, and changed address regularly whenever the rent was due. James was always borrowing from his younger brother Stanislaus (habitually shortened to a much more English-sounding Stan), which was why I found it hard to visualize him in the pricey Specchi. More likely he would have frequented some grotty little hole in the wall, some-where where he could have got sozzled for a quarter of the price. However, decades later, when it came to freshening up the city for tourism and creating the Joyce Trail, the city fathers decided that a hole in the wall wouldn't do, so it had to hand over its Joycean credentials to the smartest café in the city – or at least hadn't refuted the Specchi's claims. Perhaps it didn't miss Joyce; he'd probably been an argumentative customer who'd been slow to pay, and the owner's son was happy to let his memory go, especially when the planning permission for his new seaview villa was suddenly granted after years of being becalmed.

But maybe I was wrong. Maybe the Specchi was Joyce all over, as in 'stuff the grotty bars, I'm going to blow my wad by drinking in the smartest of them all. Stan'll see me right.'

It is hard to imagine two more different writers than Christie and Joyce. He delivering his poly-syllables right from his guts, in a shambolic life drunk on creativity, and she rarely descending below the neck, carefully manipulating her readers. One has out-sold the other by a factor of millions, but it is Joyce who is regarded as the national treasure.

There's a highbrow, anti-Agatha snobbery in the literary establishment which marks her down on the basis of limited vocabulary and characterization which rarely goes beyond the stereotype. Whenever the critics have spared her any thought, which is seldom, they have typically condemned her books as 'animated algebra' or literary crossword puzzles, ignoring the fact that she gives so much pleasure to such a huge number of readers.

It is true that lying at the core of her books is not the Great Authorial Vision of Profound Truth, but a murder riddle which the reader must read to the end to resolve. It is true that her phenomenal output reveals practically nothing about the author, but then she was almost obsessively concerned to avoid the self-revelation which is integral to being a novelist, concealing herself behind alibis and plotlines. She preferred to portray herself, disingenuously, as the conventional wife and homemaker who happened to write detective stories in her spare time, rather as other women might embroider cushion covers. She had no pretensions, gave very few interviews, was terrified of public speaking, and had good reason for keeping her private life out of the public eye.

Agatha was no child prodigy destined to write from an early age. In fact it was her sister Madge who seemed more set for a career in crime fiction, having had several pieces published in *Vanity Fair* before marriage and motherhood distracted her. Agatha certainly shared her sister's appetite for the genre, describing them both as 'connoisseurs of the detective story', but her first stab at a book was suggested to her by her mother Clara during a period of illness, and she used her debutante's experience of Cairo as its setting. A family friend called Eden Philpotts, a well-known writer himself, was prevailed upon to read the finished manuscript of *Snow Upon the Desert* and declared it full of promise. Agatha took the advice that he gave about the craft of writing very seriously, and his influence can clearly be seen on the rest of her work. 'Some of these things that you have written are capital,' he commented. 'Try and cut all moralizations out of your novels; you are much too fond of them, and nothing is more boring to read. Try and leave your characters alone, so that they can speak for themselves, instead of always rushing in to tell them what they ought to say, or to explain to the reader what they mean by what they are saying.'

These were sound and encouraging words, but in the end the encouragement was not sufficient to deflect Agatha, who was now twenty-two, from her main focus of getting successfully wed. Thereafter she wrote stories as an occasional pastime, sending a few of them off to magazines at irregular intervals but with no particular success. It was a policy later endorsed by Philpotts, who after reading another stab at a book which he once again praised, sensibly advised her that 'Art is second to life and if you are living just now (we only live by fits and starts) then put art out of your mind absolutely.' He'd sensed quite rightly that she was only pursuing writing in order to fill a temporarily available intellectual and emotional space.

Although life at Ashfield was much restricted by lack of money after her father's death, Agatha's outings in Torquay remained essentially middle-class, with tennis parties, amateur theatricals, roller-skating along the promenade with the doctor's daughters and a surprising amount of vigorous swimming in the sea (segregated beaches, of course). She must have bloomed and gained in confidence since Cairo, though, because she was by no means short of male admirers, and gently deflected three quite serious – and potentially advantageous – offers of marriage. All from men in uniform.

The first, Bolton Fletcher, a Colonel in the 17th Lancers, she met at a house party in Warwickshire. They danced together in fancy dress, and for a few days he showered her with chocolates, books and exotic flowers. But apart from him telling her how in love he was with her, they had nothing to talk about, and although she was charmed by his proposal, she clearly recognized that she was not in love with him, which in her world wasn't good enough. So when he finally sent a telegram with the message, 'Will you marry me, yes or no', she answered 'No', and the courtship ended, to her considerable relief.

The second candidate was Wilfred, a sub-lieutenant in

the Royal Navy, the son of long-term friends of the family. By contrast with Bolton Fletcher's passionate approach, Wilfred's was far more gentle and measured. They shared an interest in books, in walking and in music, and would earnestly discuss all or some of the above while taking long walks in the country. The idea of marriage crept up on the couple as much because both families thought the prospect eminently suitable as through any heartfelt emotion on either side. She liked him well enough, but in a brotherly, companionable way, and his over-developed interest in spiritualism left her cold, especially after she accompanied him on a couple of visits to local mediums. In reality, the prospect of spending her life with him filled her with boredom. So when he phoned one day saying that he had a wonderful opportunity to go to South America to look for Inca treasure, but needed her permission to do so, she told him to go, and prepared a 'Dear John' letter for when he came back.

The third possibility was Reggie Lucy, a Major in the Gunners and the elder brother of three sisters with whom Agatha did a lot of her roller-skating and amateur theatricals. Reggie, a diffident, quiet-spoken man on leave from active service in Hong Kong, had volunteered to take Agatha's virtually non-existent golf technique in hand, and the two of them had spent several happy afternoons ambling around the Torquay course. One day, while sitting under a hedge for a moment's rest out of the sun, Reggie requested that Agatha 'bear him in mind' when it came to getting married. It was an oblique, under-stated proposal completely in keeping with the unselfish, laid back attitude of the proposer, and Reggie was rather taken aback when Agatha instantly said yes. Ten days later he returned to Hong Kong with the couple unofficially engaged and Agatha rather irritated that it all hadn't happened rather quicker so that they could have got married straight away. Reggie, meanwhile, had told her that she wasn't to sit around at home moping, but to continue to lead an active social life as if she was still single. More fool him.

Not having a car, Agatha didn't often get to parties and dances outside the immediate neighbourhood of Ashfield, but occasionally such parties were of a scale that required reinforcements of female dancing partners, especially when a whole mess full of army officers was invited. On these occasions likely girls would be contacted and transport arrangements made for them. It was at one of these larger-scale affairs, in the south Devon town of Chudleigh in 1912, that Agatha Miller – licensed to keep on partying by her betrothed – met Archie Christie.

Archie was a dashing twenty-three-year-old second lieutenant who'd just joined the newly formed Royal Flying Corps stationed nearby, and had been invited to the party as a member of the Exeter garrison. He already knew of Agatha through a mutual friend, and when he'd identified her in the crowded ballroom he must have been pleased with what he saw, because the couple danced several times together and spent most of the evening in conversation. Agatha enjoyed the occasion thoroughly, but for her part she appeared not to give the young man much further thought until ten days later, when he turned up at Ashfield unannounced on a borrowed motorcycle. Agatha was away at a friend's house and she had to be summoned home by Clara to find a rather embarrassed flying officer in the sitting-room, his library of small-talk with potential mothers-in-law long since exhausted.

Archie was smitten, and he was not one to waste time. He came roaring unexpectedly up the Ashfield drive several times in the next couple of weeks, and invited

Agatha out to tea, to the theatre, to concerts and to a New Year's Ball. She was knocked off her feet by the whirlwind approach, and found his eventual proposal, 'You've *got* to marry me,' impossible to resist. Her unofficial engagement to Reggie was thrust aside, unceremoniously by him, and guiltily by her. But even in the thick of the romance, Agatha realized that their mutual attraction was one of opposites, she the timid and accomplished beauty in her impoverished country home and he the impetuous and handsome young airman who'd turned up on a motorcycle to woo her. At bottom they were fundamentally unsuited, although that incompatibility was not to be tested for some years. Archie's flying career meant that most of their engagement was spent at arm's length, communicating romantically by letter. The coming of World War I took him even further away and elevated him to almost superhero status, now in the hugely glamorous RAF. War is a great accelerator of events and the couple were married with some urgency – even Agatha's mother wasn't present – during one of his snatched early home leaves.

It was the war, not the marriage, that had the most immediate impact on Agatha's life, and it was to be another four years before the couple actually lived together. While Archie was posted overseas, and acquitted himself with the bravery suiting a superhero, she remained at home with her mother. As part of the war effort she volunteered for work in the local hospital in Torquay. Here she started at the bottom, as a Volunteer Auxiliary Nurse. The Auxiliaries were either snubbed or enslaved by everyone else in the hospital system, and Agatha had to get used to the fact that young doctors, who hitherto had been her social equals, could and did now treat her as a living towel-rail. Her experiences in coping with wounded young men were not the sort of thing one should talk about in polite society, but she stuck at it, proving a willing worker. After a while, though, she was moved sideways into the dispensary – some biographers suggest as a result of pressure from Archie, who may have felt threatened by the thought of her tending other war heroes than himself. Here she eventually ended up in a position of responsibility and acquired the in-depth knowledge of drugs and poisons which was to serve her well in her future fiction.

Agatha's spell in the hospital was her first experience of the world of work. It was also practically the first time in her life where she'd been put into an environment with a wide variety of people and backgrounds, not all of them well-spoken or well-mannered, and it must have provided a lot of food for thought for a young writer. It was during this time, in the long evenings and weekends of a young wife without her husband, that she constructed her first really successful crime story. She drew the principal weapons of the crime from her new knowledge of pharmacy, and the idea for a detective called Hercule Poirot from a group of Belgian war refugees relocated to the area around Ashfield.

After doing the rounds of several publishers, *The Mysterious Affair at Styles* was eventually published in 1920 by the Bodley Head, although the publisher took advantage of her innocence and never mentioned the subject of up-front payment, only offering her a miserly 10 per cent royalty on sales of over 2,000 copies. Agatha was too delighted over the prospect of publication to query the deal, which was airily extended to cover her next five books, and she industriously set to work to create more.

Archie, meanwhile, had come through the war with distinction and determined to leave the Air Force and start a career in the City to make some serious money. He had, wrote Gillian Gill, one of Agatha's unofficial biographers, 'the soul of a stockbroker in the body of a romantic hero'. Agatha tore herself away from Ashfield and the couple set up home in a flat in London. There they quickly had a daughter, Rosalind. For a while everything went well; Archie's career progressed, and the Bodley Head sold bits and pieces of serializations of Agatha's books, which slowly produced more money.

By 1924 the couple were sufficiently prosperous to consider moving out to a more countrified setting. Agatha wanted a garden for Rosalind, and Archie wanted to pursue his great new interest, golf, so they eventually settled on Sunningdale, because of its famous course and its rail links into the City. It wasn't Agatha's ideal location, but her mother had always warned her never to put herself or her child before the needs of her husband.

At first everything in the garden was rosy. As she wrote in her autobiography, 'I had married the man I loved, we had a child, we had somewhere to live, and as far as I could see there was no reason why we shouldn't live happily ever after.' But it wasn't long before Agatha realized what it meant to be a golf widow, spending Saturdays and Sundays effectively on her own. In Sunningdale she had none of the social contacts that she'd enjoyed in Torquay, and in any case it wasn't acceptable for a married woman to socialize alone. So she immersed herself in her writing, and it is no surprise that this period saw the creation of several new books, encouraged by an ambitious new deal with a different and far less exploitative publisher.

Over the next year or so Agatha and Archie drifted gradually apart. She'd look after Rosalind and write her books, and he'd spend his time in the City, on the train and in the nineteenth hole. His increasing absences may have been in part due to Clara, who was becoming more eccentric as she grew older; she had taken a flat nearby and was frequently in the house, and Archie and she had always eyed each other warily.

The couple's differences came to a head in 1926. This was the year of the publication of *The Murder of Roger Ackroyd*, a major commercial and critical success that truly established Agatha's reputation, and which may have put Archie's nose out of joint. He, after all, was meant to be the breadwinner; he'd been the wartime flying ace, and he'd never wanted his wife to work.

More importantly, 1926 was the year of her mother's sudden death, which Agatha found deeply upsetting. The two women had always been emotionally very close, and had grown even more so since Fred Miller's death. Archie had been away on business in Spain during Clara's last days, and so was not on hand to provide support. When the funeral was over, he suggested that they should both return to Spain so Agatha could relax while he completed his work. Agatha refused; her attention was directed towards grieving for her mother and sorting out Ashfield – which Clara had left to her – rather than working on her relationship with her husband. It was a focus which she later said she regretted, because that might have been the last opportunity to save their marriage.

After the funeral Agatha spent some weeks down in Torquay, alone, trying to sort out the family possessions and probably going through some sort of emotional breakdown. The house – for so many years her shrine, her home, her security – was in a bad state, with holes in the roof and damp on the walls, and crammed with the debris of decades of family life. She had to steel herself to consign all the memorabilia of a happy childhood to the bin, which must have been both distressing and depressing. Archie meanwhile refused to come down at weekends because he'd miss his golf, and when they finally met up again after some weeks, it was as strangers. On the telephone they'd talked of heading off to Italy for a much-needed two-week holiday, but when they actually met Archie was plainly uneasy. When Agatha pressed him, fearing something had gone wrong at work, he confessed he'd made no arrangements for their holiday. On the contrary, he wanted a divorce; he'd met a woman called Nancy Neele on the golf course, and they'd fallen in love and wanted to marry.

Agatha's first instinct was to blame herself, believing that she must have been in some way inadequate to fill Archie's life. She may have been rapidly becoming a household name for her writing but she still didn't see her books as anything other than a well-paid pastime. In her scale of things – it was something her mother had drummed into her – the relationship with her husband was far more important than anything else in the world, and now she regretted not having devoted all her attention to keeping him. 'If I had been cleverer; if I had known more about my husband – instead of being content to idealize him and consider him more or less perfect – then perhaps I might have avoided all this,' she was later to write in her autobiography. She begged him to reconsider, but she recorded his response as, 'I can't stand not having what I want, and I can't stand not being happy.'

After months of grieving for her mother, this was too much to bear. Rejection by her husband plunged her into a pit of despair, and the next few months were to play host to the most famous episode in her life.

On my second morning in Trieste I had an appointment with the Joycean-sounding Franco Gobbis, male secretary to the female chairperson of the port authority. Franco was a little tugboat of a man, a cheery puffer with a big round head which gleamed faintly with perspiration, even when it wasn't particularly hot. It turned out he'd read a lot of Agathas, and was quite an enthusiast.

'Those ten days when she went missing, eh, quite a mystery, eh. We'll never know,' he said, shaking his head in wonder. He preceded me into the high-ceilinged, parquet-floored antechamber of the port authority offices where he and his two colleagues sat, among display cases of old port equipment, ready to be summoned into chairperson Professoressa Caroli's office. La Caroli was absent at some conference or other, but from a previous telephone conversation with her I'd got the impression that she was rather a feisty lady; you'd have to be, to rise through the ranks to such a senior post in a man's world. I also got the impression that her three gentlemen-in-waiting rather enjoyed the days when Professoressa Caroli's buzzer fell silent, and didn't haul them into the darkened inner sanctum to receive further instructions.

At last Trieste looked like a functioning port. Outside the office windows, a giant white wardrobe of a Greek ferry was performing a slow turn off her berth; the gaunt, rusty dry dock was preparing to take on a coaster; the container quay was covered in coloured rectangles awaiting collection, and a roll-on, roll-off ship branded UND in giant white letters was smoking thoughtfully in preparation for departure.

'Where's that one going?'

'Istanbul. Every day,' said Franco.

Istanbul . . . so I could still take the watery route, albeit without the fine dining and the deckchair socializing. For a fleeting moment it was tempting, but I'd miss out so much on the land.

'Where else could I go from here?'

The three men consulted, nodding their gleaming domes at each other and ticking shipping companies off on their fingers. 'Greece. Turkey. Croatia. Albania . . .'

'Yes, I noticed some Albanian lorries.'

'Oh, we have a lot of problems with those Albanian ships,' sighed Franco. 'Stowaways, drugs, lots of problems. Big problems.'

'So how important is Trieste, among Italian ports?'

The three men consulted again. They were in no hurry to make any extravagant claim. 'We think we're number eight,' said Franco, finally.

We talked for a while of the glory days, when Trieste was the major port for the Eastern Mediterranean and the Suez Canal, and its fixtures and fittings were state of the art. Would there be any passenger lists, I asked, that might record Agatha's passing? The ever-obliging Franco, glad for the diversion from the normal routine, put in a call to someone he knew at Lloyd Triestino, but the news was not good. The company's archives had apparently not been considered sufficiently important by the Taiwanese to be worth keeping.

To make up for this disappointment the three men produced a set of plans of the old port, which had been constructed during the Golden Age to make the most of Trieste's Suez connection. The quays were now almost completely disused, but still very much complete, a whole slice of walled-off waterfront dating from the 1870s.

'Professoressa Caroli is planning a new purpose,' explained Franco, but when I asked what she had in mind, he shrugged. Either it had not yet been decided, or the news hadn't been released from the inner sanctum. It was to be Prof Caroli's surprise.

'Can I go there?'

The gang of three nodded vigorously, pleased to be able to grant me a permission that was in their power. They summoned a security man in his patrol van, issued excited instructions, and then we all shook each other's hands in relief that the encounter had ended to everyone's satisfaction.

It took me an hour to walk through the parade ground of silent warehouses of the old Habsburg port. Construction had started in 1868, a year before the opening of the Suez Canal, on the orders of the Austro-Hungarian parliament. The first batch of a total of thirty-five brick-built warehouses was operational twenty years later, and the contractors had still been completing the last of them in 1900 when Vienna pulled the plug on the whole project. Realizing that the existing structures were rapidly becoming superseded by the increasing size of ships and changes in port-handling techniques, they'd decided to build the new facility south of the city centre. If Trieste wanted to stay competitive, it needed to move with the times. The old port's structures had been built only with sacks and manpower in mind.

Most of the warehouses were four storeys high, in a uniform architectural style. The top floors were lined with banks of motionless cranes, giraffes in silhouette, and each floor below had a gallery of sectional steel railings which slid apart to allow loads to be hauled up and swung into individual storehouses. Those batteries of warehouses were carefully lined up behind four basins and four piers, and they no doubt had functioned excellently well in their brief moment of glory. Railway tracks ran through the cobbles between each block, and although most of it was rusted and weeded over, there was still a chuntering lonely yellow diesel shoving trucks around, like a truculent boy kicking a can.

The security man had driven me to the farthest point, dropping me off by a building housing the boilers which had provided the steam for all those cranes. The boilers' mouths stood open, like greedy fledglings in their nest, but they'd never again be fed. A charivari of shipping bits and pieces lay all around; an anchor, a giant propeller, and an old stevedores' tavern completely swallowed up in excrescences of ivy.

There was something a bit *Marie Celeste* about this abandoned city. It was hard to envisage what Professoressa Caroli could have in mind for all that bricks and mortar; you could parachute a Disneyland in here, and still have room for a university. In another place the warehouses might have made wonderful loft apartments, complete with Adriatic view, but Trieste was short of people, not accommodation.

Most of the warehouses were secured with padlocks whose keys had long since been lost, but the names of the stevedoring companies looked fresh enough. There were even faded chalked messages on some of the doors. The only block still in use was number 22, whose ground floor had been converted into pens for livestock trans-shipments. It smelled strongly of farmyards, but all the straw-lined enclosures were empty, barring a couple of donkeys standing completely motionless in one of the darker corners. Who, I wondered, was so interested in a pair of donkeys that they hauled them across the world via Trieste? Perhaps they were in quarantine? Or perhaps they were refugee donkeys whose application for asylum had been refused? Condemned to remain, stateless, in Trieste's purposeless port.

On the water itself the first basin was completely empty,

and so also was the second, but the third had a fleet of tugboats huddled in a corner, like cows nuzzling up to a wall against a prevailing wind, even though it was a completely calm, beatific day. In the basin beyond that was a rusty old Greek-flagged ferry unloading Albanian lorries, surrounded by dereliction and watched by idle groups of men who could have been customs officers out of uniform or could equally well have been stowaways enjoying their first taste of foreign soil. Either way, I walked through this little scene without being accosted by anyone, and eventually made my exit through the main gate back out into downtown Trieste without even being hailed by the policeman on gate duty. Given what Signor Gobbis had said about smuggling and stowaways, I was quite surprised at being left to walk through and away. Either security was not nearly as tight as it should have been, or I plainly didn't look like an Albanian.

Believing (incorrectly, as it turned out) that this would be the last time I'd see the sea before Istanbul, I took my time over leaving Trieste. It may be a city without headline interest, but I grew to like the matter-of-fact way it went about its business, reconciled with its diminished self. After the first day I ignored the polished and pretentious Caffè delli Specchi and took my caffeine in the Torrefazione instead, a coffee shop with a zinc-topped bar and the ambience of a betting shop where you downed your espressos standing up. It felt more real.

There were a few diversions. One afternoon I took the ferry across to Muggia, a small fishing port on the very last promontory in Italy, a short stride across the water. From the café I watched a man with a wheelbarrow cross the village square, and he watched me; we were each other's entertainment that day. The next morning I took the 100-year-old Austrian-built tram up into the hills towards Vila Opicina, which is effectively the frontier town with Slovenia. It leaves the city streets with some ceremony under the control of a uniformed driver, but once out of sight round the corner the old car drops back on to the buffers of a much newer electric locomotive, which then pushes the whole thing to the top.

The evenings I spent out on the Molo Audace, along with the lovers, the displaced Slavs and the dressed-up dignitaries who brought their guests out here for a breath of air before the opera. Around us, sinewy veterans from the Cannottieri Adria rowing club slipped past on proprietory sculling expeditions around the port before dinner, their boats moving along beneath them like semi-submerged propelling pencils.

The lack of shipping meant the water beside the Molo was clear and calm, thick with gorgeous custard-yellow jellyfish with purple-edged petticoats and long frilly camiknickers.

'Don't you think they're pretty?' I overheard one old Austrian lady say, peering into the water. 'Look at that one. It looks . . . it looks . . .'

'That's not pretty,' interrupted her companion, sternly. 'It looks like a penis.'

At sunset the Molo was the place to initiate courtships. You started from the landward end as just good friends. By the time you'd got half-way along you'd managed to insinuate an arm around her waist, and half an hour spent at the seaward tip was enough to put the result beyond doubt. As the sun dipped so did the lovers come closer together – closer, that is, until separated by the jealous twittering of their mobile phones, whose screens flickered on and off like fireflies in the dusk. Meanwhile the generous Molo pumped the heat that it had been absorbing all day back out into the rapidly cooling air, throwing an invisible blanket around all who cared to linger.

Day and night, rain or shine, the wharf pointed its unwavering middle finger into the Adriatic. It provided Triestinos with a moment of thinking space, neither properly on the sea nor properly on the land, but right in the middle of their city. Just as they were neither part of Italy, nor part of the Balkans, but right on the belly-button of the Mediterranean.

REPUBLIC OF VEGETABLE PATCHES

The Drava, when it drew into Trieste, turned out to be the ramshackle railway equivalent of Noah's Ark, with two coaches from every country it was destined for; light and dark blue for Hungary, orange and yellow for Serbia, and a rather insipid blue and white for Slovenia and Croatia. Inside, though, it was clear nobody believed the Noah story any more, for the Drava was practically empty, a forgotten train made up of forgotten rolling stock sprung like old iron bedsteads. The Slovenian coach was occupied by a handful of male passengers staring at their boots and picking their noses with the demeanour of schoolboys being sent to see the headmaster. A policeman in the corridor checked my passport, and when I asked whether any of the other coaches were any more comfortable, he shook his head. 'Railway companies never send their good ones into Serbia. They never get them back.'

A similar argument had been used by Wagons-Lits in the 1950s and 1960s, when they stopped sending the better Simplon-Orient Express rolling stock into the communist Balkans.

The Drava departed Trieste in the direction from which it came, before performing a giant doodle up on to the back of the limestone Carso, like a rider climbing carefully up on to his horse. At Vila Opicina Italian customs men came through, sniffing like bloodhounds. In the goods yard the big-chinned, macho Italian locomotive was replaced by its angular, thoughtful, beetle-browed Slovenian equivalent. It was the colour of dusty crème caramel, a colour which lifestyle programmers have been laughing at for years, and which failed dismally to co-ordinate with anything the locomotive could have pulled except rusty freight vans. It looked worried, this loco-motive; would its performance be OK? Did it fill in its timesheets? If it ditched its colour, would it become fashionable again? Eventually it summoned up sufficient concentration to haul the train a pensive three or four miles through thick woodland of black pine, hornbeam and dwarf oak to Sezana, where once again it stopped for a long think. This time it was Slovenian customs' turn to have a good look at the losers who still chose to travel by train.

Eventually we were on our way again, having com-pleted in eighty minutes what the feeblest of crows could have done in ten, and I was beginning to understand why the original Orient Express hadn't survived. Borders are far, far quicker by car.

Hills are too. The introspective locomotive was doing its best, but the forested karst had now sensed its rider's vulnerability, and it started to buck like a mustang.

The karst is where the Mediterranean and Central European ecosystems meet. It is an inaccessible landscape of heavily eroded porous limestone, where even the rivers find it easier to stay underground. A paradise for sparrow-hawks, horn-nosed vipers, and blind lizards which dwell in the complex cave systems, it is not an easy place for man to move around. Huge numbers of soldiers were killed here during World War I, in two years of attritional trench warfare between the Italians and the Austrians. For many decades thereafter the karst was the natural barrier between the communism of Eastern Europe and the democracy of the West. Now it was making it plain that the railway was unwelcome, hauling it this way and that like an angler playing a fish.

Occasionally we got a glimpse of a pleasant, cultivated valley with a suggestion of vineyards, and a fortified hamlet dribbled like red beans into a furrow in the hills. Probably there'd be an *osmizza* or two, a tavern where farmers sold the wine they produced themselves. But just as soon as it appeared in one window it disappeared in the next, and the line was hoicked away into territory where only the resolute survived. 'You really want to get there?' it seemed to say. 'Then you really have to earn it.'

I found the restaurant car in the Hungarian part of the train. It was upholstered in streaks of beige and brown with insipid grey curtains pinned to the walls, but each of the empty tables was covered with a carefully laundered white tablecloth. Unfortunately this brave attempt at starched whites was ruined by the polarized window glass, blotched on the outside with mud; the light filtering through those windows transformed the immaculate white tablecloths to a dirty grey pebbledash.

The restaurant was presided over by a Hungarian with a shock of black hair and sad eyes. A tragedian, for sure. He was deep in negotiation with a couple of olive-skinned young men when I arrived, but they departed almost immediately, commenting loudly, in a mix of English and German, 'Yes, when we come back we will have an omelette.' Oh yes, and I bet there are no bananas.

The glum Hungarian brought me a thick, strong coffee. It was instant, but with added earth.

'No customers?' I asked.

'No, nobody has any money.'

I got out my books and boned up on how the karst, which covers 44 per cent of Slovenia, had offered refuge for the Yugoslav resistance in World War II. Holed up in the limestone caves, they had vexed the Germans to such an extent that the latter created a special Karstwehr force, trained to cope with the terrain. Yugoslavia may have been quick to fall as a whole, but the underground resistance tied up so many troops and so frustrated Hitler that he ordered 100 local civilians to be executed in retaliation for every German soldier killed. But despite this huge price in wasted lives the Partisans achieved heroic status in local eyes. It was their status as defenders of the nation, as much as their communist ideology, which won them so much national support in the elections that followed the war. Their leader was one Josip Broz, otherwise known as Tito.

At this point in my reading the train tackled a tunnel, but the beetle-browed driver hadn't remembered to turn on the beetle-browed lights. Total darkness was followed swiftly by a huge crash alarmingly close at hand. It could so easily have been an act of Partisan sabotage, but the return of daylight revealed the glum Hungarian struggling to right a supermarket trolley full of beer bottles he was just taking for a walk.

Nearing Ljubljana we finally stepped down off the karst into far more gentle, populous countryside, where every house had its carefully tended vegetable patch, and everything was neat, orderly and uneventful. The loco-motive seemed to have resolved its anxieties, the limestone barrier had been surmounted and the extrovert unruliness of Italy had been replaced by the introvert orderliness that resulted from 1,200 years of Germanic rule. This was Slovenia, the country that spent its childhood under the Holy Romans, was schooled by the Austro-Hungarians, and graduated into the grand communist enterprise called Yugoslavia. It is now the Switzerland of the Balkans.

Ljubljana is a pleasant, pocket-sized little city, in a pleasant, pocket-sized little land. The river Ljubljanica threads right through the cobbled centre, a lurid green ribbon perpetually bandaged by little bridges. At its heart the city is reminiscent of Salzburg: cobbled, tea-shoppy, with flurries of art nouveau and overlooked by a castle on an outcrop of rock. Most of its grandeur – all that street furniture of pillars, obelisks and pyramids – is the work of one man, Jože Plečnik, who studied in Prague. For two decades in the early twentieth century Plečnik was given a free hand in dressing up a country town to make it look like a capital.

Plečnik's endeavours notwithstanding, this still doesn't feel like a place where serious money-making takes place, even though the Slovenian economy has hugely out-stripped the other states that once belonged to the Yugoslav federation. On weekday evenings the crowds thronging the centre are young, slightly intense, jeans-wearing, guitar-strumming, bicycle-pushing students. There's something a bit hippy and sleepy about them, their language sounds sippy and slurpy to the untrained ear, and they don't seem to care over-much about their appearance. Physiognomies are blunter here than they are over in Italy, as if the wave of limestone has washed over the genetic make-up of the southern European and smudged all its finer features. It's a case of too much nose, not enough chin, legs too thin and way too much crimson in the hair.

I was in Slovenia for a close encounter. If I'd been Poirot, my moustaches would have been twitching with the anticipation of nearing my quarry, and I was encouraged by a good omen in the weekly street market. Among the portraits of Tito and the Partisan rifles was a whole box full of Agatha hardbacks, in Slovenian, next to a framed painting of Jesus Christ.

'Oh yes,' said the stallholder. 'Everyone here reads Agatha Christie.'

It was one of those fans, a student called Mateja Skoda, who had given me the low-down on Agatha's visit to Slovenia. I'd no idea whether Mateja was one of the jeans-wearing crimson-haired, because I only knew her through her Agatha Christie website. In its pages I'd read how Agatha came to Slovenia's Lake Bohinj, hoping for a little privacy on a holiday in the sun, in 1967. Nearly forty years after first setting out on the Simplon-Orient Express.

This was to be the first time my journey overlapped with Agatha in what she herself designated her 'Second Spring', the second half of her life, so it was effectively an encounter between the front end of my narrative and the back end of hers. She'd lived an awful lot of life in those forty years, and a lot of it still lay ahead of me further down the tracks, but by the time she returned to Slovenia on holiday her story was nearing its end. She was in her late seventies, had written eighty-seven of her 105 books, and had been translated into 112 languages. According to UNESCO that ranked her second in the world after the Bible (171 languages) and ahead of Shakespeare.

She had also been married for thirty-seven years to her second husband. The 'Max' I'd first heard mentioned in Aleppo had turned out to be neither a vintage car nor a faithful dog, but an archaeologist called Max Mallowan whom she had met at Ur. It was that chance meeting which had completely altered the complexion of her life, and for thirty years thereafter the couple had spent every winter in the deserts of either Syria or Iraq. It was an unlikely transformation for the doyenne of vicarage and village green fiction. The woman who had been the golf widow of Sunningdale in her thirties was still sleeping in tents in Arab and Kurdish wildernesses at the age of seventy. A few years before coming to Bohinj she'd also made a 3,000-mile journey through the Khyber Pass to Bombay, a particularly vigorous enterprise for anyone, let alone a septuagenarian.

By the time they'd come to Slovenia, however, the couple had drawn in their horns. Even Max, thirteen years younger than Agatha, was in every appearance the distinguished elderly professor, and about to be knighted for his services to archaeology. They were meant to be travelling incognito; Agatha had a deep-rooted distrust of the press dating back to her break-up with Archie, so the couple used their married names of Mr and Mrs Mallowan. But in those days she was famous even in Slovenia and it wasn't long before she was recognized and pursued by journalists. I'd read a couple of the resultant interviews on Mateja's website.

I'd e-mailed Mateja just before I left home, suggesting that we meet up to talk about Agatha over a coffee, but the poor girl got cold feet. 'Due to some personal reasons I am unable to accept your invitation,' she'd e-mailed back. 'In any case I am not as interested in Agatha Christie as I used to be.' I don't blame her. For all she knew I could have been a Net lurker, using Agatha-lust as an excuse. It would have been good to meet an example of the new generation of reader, but in the meantime her website had helped net me a bigger fish in the shape of

Janez Cuček, one of those pursuing journalists whose interviews I'd read.

I'd arranged to meet Mr Cuček in the Pen Club, the restaurant on the top floor of the Slovenian Writers' Association. From the villa's location in the leafy, prestigious area of town between the opera house and the American Embassy it was clear that writers were ranked with ambassadors hereabouts. In the downstairs rooms groups of earnest-looking people waggled their heads pensively over putative festival programmes, before retiring upstairs to the restaurant balcony for *kraški pršut* (air-dried Karst ham) washed down with a few glasses of Laški Riesling . . . which makes *kraški pršut* one hell of a lot easier to say.

Janez turned out to be a tall, lean sixty-six-year-old who spoke English wonderfully well and was very curious as to why he'd been summoned out of retirement.

'How on earth did you track me down?'

As we settled on the Pen Club balcony I pulled out a printout from Mateja's site, headlined 'Bohinj is too beautiful for a murder'. He scanned it, his eyebrows climbing into his bald patch.

'It is my headline, and my name is here,' he said. 'But this is not my article.'

Over a bottle of Cvicek, a light red from the southern Dolenjska valley, he told the story.

'I'd only been working as a reporter for a couple of years when the news came through that she'd arrived. She'd said no journalists, no interviews, which was probably why the editor chose me. You know, young, keen, do anything. I caught the next train up to Bohinj, speed-reading *Murder on the Orient Express* on the way. I'd never read anything of hers before, you see.

'The couple had chosen a hotel away from the road up

in the trees, presumably for more privacy, but when I arrived there were already a couple of other journalists sniffing around. So I just pretended to be a normal customer and persuaded the receptionist to give me the room next door to hers. You have to remember that those places had no experience of celebrity visitors in those days. Then I bought some flowers, and when I could hear through the wall that they were in their room, I simply stepped across from my balcony to theirs.'

'I bet they were pleased.'

'*He* was very cross. Very cross. You know, this cross.' Janez opened his eyes wide and held his breath until the blood vessels stood out on his temples. 'But she was cool,' he continued, exhaling. 'He wanted to call the police, but I presented her with the flowers, and she said I could stay and that she would answer a few questions. He still wanted to call the police.'

'So what did you talk about?'

'It was polite stuff, really, and I don't remember any detail. About her books, how she got her inspiration, that sort of thing. She asked me the names of some of the mountains, so I asked her whether she was going to use Bohinj as a setting in a book, and she said that line about it being too beautiful for murder. Oh yes, and I remember her saying something about not seeing herself as a great artist. She'd never wanted to be famous, she said. She'd always wanted to be just an ordinary person. And she didn't generally like journalists. I think she'd had a very bad experience.'

I murmured something in agreement. It was fair to say that she had.

Our glasses were refilled, and Janez ran his eye down the printout I gave him. 'The rest of the article was basically about what the Mallowans did while they were there, which wasn't much,' he said. 'They hired a car, which was virtually unheard of in those days, and it had to be a French one, I remember that. I suppose because of the war, they didn't want German. The driver told me that they always went to the same place, some caves I think, and he'd had to wait around for hours, but I don't think he was complaining.'

He placed the printout back on the table.

'It was quite a scoop at the time. Good for my career.'

A small crowd of opera-goers passed by under the balcony. 'This country seems to hold writers in great esteem,' I said.

'Completely. There's a film on here at the moment about Virginia Woolf – British one I think – and more people will go to see that than will go to anything starring Sylvester Stallone.'

We ordered goose liver and truffles, and conversation moved away from Agatha.

Janez's career had progressed from newspapers to television news, and he'd spent many years in the select press corps which followed President Tito around the world.

'The Non-Aligned Movement was wonderful for me. All those conferences, wonderful. I felt so privileged. I remember having an affair with a diplomat's daughter on a trip to Brazil. When I asked her why she chose me, she said it was because she wanted to experience love with someone old. Old! I mean, I was only in my thirties!'

'And Tito? How was he?'

Janez shrugged. 'He was not corrupt, and his Yugoslavia was a good idea in its time. You have to know some of the history of what went before to realize what it meant to us. Slovenia, Croatia, Serbia, Bosnia, Montenegro – we'd had hundreds of years of being bullied around by Turks, Austrians and Hungarians as parts of their empires. Yugoslavia literally means the "kingdom of the south Slavs". It made sense for us to club together; we all speak the same language, have the same origins, live in the same region. I mean, there are only two million of us here in Slovenia. What chance had we of going it alone?'

Originally the southern Slav nations had combined for the sake of self-defence against bigger external forces. Then they had committed to that combination because it was a noble idea. And finally they'd stuck with it because of the personality of Tito and the refreshing peace that came with communism. It was only when Tito died and communism faded that the individual nations started to look more closely at each other and realize they were conjoined with marriage partners with whom they were fundamentally unsuited. Unfortunately, by that time they were all living in each other's houses.

The mention of houses took Janez off on another tangent.

'When I built mine, the others all around me were being built by normal, working people. I suppose the very able Slovenes probably got frustrated and left, but in those days ordinary people had opportunities they'd never be able to afford today. It was a successful form of communism, the Yugoslavian one. We could travel. Lots of foreigners came here on holiday. The economy was healthy. We had liberty.'

'And could you write what you wanted, without censorship?'

'Not Tito, the army or the Non-Aligned Movement. They were sacrosanct. Everything else, you could say. When I was still on the newspaper I wrote an article which accused a hero of the Partisan movement of pocketing money intended for a housing project, and the man himself turned up in the newspaper office the next day waving a pistol and demanding to see me. My editor told him I'd gone away. Anyway, it went to court – and the hero lost. I think he thought his status put him above the law.'

I asked him what he thought had subsequently gone wrong.

'In the end the differences between the peoples – Slovenes, Serbs, Croats, Muslims – proved too deep. When we didn't have any outside force opposing us, or any strong internal leadership to bind us together, it all fell apart.'

Slovenia had gone first. As a fundamentally prosperous, hardworking nation it was tired of supporting the poorer regions of Yugoslavia. Communism had never come naturally to it. On 25 June 1991, eleven years after the death of Tito and two years after the fall of the Berlin Wall, the tiny state had declared its independence. It was a bold, insolent move, and it greatly offended those who were committed to the idea of Slav togetherness – i.e. Serbia. There was a brief stand-off while the Serb-dominated Yugoslav army rolled in across the border, but threats of immediate sanctions from the European Union made Serbian President Slobodan Milosevic think twice, and anyway he was faced with a far more difficult problem at home, because the much larger Croatia was also declaring independence at the same time. There were Croats in the Yugoslav army, and to have fought a war in Slovenia would have necessitated maintaining supply lines across Croatia. The ramifications were too risky, so Slovenia was left to go its own way in peace. In this way the small, powerful tugboat had disconnected itself early enough to be well clear of serious danger once the Yugo mother ship started to founder on the rocks.

'Some crazy stuff has gone on, but the Serbs were never

our enemies,' Janez added, suddenly watery-eyed as he recalled friends and former colleagues in Serbia whom he was unlikely ever to see again, and whom he knew to be struggling to make ends meet. Their careers had been brought to a sudden and premature end by politics.

'These last few years we've moved a long way away from the others. Our news programmes are full of Bush and Blair, not Milosevic. We don't look that way any more, we've moved on. Our per capita income is ten times higher than Croatia's, so now we're joining the EU.

'It's another mother ship,' he concluded, wistfully. 'But we've got no choice, have we?'

The following day I set out for Bohinj myself, on a daily four-country express which had started in Croatia and was heading for Germany via Austria. It may only have been three coaches long, but it was smooth, efficient and comfortable, and in a totally different league to the manky old Drava. It only needed to breathe out and it had reached Jesenice, just before the Austrian border. There I changed on to a little two-coach number pulled by a long-snouted diesel, and we set off for a scenic trundle through the southern slopes of the Alps.

In Slovenia everyone has a foot in the countryside. On Friday afternoon Ljubljana empties like a gurgling jug, standing empty most of the weekend until the taps begin to flow again on Sunday afternoon. As a result this little train was full of students returning home for the weekend, the air rank with the smell of dirty washing emanating from their rucksacks.

The passengers on this route used to be much, much grander. The line was originally specially constructed by the Imperial Court in Vienna to provide easy access to the lakes at Bled and Bohinj, exclusive holiday resorts for the royals, and to the distant vineyards at Gorizia. *En route* the line carved through forty-three tunnels, criss-crossed tumbling rivers and ran through orchards and alpine meadows where drying racks were hung with scythe-cut hay, stopping at every station on the way. Every house in these valleys had a woodpile, a couple of apple trees and the obligatory vegetable patch. Every butter-coloured village was full of chickens, and every landscape had a perched onion-domed church, a cluster of brightly-painted beehives and a granny struggling uphill with a zinc bucket to find her cow. It was far more intimate, and far prettier, than anything I'd seen out of the windows of the Orient Express.

I'd expected Bohinj to have changed enormously since 1967, but clearly it had hardly changed at all. The lake was cupped in a timelessly beautiful glacial valley, surrounded by a ring of peaks that would soon be covered in snow. Contrary to accepted practice in all other countries with Alpine lakes, there were no hotels whatsoever on the lake shore. The Bellevue, where Agatha and Max had stayed, was still in operation in its secluded spot up among the trees. Built out of dark wood in the shape of a giant A, it was sombre, quiet and smelled of old soggy biscuits. Its principal decorative features were framed tourist-board posters showing exactly the same view as you could see through the windows, which seemed rather pointless. Perhaps they were helpful on foggy days.

The Bellevue may have been the exclusive address in its time, but in the years since then it had become deeply, deeply out of fashion, and only three rooms in the entire hotel were let. It was the sort of place which, if you were under sixty and in any remote way metropolitan or sophisticated, would fill you with horror. Meanwhile over-sixties who were careful with their money would probably see its good points.

The hotel management had tried to capitalize on the Agatha connection by redecorating room 204 with older furniture, a valve radio and a dismal picture of the author at a very advanced age, very thin (Agatha had been overweight for most of her life), and therefore probably near death. There were more flattering pictures of her in the library downstairs, along with a cabinet containing some of her books, and a more interesting set of photographs recording the visit to Bohinj of 'Prince Haile Selassie'. The Prince had turned out to be a local lad who'd dressed up and blacked his face with polish, fooled all the insignia-wearing dignitaries and been treated to a right royal buffet at the Bellevue, where his dancing style finally gave him away. It was hard to be critical of the locals' credibility; this boot-polished buffoon was probably the first 'black' man the area had ever seen.

My set dinner was chicken in breadcrumbs with a garnish (lovely word, garnish) on the side. It was served on lime-green tablecloths in the empty dining-room, where a radio behind the bar had been switched on to fill the silence. As I rearranged the garnish, and then arranged it again, I decided that the lake itself may have been too beautiful for murder, but the hotel had distinct scene-of-crime possibilities. It was the sort of place which might have been chosen, as a backwater, by someone with a history to conceal who didn't want to be recognized. A fatal mistake, because backwaters are far too full of people who know each other very well. It makes a stranger more noticeable, not less so.

I pottered around the lake for a couple of days, enjoying its peace and clarity, and the sight of scores of small, sipping trout in the shallows. My furthest expedition was up to Slap Savica, a giant waterfall which erupted from a hole mid-way down a huge cliff, creating its own little vortex of wind and mist. This was the beginning of the Sava river, and in the course of the next couple of weeks I was to follow it from its birth at Slap Savica to where it finally buried itself in the Danube, in Belgrade.

Back at the Bellevue I'd spend my evenings on the balcony of what had once been Max and Agatha's room, where Janez Cuček had done his imitation of the man from Milk Tray. From here the view was divided into three, with the lake below, the mountains filling the middle space and the sky above. Once the daylight had departed, these three elements were powerful, silent bands of different intensities of grey – the sheet of water, the face of rock, the tent of sky, and an occasional car headlight nosing its way tentatively through the valley bottom. In the cooling evening the hotel's wooden framework shifted and groaned like an old dog curling up in its basket. Someone moving on the other side of the building caused a board to spring and a floor to quiver, and indistinct voices ran in crotchets along the beams.

I felt a gust of sympathy for the Bellevue, the sort of sympathy you might feel for a family pet on its last journey to the vet. I was glad to have caught it before it went. It was clean and honest, but too far gone for modern living. I was pretty sure it wouldn't survive.

Lakes Bohinj and Bled were put on the map for the discerning general public back in the 1860s by a Swiss water healer called Arnold Rikli. Rikli prescribed boots-only hiking in the mountains and *badehose*-less bathing in the lake, although for much of the year this was probably less scandalous than it might sound, because the water was cold enough to make the sexes virtually indistinguishable.

There's not a lot more to do at Bohinj today than there was back then. Bled, however, has moved on, with an eye to what the outside world might want from it. The lake is much more chocolate-box picturesque than Bohinj. It is surrounded by deciduous trees and overlooked by an eleventh-century castle standing on a bluff of limestone. At its centre is a church-crowned island popular for upmarket weddings.

Most of Bled's lake boats are *pletna*, a local design which is sculled from the rear by the descendants of twenty poor local families who were originally granted their licences by the Viennese court. No motorized boats are allowed on the lake surface, and there's the same purity of water and clarity of silence here as there is at Bohinj, with the slap of swan's wings and the tolling of church bells, and pike hanging in the watery shadows like dead branches. Behind this unchanged shop window, however, you can gamble, play golf, and eat and drink well, so the tradition of the place as a retreat for the great and the good has been to some extent revived. Particularly at one of Tito's former residences.

I arrived in Vila Bled in the wake of Hollywood actors Jeff Bridges and William Hurt, the latest in a long line of important guests to stay in what was once a presidential palace and is now a luxury hotel. The Vila is a monumental summer house built by Marshall Tito in brutalist style out of the same white marble from the Dalmatian island of Brac as was used for the White House in Washington. It was originally intended as a guest house to impress Tito's ideologically sympathetic visitors, such as Khrushchev, Nehru, Indira Gandhi, Nasser, Bokassa and Kim Il Sung.

The Vila has a lot of history. Its location, set back a bit from the water's edge (even Marshall Tito respected the public right to walk all around the lake) was the site of an earlier mansion built by an Austrian noble called Duke

Ernest Windischgratz. When the Duke no longer felt welcome in the new between-the-wars kingdom of the Serbs, Croats and Slovenes, he sold it to King Alexander Karageorge, one of whose sons was born here. Then, when the Karageorges fled the country at the beginning of World War II, the site was earmarked for a new palace by the Germans, but Tito's Partisans never left them alone for long enough to get started, and ultimately it was re-developed by Tito himself in 1947. So Vila Bled has tasted everything on its thirteen-acre plot: Austrian imperialism, Slav nationalism, Nazi occupation, Yugo communism, and now the new Slovenia, embracing capitalism and about to embrace the European Union with mixed emotions.

Most of the Vila's fixtures and fittings were originally ordered in the 1950s and 1960s by Tito himself. Ironically, their rather understated, functional, minimalist style is now deeply fashionable in modern designer hotels, so by sticking to its guns, unwaveringly maintaining its clean and uncluttered look from the 1950s, the Vila Bled has become trendy. Now Hollywood stars sit in the same seats that once supported communist dictators.

For nineteen years – in other words for most of its career as a luxury hotel – the Vila has been managed by Janez Fajfar, a colourful, unconventional Slovene with a chubby, gleaming moon face anchored by a little beard, like a magnetic pole. A local man, he still lives simply, in a house he shares with his brother ('He grows the vege-tables, I grow the flowers'), and is unashamedly nationalistic.

'When we were still part of Yugoslavia,' he said as he took me around the hotel, 'I used to have pompous Serbian guests who'd sit on the terrace here and say, with a sigh, how beautiful *their* country was. That really irritated me; this wasn't their country, it's ours.' He harrumphed. 'My grandmother ran a *pensione* in Bled during the early part of the twentieth century, when we had Austrian Emperors then Slav Kings and then Nazi Germans in quick succession. She used to say, "They come, they go, we stay".'

Janez wanted to show me a fresco that Tito had commissioned for the Vila's meeting room, but a visiting group of screenwriters had locked the room while they had their lunch. Typical writer paranoia.

'It's a picture of the liberation of Yugoslavia, and it was done by a local church painter,' he explained, momentarily flustered. 'But the painter had the last laugh. If you look at the feet of the female figure which represents the Yugoslav army, you can see she's wearing Serbian shoes.' I couldn't personally see why that amounted to the last laugh, but for him, this was a vitally important detail. It showed that, even when Slovenia was supposedly a happy part of greater Yugoslavia, the Slovenes were still careful to mark the distinction between nations, especially when it came to anything militaristic.

'So what was it like when Serbia was effectively in charge?' I wanted to see how deep his distrust of everything Serb actually went.

Janez needed no prodding. 'Front is everything. They have to look cool. And they have to have a good time. You go to Belgrade on business and you get plied with food and drink until you sign a piece of paper, and you only realize what you've done when you get home. If that doesn't work, they'll use a Serbian woman' – here he whistles – 'and they really are very good in bed. They're obsessed by sex. Even in their conversation, they use the names of sexual organs instead of punctuation. You know what Serbs say when they *really* want to insult you? "I fuck your mice" – it means "I fuck everyone in your house from the mice upwards."

'You know,' he continued, 'they're all bosses, the Serbs, everyone is the best. Their mothers tell them they're the bravest, handsomest, cleverest, so of course they never do any work; that's for people who are not brave, handsome and clever. They're like mayflies. A brief glorious period in full plumage, have sex, then die. When they're young, they rely on their parents to keep them, and when the parents get old and can't work, then they're all poor, and they look for someone to blame.'

'Isn't that something Slobodan Milosevic was quoted as saying? "If we're not much good at working, at least we know how to fight"?'

'Sounds like him. You remember the story of that sniper – where was it, Srebrenica? When he was asked why he did it, why he killed all those civilians, he said it was to be sure of getting a military pension. Crazy!'

By now we were sitting on the terrace, looking out over the lake. Janez was in full flow.

'Tito told us not to hate, so I don't bear any hatred, but we're very different, all the Balkan nations. It's surprising we lasted as long as we did. I mean, it was as recent as 1912 that the last camel caravan arrived in Macedonia! And we were supposed to be part of the same country! Economics are different, character is different. Compare us to the superlative Serbs. In Slovenia, we don't want to lead, no one jumps up high, his neighbour will pull him down. And we like to keep everything to ourselves. I know we're going into the European Union, and we will have to open up a bit, but I don't think a true Slovenian should ever sell an inch of his land to a foreigner. Not an inch. The reason we were able to withdraw from Yugoslavia comparatively easily is that we were always at least ninety per cent Slovene. That purity is what allowed us to simply move away.'

Janez drove me back to the station. On the way he offered a lift to a fiftyish man waiting for a bus outside the doctor's surgery. Dropping him off at his house, where his wife was waiting, necessitated accepting an invitation for a glass of home-made plum schnapps in a very pastoral setting at their garden table under a fruit-heavy cherry tree. From what I gathered, once we were seated, Janez launched into an explanation of my Agatha Christie quest. My role was to nod, smile, savour the setting and the kick of the schnapps, and given that the sun was warm, the birds were singing and there was plenty of time until the next train, I was very happy to do so. But then Janez was up on his feet again, and we were on our way quicker than I expected. He explained why when we were back in the car. 'Very sad story. His wife is half paralysed from a stroke two years ago, and today the doctor has just told him that he has inoperable cancer. Now he has to tell her. So you can see, knowing that, that I did not find this an easy moment to make conversation.'

I took the Mimara from Ljubljana to Zagreb. Like the train I'd taken up to Bled, it was relatively sophisticated, clean, air-conditioned and with polarized windows, although the automatic doors were broken at one end, and the toilet at the other end was locked, so it was not a coach for people with prostate problems. Once we'd crossed the border into Croatia, however, a new guard came aboard and unlocked the toilet, and thereafter it was in almost permanent use almost all the way to Zagreb. It seemed that Croats, like cats and foxes, like to mark their own territory.

The Mimara was on the last leg of its journey from

Berlin, and it started out from Ljubljana with great enthusiasm, keen to emphasize its importance to the dwellers of the suburbs. A few minutes later, however, we were banging along like a car with a flat tyre, hugging the banks of the river Sava and bouncing off the valley walls with the wheel flanges grinding hard against the rails. In days to come the trackwalkers on that stretch of line would curse the blessed international expresses, and their perennial need to impress.

By now the Sava had matured radically from where I'd seen it first burst from its mid-cliff womb in the mountains above Bohinj. In places it was broad and generous and lined with birch and ash, and in others its valley narrowed into a canyon, turning it into a violent torrent. I fell into conversation with two young Americans who were sitting a couple of seats away; as Paul Theroux wrote in *Great Railway Bazaar*, 'You may be alone on a train, but you are never lonely.' They told me they were headed for Sarajevo, so I expected some enlightened conversation about Balkan history or family or army connections with Bosnia, but it turned out they were only heading there because friends had told them it was a cool place to send e-mails and to buy cool T-shirts with real bullet-holes. As far as the rest of Bosnia or even Serbia was concerned, they considered it off-limits to anyone from the US. Our conversation ended with them telling me about great places to eat in Arizona, which always seems to happen to me when I meet Americans.

It is immensely difficult getting a grip on the Balkan whirlpool. The two books I had with me, Misha Glenny's *The Balkans* and Rebecca West's *Black Lamb and Grey Falcon*, were respectively 708 and 1,175 pages long, and still they only scratched the surface of the complexities of Balkan history. Glenny, who was the BBC's correspondent through most of the Balkan crisis, kicked off his analysis with an angry stab at the typical outsider's characterization of the Balkan Slavs as 'congenitally irrational and bloodthirsty mobs, never happier than when they are slitting the throats of their neighbours'. So far I could only agree with him, because I'd seen no sign of bloodthirstiness among the cultured, Stallone-hating, vegetable-loving Slovenians. For them the break with Yugoslavia had been a fairly natural one, fairly easily achieved, and hadn't left a particularly nasty taste in anyone's mouth.

That wasn't to say that the Slovenians felt much sympathy for their neighbours. Few whom I had spoken to had much good to say about the Serbs, but nor had they all that much compassion for the Croats. 'At least the Serbs will stab you in the front,' they'd said. 'The Croats will stab you in the back.' Clearly, Slav history is full of back-stabbings and in their worst moments those stabbings have totalled hundreds of thousands. This region has been at the epicentre of so much conflict, for which the back-story is usually too complex, and too open to interpretation, for most disinterested parties – and I include myself among them – to comprehend. Especially if it means wading through 1,175 pages. It is far easier to simply label the Slavs as 'congenitally irrational and bloodthirsty mobs', and to blame them for starting World War I.

John Gunther, an American journalist and author in the 1940s and 1950s, summed up popular feeling towards the Balkans, then and now, in his popular book *Inside Europe*, which was published at the beginning of World War II. 'It is an intolerable affront to human and political nature that these wretched and unhappy little countries in the Balkan peninsula can, and do, have quarrels that cause world wars. Some hundred and fifty thousand young Americans died because of an event in 1914 in a mud-caked primitive village, Sarajevo.'

To understand quite why these countries have had so many quarrels, you have first to understand their closeness. Even in our 'civilized' countries, most murder victims know their murderer, and more often than not it turns out to be a family member. It's just that the Balkans have more extended families than most.

At bottom, the people of the former Yugoslavia belong to the same ethnic family. They share a common origin and a common language, but they have spent very little time sharing the same bed. Interference from outside has meant that two major factors divide them: religion and imperial overlords. The religious divide places Croatia and Slovenia in the Catholic corner, while Serbia is Orthodox, and Bosnia partly Muslim. Those religious divides are largely down to the influence of two different imperial powers. Croatia and Slovenia (and briefly Bosnia) were part of the (Catholic) Austro-Hungarian Empire until World War I, while Serbia spent 350 years on its knees to the Muslim east, under Ottoman rule until 1867. Nature may have created them the same, but nurture certainly brought them up different.

For the Serbs, the period of Ottoman domination left the largest scar on their psyche, partly because of the way the Turks treated them and partly because their strong sense of nationalism was deeply insulted by the Turkish occupation. While the Croats and Slovenes were not too unhappy under the Austrians – Croatia, in fact, offered its throne to the Austrian royal family in the sixteenth century as a way of insuring itself against Ottoman invasion – the Serbians still mark their original defeat by the Turks (the battle of Kosovo Polje on 28 June 1389) as a day of national mourning.

Bosnia, a collection of diverse villages in the mountains, is where all these variations were – and still are – polarized. In the same way a British expatriate becomes almost a caricature of Britishness when overseas, running the Union Jack up the flagpole at dawn, so do the Croat, Serb and Muslim villagers in Bosnia cling extra fervently to their nationalist identities, each feeling threatened by their neighbours.

Accordingly it was a staggeringly provocative act for Archduke Franz Ferdinand, heir to the Austro-Hungarian Empire, to choose the Kosovo Polje day of mourning in 1914 to make an official state visit to Sarajevo, the Bosnian city which had a particularly large Serb minority. The message his presence implied was that here was the heir to the current imperial power, come to swagger around his estates, and he couldn't care less about the feelings of a certain culturally inferior section of the community. The shots that killed him and his wife were predictable, although what was more of a surprise was how one simple hot-headed event precipitated such a universal conflagration.

At the time Austria was looking for an excuse for military action against Serbia. After fifty years of post-Ottoman independence and iffy monarchs, the Serbs were entering a healthy nation-building phase and rapidly becoming a worrying force on the Empire's south-eastern flank. The other Slav states still under Austrian control – Bosnia, Croatia and Slovenia – were looking with envy at the strengthening Serbian nation, and Serbia in her turn was tacitly encouraging them to kick free. So Austria accused Serbia of being behind the assassination of the Archduke (partly correct: assassin Gavrilo Princip was a

Bosnian student but the organization he belonged to was Serb), made several draconian demands, set a forty-eight-hour deadline for compliance, and when Serbia actually complied, declared war anyway. A series of international alliances then brought in everyone else. Hey presto, World War I.

The war was a gruelling time in the Balkans. For the first time for centuries Croats, Serbs and Slovenes were lined up together against a common Teutonic enemy, but their fighting men were ill-equipped, ill-disciplined and easily defeated. Put on the back foot straight away, the Serbian army retreated to link up with British and French reinforcements arriving on the coast of Montenegro, but to reach them they first had to scale the Montenegrin mountains in the teeth of the winter. Around 100,000 died in the retreat, many from starvation and cold, and when they reached the other side they found the Allies hadn't yet turned up. Even a food ship sent to resupply them had been torpedoed, leaving loaves of bread floating on the water. It is a measure of these men's desperation that they jumped in to retrieve those loaves, but with no knowledge of how to swim, many drowned.

With the war eventually resolved, the Slav nations found themselves on the winning side for the first time in hundreds of years. They were finally in control of their own destinies after centuries of being controlled by others, and it was a natural choice to decide to stick together, for the sake of their continuing security. From a variety of possible governments they opted for a monarchy, ruled by the dynastic Karageorge family, who had first risen to prominence as the defeaters of the Turks. The new nation started out with the title 'Kingdom of the Serbs, Croats and Slovenes', and was later mercifully shortened to 'Yugoslavia'.

The country had fundamental problems from the start. Its population was effectively two different sorts of Slav, and they were as different as the panther from the lynx: the Roman Catholic Slav, who'd been part of the western bourgeois system and who looked to Austria for leadership (i.e. the Croats and the Slovenes), and the Slav who belonged to the Orthodox church, who subscribed to the view that all men should be heroes, who'd spent all those centuries under the cosh of the Turks (i.e. the Serbs).

Serbia's profile as the largest and most populous republic and traditional seat of the Karageorges made its capital, Belgrade, the obvious choice for the focus of political and economic power, but that quickly fuelled resentment in the other states, who considered their capital cities equally deserving. The Serbs were fierce believers in the pro-Slav ideal, and they thought that to criticize the concept was the work of wickedness, so they had a tendency to be heavy-handed with any dissent. Such heavy-handedness was bound to produce a reaction, and the inter-war years saw the foundation of the nationalist Ustashe in Croatia, a prototype terrorist organization which was dedicated to the overthrow of the Serb-dominated Yugoslav state and the Serb-majority Yugoslav army. It was the Ustashe who were behind the assassination of King Alexander Karageorge in 1934, while on a visit to France.

By the time World War II broke out the Yugoslav state was deeply divided along nationalist lines. For the first eighteen months of the war Yugoslavia managed to maintain its neutrality, until the Axis powers persuaded the reluctant Karageorges to sign a cooperation agreement. At the time it was an expedient move to save the country from being over-run, but the population as a whole was horrified by the capitulation, and two days later a group of Serbian air force officers, supported by the church and the communists, staged a coup, replaced the King and withdrew from the pact. Hitler's response, on 6 April 1941, was to send 800 aircraft to destroy Belgrade, killing 24,000 people in a single day. He summoned his ally Italy to attack from the western side, and within ten days Yugoslavia was completely overwhelmed. But by no means finished.

At the time Winston Churchill described the Serbian defiance against hugely unequal odds as 'valiant', and a 'heroic gesture', and the resistance that followed it was immensely valuable for the Allied war effort. But it was at great cost in terms of human life.

The freedom fighters fell into two camps, the Cetniks and the Partisans, where the Cetniks were largely Serbian pro-royalists who supported the government which had gone into exile in London. The Partisans, with Tito as their leader, had their base among the communists and were fighting for liberty both from the invaders and from the old royalist system as represented by that same government in exile. These two organizations were up against both the Germans and those Croats who'd joined the fascist Ustashe, and who were now effectively ruling Croatia as a Nazi puppet state. And they also fought each other.

So if you were a Slav freedom fighter, you had a choice of enemies.

Huge numbers died in the mêlée. The Partisans are thought to have murdered up to 100,000 of their opponents, and the Ustashe set up death camps such as the infamous Jasenovac, the third largest such camp in the whole of World War II, to rid Croatia of Serbs, gypsies and Jews.

The blood-letting was unstinting. In all some 1.7 million Yugoslavs are supposed to have died in the war, or one tenth of the total population – and 500,000 of those are thought to have been executed in Ustashe camps, although these figures are still hotly debated. The majority of the executed were Serbs, and many of them were forced to renounce Orthodoxy in favour of Catholicism before being killed by the Croat Ustashe with mallets and axes. The Ustashe solution for what they perceived as the Serb problem was to ensure that one third were exiled, one third were converted, and one third were killed. In Bosnia, they threw Bosnian Serb women and children off cliffs.

The whole history of the Ustashe and its programme of extermination is one of the most chilling, and least written about, of the war. And although the numbers vary widely depending on who you're talking to, it is fair to say that far more Serbs were killed by Croats in World War II than vice versa in Balkan crises ever since.

Once the war was over, the majority of the Ustashe melted away back into the populace and the organizational power of the communists set about making sure of winning the peace. Marshall Tito took control and embarked on his ideal of a southern Slav federation, as had been tried between the wars, but this time with a communist foundation. For many years the experiment was successful; thanks to Tito's adept footwork and his foundation of the Non-Aligned Movement distancing himself from Stalin, the Yugoslavs experienced few of the personal restrictions deployed by communist Russia and benefited from a pretty prosperous economy, much helped by tourism. On the surface, everything was rosy, but underneath, all the old resentments were still festering, and the war wounds in particular went unhealed.

Tito, who had a Croatian father and a Slovenian mother, was only too well aware of the dangers of the ethnic divides in his new federation. He realized that

Serbia, the biggest and by far the most populous nation, was far too dominant, so he divided it up, creating self-governing provinces of Kosovo in the south and Vojvodina in the north. He also encouraged the various ethnicities to settle across borders, in the hope that those borders would disappear and differences would be forgotten once they'd lived long enough side by side. But either that coexistence wasn't long enough or the differences ran too deep, because nationalistic squabbling grew increasingly serious after his death. Once he'd gone, the Yugoslav federation started a system where each state took it in turns to be in charge, but that only served to accentuate the national differences and fuel the resentments.

The catalyst for crisis came in 1989, when the Berlin Wall fell. Communism was discredited and all former communist states started the move towards capitalism, democracy and independence. Slovenia and Croatia wanted to do the same. Serbia, however, was still committed to the pan-Slav ideal, and received the support of Britain, France and Russia, who feared the consequences of the break-up of the state. In so doing they were allying themselves to an emerging Serbian leader called Slobodan Milosevic.

Milosevic didn't have a great start in life. Both of his parents committed suicide before he was eighteen. And he had none of Tito's tolerance or vision. He first became President of the Serbian League of Communists in 1986, and within a year had radically changed its liberal stance towards other ethnicities. He was the only politician in the Serbian government of 1987 who tacitly endorsed a provocative memorandum published in a Belgrade newspaper which declared that the lives of the 600,000 Serbs living in Croatia were threatened.

Accordingly, when Croatia started talking about independence, he saw red. He quickly rescinded the autonomy of the Tito-created provinces of Vojvodina and Kosovo lest they show any temptation to secede too, and thereby created a bigger and more powerful Serbia to give him an automatic majority in the Yugoslav federal parliament. Working through the more right-wing newspapers, he whipped up fear of the return of the Serb-exterminating Ustashe, moving towards a creed of 'Kill before you are Killed.' He didn't do this entirely unopposed, however, and in March 1991 hundreds of thousands of people took to the streets of Belgrade to voice their opposition to the direction in which all this nationalist propaganda was taking them.

When Croatia finally made its move in June 1991, its large Serb minority, many of whom had originally been encouraged to settle in Croatia by the Austrians as a bulwark against the Turks, responded to the Croat demand for secession by proclaiming their own, independent, Serb state of Krajina. The next few months witnessed dreadful scenes as neighbours who had been living peacefully side by side for 150 years turned on each other, and 13,000 Croats were killed. The Krajina Serbs had Milosevic's support and the firepower of the Yugoslav Army on their side, and they steadily 'ethnically cleansed' up to a third of the Croatian land-mass until brought to a halt by a ceasefire brokered by the United Nations. This, plus headline-grabbing distractions in Bosnia-Herzegovina, where the Serbs were taking ethnic cleansing to new heights, allowed the Croats time to regroup. In 1995 in Operation Storm they pushed 150,000 Krajina Serbs back across the borders into Serbia, creating the largest single movement of refugees in Europe since World War II.

Although Milosevic has been condemned as the big bad

wolf of the Balkans, Croat leader Franjo Tudjman was almost as nationalistic and intolerant, but he was better at courting world opinion and at portraying the Croats as the wounded party. Like Milosevic, he wanted to build an ethnically pure empire, a Greater Croatia that would rival Greater Serbia. So while the Serbs were carrying out their ethnic cleansing of the Muslims in Bosnia, sponsored by Milosevic, the Croats were doing the same, backed by Tudjman. It has since been established that during these difficult years when they were supposedly at loggerheads, Milosevic and Tudjman actually met in secret to sound each other out, and had effectively agreed between themselves to split Bosnia down the middle.

In the end it was Bosnia-Herzegovina and Kosovo, where the complexity of the conflicts was deepened by the persecution of Muslims and the introduction of Albanians into the Serbo-Croat mix, which brought the world down on Milosevic's head. The worst atrocities since World War II were perpetrated here. The massacre of Srebrenica in 1995, where 8,000 unarmed Muslims died, was one of the major triggers for renewed diplomacy that resulted in the Dayton Agreement and the deployment of NATO peacekeeping forces. It was Milosevic's refusal in 1999 to allow those peacekeeping forces across into Kosovo when fighting intensified there, with Kosovar Albanians seeking independence, which eventually provoked NATO to take the drastic action of bombing Belgrade.

Belgraders were gobsmacked by the unprovoked attack. Few had seen it coming. The local press, heavily censored by Milosevic, had failed to report the realities of the Kosovan crisis. The main dispute was effectively outwith their borders, and many more civilians had been killed during the crisis in the early and mid 1990s without provoking any such reaction from the international community. In the end it became a question of NATO needing to make a stand in the world's eyes, to maintain its credibility, and Belgrade got it in the neck.

That NATO bombing of 1999 had a significance that reached far beyond the borders of Serbia: it was the first time that war had been declared by a group of countries whose sovereignty was not threatened, but who intervened through political expediency and concern for human rights. And as such it was a turning point in world history. Within a couple of years many of the same arguments were being rehearsed, and many of the same waves of bombers were being released, first in the skies over Afghanistan, and then over Iraq.

CITY OF INNER DEMONS

For the city with the ugliest name on the planet, memorable largely for its points potential in Scrabble, Zagreb is a handsome place. It rises out of an unprepossessing smudge of half-finished brick houses and a ring of graffiti and girders. Nestling at its heart is a mini Vienna, with parkland, bandstands, coffee houses and plenty of swirly stucco with butter-yellow walls and Red Leicester roofs. After Ljubljana, where urban life was basically something that essentially country folk had to tolerate to earn a living or acquire a degree, this really felt like a city.

Glavni Kolodvor, the railway station, makes a huge and formal front door to Zagreb, spreading its arms wide as if taking a deep bow. And justifiably so, because much of the late-nineteenth-century city that is laid out in front of it was created on the back of the prosperity brought by the railway. Beyond the station forecourt stretches a long, broad formal garden modelled on Munich's *Englischer Garten* which penetrates right up to the city centre, Ban Jelacic Square, a seething rectangular bead of people threaded by clanging strings of colourful trams.

A giant produce market, the 'belly of Zagreb', sits directly behind the square, up a short flight of steps. Margaret Thatcher, who for a while was an unlikely icon for emerging Eastern European countries, came here in the early 1990s to be presented with a nice set of plums by the gossiping farmers' wives. The fruit and vegetables are upstairs in the open, while the butchers are all lined up in an underground hall below, their heads disappearing into a hanging forest of hams and sausages. In a dairy annexe white-coated ladies in hairnets preside over cream cheeses which are so fresh they are still quivering on the muslin. And all these stallholders fix their prices in quantities of pine-martens or Kuna, the shiny new Croat currency, symbol of the newly-independent state.

Zagreb's once-fortified Old Town is pretty enough to have been made out of gingerbread. It rises above the nineteenth-century city like a Montmartre without the souvenir shops, where national coats of arms are laid out in coloured roof-tiles and a lamplighter still does his rounds. It's so quiet and quaint up here that St Mark's Square could be a village in Tuscany at siesta time, but the occasional scurrying figure is a politician, not a peasant, and there are more loitering policemen and swanky German-made limousines than most Tuscan villages would see in a lifetime. The business of government is carried on here among the woodsmoke and turtle doves.

Between the Old Town and the market runs Ul Tkalciceva, along a small valley that was once a riverbed. These days Tkalciceva is what the Croats like to refer to either as the longest café in Europe or Zagreb's front room. It's a pedestrian street lined with open-fronted bars, the venue for evening strollers. Sitting here, with a local beer to hand, you can watch the whole reproductive process play itself out: the singles all dressed up ready to

party, the courting couples, the round-bellied mothers-to-
be, and finally the proud couples pushing the baby in a
pram, who return to Tkalciceva out of a sense of
nostalgia, because this was the place that set the mating
in motion.

Agatha came through Zagreb several times on the
Simplon-Orient Express but there's no evidence to suggest
she did much more than look out of the window. A handful of years after her first transit in 1928 she chose to set
the main action in *Murder on the Orient Express* on
Croatian soil, grinding her train to a halt in the ancient
forests between the towns of Vinkovci and Slavonski
Brod. And she was to return to the region for her
honeymoon with Max, travelling down the Croatian
coast, spending some days in Dubrovnik, and then taking
a boat to Patras in Greece. Decades later she was back in
the city, briefly, in 1967, according to the account of one
of the journalists – a Croat working for a Croatian
women's magazine – who'd tracked her down to Bohinj.
But she never mentioned it in her writing.

When she passed through back in 1928, Zagreb was in
its prime and the regular call of the Simplon-Orient
Express confirmed the city's sense of having arrived. Rich
bankers and industrialists used the train to set out to see
the world, buying a ticket to Trieste where they'd transfer
to a Lloyd Triestino sailing for America. In 1925 a locally
owned company constructed the grandiose Hotel
Esplanade, right by the station, specifically for the Orient
Express customers, and the combination of luxury train
and luxury hotel brought an injection of millionaires, bon
vivants and adventurers to the Croatian capital.

The Esplanade offered hot and cold water in every
room, French cuisine, liveried porters and the chance to
gamble and meet young ladies. It quickly became the

epicentre of Zagreb social life. The Officers' Ball, the Doctors' Ball and the Journalists' Ball all took place here, in the mirrored and marbled Emerald Ballroom, with invitees who included members of the royal family and 1,500 guests from all levels of society. As the local newspaper wrote at the time, 'The visitors from abroad were impressed and expressed their amazement that a city the size of Zagreb, which by European standards is an ordinary provincial town, judging by the number of its inhabitants, could organize an event of such high standard with so much taste and style.'

There was plenty of eccentric behaviour, too. The Italian consul, a confirmed bachelor and admirer of the fairer sex, gave a banquet to which he invited all the well-known ladies of the town. The guest list totalled eighty women and just ten men, and by the early hours all the men were lying under the tables, so the hotel staff stepped in to 'entertain' the ladies. One of the hotel's most loyal guests was local artist Fedor Vaic, who came to the Ruby Restaurant every day for more than fifty years. Vaic was so short that his head hardly appeared above the tablecloth. He was also a real loner, but he made friends with the hotel staff. In the restaurant he'd drink constantly and regularly fell asleep between courses, his head swaying slowly backwards and forwards, until the waiter arrived with the next dish and touched him gently on the shoulder with his serviette to wake him up again. When Vaic died, one of his newspaper obituaries was written by the hotel staff.

Unfortunately for the reputation of the Esplanade it became the residence of choice of the Wehrmacht and the Gestapo during World War II, and it was here that the leaders of the Ustashe-based puppet regime would come to receive their orders and to consume a few glasses of schnapps with fellow Fascists. After the war, in the new milieu of the communist regime – which didn't endorse the hotel's concepts of luxury and privilege – it suffered heavily. Meanwhile the Simplon-Orient Express no longer drew up at the hotel's doorstep with coachloads of glitterati. The war had rendered nearly 300 coaches unrepairable, and the remaining stock of 200 had been partially rearranged with three classes of sleeping compartment all within the same coach, to try to cater for a much more mixed clientele. And 'mixed' it most certainly was. The train filled up with refugees, soldiers, black-marketeers, Nazis on the run, and large numbers of passengers pretending to be something other than what they were. It quickly acquired a reputation as the spy's transport method of choice, although this was probably more apocryphal than actual. The only documented on-board spy murder took place in 1953, when the US naval attaché in Bucharest was hurled off the train in a tunnel in Hungary. But because the train connected alien ideologies and economies, it was distrusted by every state it crossed, resulting in prolonged stops on the borders. The discovery of even the most trivial of illegal goods could have the whole thing shunted into a siding for hours.

The Hotel Esplanade persisted in holding occasional Orient Express parties, but when the train effectively died in 1962 (a pale version of it limped on as the Direct Orient until 1977, full of Turkish *gastarbeiters* returning home), it tried to emerge from under its shadow with the slogan 'The Orient Express is gone; the Esplanade is forever.' In the 1970s and 1980s it made headlines by introducing Zagreb to the kiwi fruit and the CD-ROM, and today it is trying to make a comeback with a complete interior redesign. Whether Agatha ever stayed here or not I cannot say; the Emerald Ballroom where the Italian consul ended up under the tables, no longer able to entertain his lady friends, is wonderfully intact, but the hotel has not preserved its guest lists. Given its mixed history, they may not have made comfortable reading.

Agatha Christie may not have written anything about Zagreb, but Rebecca West's *Black Lamb and Grey Falcon* was published only a few years after Agatha first passed through, and its first chapter begins on the platform of Glavni Kolodvor. West, like Agatha, was embarking on her journey at the end of an emotional crisis. The well-connected daughter of a journalist, she'd just come to the end of a torrid ten-year affair with the author H. G. Wells. Even though her book was written fifty years in advance of the final disintegration of Yugoslavia, the country she describes was already riven with ethnic divisions. 'I had come to Yugoslavia to see what history meant in flesh and blood,' she wrote. She too arrived here on the Simplon-Orient Express, although in her case she had a husband in tow.

Waiting for her on the platform were three men she counted as friends – a Serb and two Croats – none of whom liked each other. Over the days that followed she realized that other Croats would often refuse to meet her if she was accompanied by her Serb friend Constantine, and if they did they argued constantly, usually along ethnic divides. 'How can we let the Croats be officials? They are not loyal,' said Constantine when the conversation turned to the inevitable dominance of Serbs in high positions, even in Croatia; his line was that the Croats were only interested in looking after their own. For their part, the Croats maintained that Serb management was incompetent, pulling the Croat schools down to Serb standards. To which Constantine replied that it was more important to have relatively good schools everywhere than a few very good schools just in Croatia. Etcetera.

This, concluded West, was the essential difference between them. The Croats were thinking of the good of Croatia, but the Serbs believed they were working for the benefit of everyone. They saw themselves as having given the Slavs their freedom, and now they wanted to improve the life of the Slavs in Macedonia as well as those in Zagreb and Belgrade. In part, this was the arrogance of a nation which liked being in the driving seat, implementing an ideology, but in part it was also their heroically romantic image of themselves, trying to complete the 'poem of their existence', as West put it. 'These people hold that the way to make life better is to add good things to it, whereas in the West we hold that the way to make life better is to take bad things away.' In a way this concurred with Janez Fajfar's description of the Serb's mayfly-like existence, although his had a far less positive spin.

West's few days in Zagreb amounted to a seamless set of encounters with all of the great and the good. Wherever she went she found a poet and a playwright waiting for her, in order to discuss Conrad and Tolstoy and Nietzsche's attitude to music. Personally, arriving in Zagreb with a couple of phone numbers to call, I was not expecting a similarly high-octane experience, and I hadn't swotted up on my Nietzsche. But within a couple of hours of dialling the first number I had already been to a book launch and shortly afterwards I found myself sitting on a hand-carved hardwood chair in what my host called his salon, a private room on the upper floor of Zagreb's Archaeological Museum.

Ivan Mirnik, who was in his mid-fifties, was the museum's deputy director, charming, impish, urbane, and very dapper in a suit of grey silk. He was one of those people who took great delight in the art of conversation, and in holding court to an agreeable audience of young men.

'Tell me about your life, dear boy,' he said, when we met, reminding me instantly of the sort of gossipy professor you'd find in the quadrangles of Oxford or Cambridge. When I complimented him on the flawlessness of his English he pointed out that he had been to thirty-seven performances at the Royal Opera House, Covent Garden. 'Don't underestimate us,' he seemed to be saying. 'We Croats are deeply cultured people.'

The launch, in the Austrian Cultural Institute, had been in honour of a book profiling Austro-Jewish dynasties from Croatia between the wars, many of whom had later died in Jasenovac at the hands of the Ustashe. Two descendants of the survivors – one intense-looking and middle aged, and the other a grinning young lawyer – had returned with us to Ivan's salon. Ivan, it seemed, was very well connected.

'Dado's family had assets which were the equivalent of the annual tourism revenue of the whole of Croatia,' he explained, indicating the intense middle-aged man. 'Of course it was all taken away by the communists after the war. And now he wants it back.'

Dado explained haltingly how he had been writing open letters to the government for a couple of years, and how the newspapers had recently started to ask him for money to publish those letters.

'Money? For printing a letter to the editor? Crazy. I refuse. So they put my letter in the sport pages.'

'How wonderful,' joked Ivan, 'then everyone will read it.' More seriously he added, 'Of course, a lot of people are making very big, unjustified claims. Opportunists.'

It turned out he too had been writing to the newspapers

on the subject of a certain family living in west London who claimed to be Croatian princes, and also wanted their extensive landholdings and titles returned.

'I wrote a piece pointing out that the last of that branch of the family had died 350 years ago.'

'Did they pay you any attention?'

'They? You spit in the face of a whore and she will say it is raining.' Ivan smiled and brushed lightly at his silk shirt.

I turned back to Dado. 'And do you have any prospect of getting anything back?'

He shrugged. 'Depends who lived there after my family, on the strength of their claim. And whether the papers are complete. Very little property is really "clean". The government has to decide who has the best claim.'

It turned out that 'clean' was a crucial concept in post-Yugo Croatia. Properties that were 'clean' were those whose ownership history had been properly legally recorded, whose owners had not been discredited by any of the regime changes, or who did not have some Serbian connection. Properties which were not 'clean' – a very significant proportion of the urban housing market – could not be bought or sold until their ownership issues had been resolved.

'Our society is full of suspicion,' Ivan said. 'Everyone is hiding something.' Serbs and Croats had lived together for so long that everyone had Serb blood, Serb relatives or Serb business connections, but nobody liked to admit to it. 'Whoever ends up with the legal title to a house or a field, whether it be the pre-war landowners, private owners during the communist era, or the new entre-preneurs who are buying stuff with wads of cash, somebody else is going to be very disappointed. Very. And there are bound to be unpleasant allegations. Briber of politicians! Ustashe! Serb! Communist!'

Ivan paused and the others waited, knowing him well enough not to interrupt when he was in full flow.

'It is impossible to satisfy everyone. Do you know that Bosnian fable about the man, his son and their donkey?'

I shook my head.

'A man comes into a town sitting on his donkey, led by his son. "Oh, how could you make the poor boy walk like that!" say the people in the outskirts. So the man changes places with his son and leads the donkey himself. "Oh, what a fool!" comes the reaction from downtown. "The boy plainly needs the exercise." So they both climb on the donkey. "Heavens, look at that poor animal," says the crowd in the marketplace. "Being made to carry such a load!" So the end result is that the boy and his father end up carrying the donkey themselves. In an attempt to please public opinion. Ridiculous!'

The others then chipped in, agreeing that the ownership issue was fundamental to the forward development of the country. 'The land registry is a real dog's dinner. You can't start an enterprise unless the land it's built on is clean,' said Branko, the young lawyer. 'There's not enough security to get outsiders to invest. It will slow down our entry to the EU.'

'That and the tycoons,' interrupted Dado.

'The tycoons?'

'Yes, we call them that,' said Ivan. 'About a hundred of them. Some of them were warlords, including some Bosnians. During the early 1990s they were allowed by government to make interest-free withdrawals from the Bank of Croatia. The EU won't let us join until there's an explanation, until that money is accounted for. Of course we all know who they are – they've all got big villas with pools – but no one will say. Sure, the government has changed its spots since those days, but in essence they're still the same people and they're all holding hands under the table. We've changed from a socialist society to a capitalist one, but we have no capitalists. To be a capitalist you have to haul yourself up above other people, and most Croats are not ready to do that. We've got too much self-doubt.'

'It doesn't sound as if a lot has improved since Croatia struck out on its own,' I ventured.

Ivan looked momentarily disconcerted. 'Don't get the wrong impression. The economy may be sinking, but at least we have the freedom to say exactly what we want. We live well, intellectually. The cultural life has done very well. Lots of new money has been spent. Here in the museum we've got wonderful new cabinets, computer systems and even a security guard. The theatre is good, dance is good, and it's cheap. Literature is flourishing. By the way, have you read Rebecca West?'

I acknowledged that I had.

'You know, of course, that she had a love affair with a Serb?' He said it as if it explained everything.

'I didn't know that. I am saving the chapters which describe Serbia for when I get there; it is practically the only bit of travel writing about that country I've been able to find. Even in Zagreb.'

Ivan grunted. 'Don't go asking for a guidebook to Serbia in any of our bookshops. They'll box your ears.' Even the libraries had, apparently, relegated books by Serb authors to the basement. 'City people can talk about Belgrade readily enough, but that's because we didn't have any fighting here. In somewhere like Vukovar it is very hard to live alongside the man who killed your family, and see him every day in his garden. Very hard.'

From there conversation turned towards the arts scene

and some family gossip was exchanged, and I reckoned it was time to go. As I took my leave, Branko drew me aside for a word of warning about my onward journey. 'Be careful,' he said. 'The Serbs will take your possessions. Your life is safe, but nothing else.'

Over the next couple of days I sat around in cafés, watching, listening, reading, and dipping in and out of Zagreb cultural life. The monthly diary of arts events listed many pages of museums, but when I read how many exhibits they had in total – 3.6 million – my enthusiasm for visiting them evaporated on the spot. The more popular end of culture was represented by rock bands Leftover Crack and Pungent Stench. The sixteen different theatres had a choice of productions with titles like 'Pond Scum, or Old Woman's Porridge', most of which – when you read the small print – turned out to have the same 'how I survived Yugoslavia' theme. In the bookshops I browsed for titles on Serbia, but instead found heaps of introspective volumes with snappy names like 'Stjepan Radic, the Croat Peasant Party, and the politics of mass mobilization 1924–28'.

It wasn't just the arts scene which was picking over the bones of recent history; everybody was doing it, in the streets, in the markets, in the cafés. One of the first notes I had made when I arrived was that the citizens of Zagreb looked like a tribe of Latin teachers, well-meaning, socially unsure of themselves and a little off-fashion, and very expert in a subject which was largely irrelevant to today's world. Now I realized they also looked troubled, possibly by the arrangements for next year's school trip – but more likely because their nation had been disembowelled, its bodily organs tugged out for examination, and some of them replaced, but nobody really knew if they'd been put back in the right order.

Theirs was a country with a stomach-ache, and they didn't know whether the pain was post-operative healing or a warning of new trauma to come.

As individuals they seemed to be wrestling with inner demons, as if they'd just gone through a divorce where both parties were still unsure of who had actually committed adultery first. Some of them were plainly worried by their new status as an independent entity, and others were much more hardline about it. The receptionist in the Hotel Astoria, for example, asked me one morning whether Scotland and Wales were going to secede from England.

'I doubt it. They'd lose too much.'

He was emphatic. 'Then they are cowards.'

I pointed out that a lot of English lived there, too.

'Ah,' he said. 'Difficult.' The idea of ethnic cleansing passed between us, like a fart at a cocktail party.

The second friend-of-a-friend telephone number I called was for Andreja Radic, an architectural historian whom I adjudged, when we met, to be in her early forties. She was big-boned, straw-blonde, attractive in a lugubrious sort of way, and deeply immersed in her subject. As luck would have it, the era in which I had professed an interest over the telephone – late 1920s, when Agatha first came through – coincided with her own speciality of the new Croat school of architecture of the 1920s and 1930s, so she agreed to walk me through the city pointing out significant buildings.

To be honest, I was more interested in people than architecture, so much of what Andreja showed me was too specialist for me to appreciate. The general picture was clear, though; the late 1920s were something of a golden age for Zagreb, with a social life which revolved around jazz bars, performing arts, society balls and rapidly increasing overseas travel. In this context the new wave of locally qualified architects wanted to create a cultural identity for the city which was to be quite distinct from the traditional mini-Vienna that Zagreb had always been. Their work was essentially form-and-function, logical in its structure.

'There were lots of well-off families looking to build,' Andreja told me. 'The husband would have been an entre-preneur, or working in administration or banking. By the 1960s these families would have had a house in town, a small farm somewhere nearby, and a summer house down on the coast.'

'Very civilized,' I murmured, but I was not surprised. This was, after all, the nation that gave us the necktie and the propelling pencil, both of them symbols of sophistication.

I tried a cheeky question. 'Does anyone still live like that? You, for instance?'

Andreja grimaced. 'Yes, both my grandparents built houses in the 1930s, but in the 1960s my parents lived in a flat in the city and spent their extra money on foreign travel instead. The rich of thirty years ago are not the rich of today. There's no such thing as old money in Croatia. Both my parents are long past retirement age, but they're still working.'

'So no house at the seaside for you?'

She seemed almost embarrassed to admit it. 'My husband's family has a summer house on one of the islands. We don't like it particularly, but the children do. At the weekend the place is over-run with people from Zagreb.'

She led me inside an apartment block designed by one of the Croatian school of architects, to show me how the window frames had all rusted over and the communal areas had been cruelly neglected. 'There's probably an argument about who owns this one,' she said. 'So nobody takes responsibility for it.'

As we walked across town to look at the exclusive villa district, she admitted, as Ivan had done, that the new Croatian nation-state had had its benefits for her. 'In the former state the scholarships and bursaries reached Zagreb very rarely. Now, with direct international contacts, I get to spend a few months every two or three years abroad.' Her brother lived in Germany, and she would have liked to do the same if she could, 'but my subject is the city I live in. It would be very hard to study it, or find a market for my studies, anywhere else.'

'Why leave, if there's more money for you now?'

'Because there's no continuity. You constantly have to re-prove who you are, with endless papers, in order to stand still. We have what amounts to an illness of society in transition. Everyone is suspicious of everyone else, you know, "What percentage of Serb are you?" '

For a moment I wondered whether Andreja herself might be some percentage Serb, but I didn't know whether that was the sort of question I could ask.

'The priorities are wrong,' she was continuing. And I could see it upset her. 'Thanks to the Ministry of Science the research foundation I work for is secure, but my children's school has holes in the roof.'

From the villa district, where there was every indication that some people were still living pretty prosperously, we climbed up into the Old Town to attend another launch party, this time for an exhibition of the work of one of the 1930s school of architects, which was being curated by one of Andreja's protégés. The crowd which was gathered in the museum courtyard for the opening speeches looked like the sort of launch party grandees you'd find anywhere in the world; a sprinkle of academics and intellectuals and the rank and file of the comfortably-off who like to be seen at such events. Although they were her sort, and she was greeted by several, Andreja was clearly uncomfortable among them. And again I wondered whether it was something in her lineage, or whether she was simply shy.

Once the speeches were done, I was propelled around the exhibition by the chattering human tide. It all seemed very well presented, if a touch obscure – but then the celebration of home-grown talent is what new-found nationalism is all about, no matter how minor that talent may be. The exhibition, as with the renewal of Ivan's computers and the funding of Andreja's foundation, was part and parcel of the process of national rebranding, even if it meant rewinding the clock and papering over fifty years of history to pick out obscure architects from the years that came before. In this case the result may have been a trifle dull and specialist to a visitor like me, but at least the architect was a product of the clean, safe 1930s, and I was prepared to bet that he was also a nil-per cent Serb.

Although Zagreb had been welcoming and what lay ahead – Belgrade – was potentially hostile, I was pleased when the time came to move on. The longer I'd stayed, the more I'd stopped noticing the glamorous Croats with their self-confidence and their mobile phones, and the more I'd started picking out the worried ones who preferred not to meet your eye. I'd started to home in on Andreja's 'illness in society'.

It even seemed to infect visitors, if the occupant of the Astoria's room 142 was anything to go by. At first I assumed that the repetitive groaning that seeped under my door, late at night, meant that the person across my corridor was getting an enviably regular diet of sex. But then on my last night I went to a performance of Prokofiev's *Romeo and Juliet* in the glittery, gilded Austrian-built National Theatre. When I returned to the hotel and put my key in my door I heard him moaning quite audibly, and clearly there were no other voices involved. In other circumstances I might have made an assumption about enthusiastic onanism, but this time, standing in the corridor, I could make out some words, and they were definitely English and far from ecstatic. He was repeating the same litany again and again, bits of which I could just make out. 'I can't . . . I won't . . . I can't . . . I won't . . . go away, go, go.' He went on, and on, and on, and even after I'd turned out the light I could still hear him, quieter now, but droning away into his pillow. The angst of Zagreb was tightening its grip.

Agatha's life hit its lowest point in early December 1926, with a mysterious and celebrated ten-day disappearance which was to dog her for the rest of her days.

Her mother had recently died and her marriage was on the rocks, although she was holding out against divorce – still a real stigma in those days – in the hope that Archie might change his mind. He, meanwhile, had practically moved out. He was living in his club in London most weeks, and spending weekends with mutual friends where his new love and golfing partner Nancy Neele was also a house guest. The lovers were careful that they should not spend the night together alone, out of concern both for her reputation and for his; within the close-knit and conservative world of the City anything that could be construed as racy behaviour was bad for business.

There are several accounts of the day she went missing. According to one, Agatha had taken Rosalind with her and visited her mother-in-law – with whom she'd managed to maintain a reasonable relationship – during the day. When the latter noticed she wasn't wearing her wedding ring, and asked her why, Agatha 'sat perfectly still for some time, gazing into space, and giving a hysterical laugh, turned away and patted Rosalind's head'. Another version has her having an argument with Archie.

That evening she'd come downstairs at eleven o'clock, got in her car, and driven off, watched by an anxious maid. The car was found at 6 a.m. the following morning, off the road but otherwise undamaged, by a beauty spot called Newlands Corner, less than an hour's drive away. The car doors were open, the battery flat and the police report described it as 'found in such a position as to indicate that some unusual proceeding had taken place, the car being found half-way down a grassy slope well off the main road with its bonnet buried in some bushes'. There was no sign of the author. A search was instigated, 15,000 volunteers joined in, and a nearby lake with a reputation for romantic suicides was dragged. Her secretary Carlo had told the police that Agatha had not been well for some weeks, and that her family were worried about her mental state.

The press soon got wind of the couple's estrangement, and Archie was not unnaturally suspected of having done away with his wife. His public profile was not helped by his curt, dismissive attitude towards journalists; his reported view was that her nerves had 'completely gone', and that she had gone away for 'no real purpose whatever'. He was later to famously add, in an in-depth interview in the *Daily Mail*, that 'my wife had discussed the possibility of disappearing at will. Some time ago she told her sister, "I could disappear if I wished and set about it carefully" . . . that shows that the possibility of engineering a disappearance had been running through her mind, probably for the purpose of her work. Personally, I feel that is what happened.' If Archie was trying to dampen down speculation with such a statement, it didn't work. His suggestion prompted even more questions and the case was followed with great interest by all the major newspapers, with rewards offered for anyone who could find her.

After a week of false trails the press was still full of speculation about what had happened to the authoress in her own real-life whodunit. According to 'friends of Mrs Christie' quoted by the *Mail*, Agatha had said, 'If I do not leave Sunningdale, Sunningdale will be the end of me.' Various fanciful eye-witness reports were printed describing a woman in a frenzied condition staggering around Newlands Corner in the small hours, her teeth chattering with cold. The tabloids filled the void with reports that she'd been seen living in London dressed as a man, and Berkshire police were working on a theory that she'd called Archie away from his dinner party and arranged to meet him at Newlands Corner. With no body and no clear clues, though, nobody was any the wiser, least of all the police.

One select group, however, was beginning to have its suspicions. The chambermaid of the Hydropathic Hotel, a teetotal establishment which promoted genteel recuperation in the Yorkshire spa town of Harrogate, had first spotted the resemblance of a quietly-spoken new guest to the photographs being printed in the newspapers. This guest had checked in as a Mrs Theresa Neele (Agatha had borrowed her rival's surname), who'd recently arrived from South Africa. She'd even placed an advertisement in the newspapers asking for relatives and friends to get in touch. The chambermaid mentioned her suspicions to the members of the Harry Codd band, who played every teatime in the Hotel's Palm Court. The members of the band had plenty of time to observe the assembled guests over the top of their instruments, and they agreed that the profile of the reserved guest sitting in the shadowy corner of the room doing crosswords bore a similarity to that of the authoress which was too close to be ignored. They took their suspicions to the police.

Ten days after Agatha had first disappeared, Archie marched into the Hydropathic Hotel and confirmed that 'Mrs Neele' was indeed his wife. He stayed in the hotel that night, albeit in a separate room, and great precautions were taken to keep all the newspapermen at bay. What the reunited couple said to each other behind closed doors is not known, but the absence of any official explanation beyond a short announcement to the effect that 'Mrs Christie is suffering from a loss of memory' meant that press interest in this new twist to the story reached fever pitch. The next day the police used a decoy vehicle at the front entrance to distract attention while the couple were bundled into a car outside the back, but it didn't work. Journalists and photographers threw themselves at the unhappy couple at every turn as they made their way to the station, and it was only once they reached Cheadle, where Agatha's sister Madge lived, that the gates could finally be shut behind them.

No entirely satisfactory explanation has ever emerged for Agatha's ten-day disappearance. In her autobiography, she herself skates quickly through the end of her first marriage without mentioning the most famous episode in her life at all. Her official biographer Janet Morgan follows the line taken by the family at the time – and they'd produced doctors to vouch for it – that the author had suffered an 'unquestionably genuine loss of memory', as a result of the emotional strain she'd been under.

But elements of the story do not accord with this suggestion of a breakdown. Before she'd disappeared, for example, Agatha had apparently written to Harrods asking to have some jewellery, which was being repaired, forwarded to 'Mrs Neele' at the Hydropathic Hotel, although Harrods later declared they had no such letter in their files. She'd also taken with her upwards of £500 in a money belt and even written a note to Archie's brother saying she intended to take a short holiday in a Yorkshire spa. So why abandon the car, so melodramatically, at Newlands Corner?

Edgar Wallace, writing in the *Daily Mail*, theorized that Agatha had faked her own disappearance simply to spite her husband, and was far too overwrought with emotion to consider the possible consequences. 'The disappearance seems to be a typical case of "mental reprisal" on somebody who has hurt her . . . that she did not contemplate suicide seems evident from the fact that she deliberately created an atmosphere of suicide by the abandonment of her car,' wrote Wallace.

However deliberate the plan, and whatever the motive for her disappearance, it is fair to say that Agatha was certainly not prepared for the huge amount of media coverage it would receive. She may have been hoping to engineer a reconciliation with Archie, but the very public outing of their marital disharmony on to the front pages of so many newspapers for so many days meant that there was no way back. And indeed, after Archie picked her up from Harrogate, she was never to see him again.

The whole ten-day episode inflicted deep pain on Agatha. From that moment on, the author shunned any kind of publicity or public speaking engagement and she avoided the press for the rest of her life. The episode's complete omission from her autobiography indicates that it was still a raw and undiscussable option forty years on.

Eventually the divorce was settled, and Archie re-married within three weeks. Meanwhile Agatha extricated herself from the Berkshire golfing community and set up home as a single mother in a flat in London. She was under considerable financial pressure, but for once she found herself unable to write until liberated by the anonymity of a holiday in the Canary Islands. There, with an odd prescience of what was to come, she completed *The Mystery of the Blue Train*, a story which features a single woman in her thirties who sets off by train to see the world, and becomes caught up in a crime. *The Blue Train* was followed quickly by a couple of other mysteries and a much heavier novel, *Giant's Bread*, the first book she wrote under the pseudonym Mary Westmacott, whose characters were full of personal pain.

Having dragged herself, through her writing, out of the mire towards a financial, and spiritual, equilibrium, Agatha now decided that she deserved a holiday. By this time Rosalind was securely lodged in the upmarket girls' boarding-school at Benenden in Kent, so she had the freedom to absent herself for longer periods. Accordingly she was planning a trip to the West Indies to set the seal on this whole ghastly episode in her life, when a conversation at a dinner party with a recently returned naval couple introduced the whole idea of Baghdad.

From this distance Iraq seems an unlikely choice, but at that time there was a lot of coverage in the UK press of Leonard Woolley's amazing discoveries in the Royal Tombs at Ur, which had come hot on the heels of

Carnarvon's at Luxor. As an added attraction there was the prospect of a long journey on the Orient Express, and Agatha had always loved trains.

So, in the screenplay of Agatha Christie's life, these were the two pivotal moments: the ten-day disappearance which ended the first half, and the subsequent journey on the train which was soon to provide the setting for Hitchcock's *The Lady Vanishes*, which was to trigger the second. Those two halves were strikingly different.

LOVE AND DEATH AMONG THE SERBS

The rail link between Zagreb and Belgrade follows the course of the Sava river, just as it does from Ljubljana to Zagreb, but here the Sava floodplain has flattened out and been subjected to a merciless beating by the sun. At some stage earlier in the year it had probably been fertile, but the last shudder of agriculture was a distant memory and all that remained was the barely recognizable afterbirth, stirring in the dust. Only the houses still had short skirts of green. Lonely, barely adolescent trees stood back to back in small groups, preparing to defend themselves until the last. And somewhere in the near distance, beyond the white, gleaming skeleton of a car, picked clean by human vultures, ran the difficult border with Bosnia.

The train was hauled by a Croatian locomotive painted in rugby-shirt stripes of red, orange and white, to make its shoulders look broader to the enemy. It had started out from Salzburg as an important express, and every time it stopped it had been patrolled by wheeltappers ringing out the kilometres. By this stage in its journey, however, it was relegated to village bus, full of big women with bags of vegetables offering each other boiled sweets. They reminded me of a story told by Croat journalist Dubravka Ugresic, where a sex education lesson involved a teacher drawing a naked woman on the blackboard. The progress of the sketch was followed in complete silence by the class, but when she'd finished a hand went up at the back. 'Please, miss,' said a voice. 'Where are the mummy's plastic bags?'

Ugresic's book *The Culture of Lies* doesn't have many light-hearted moments. The journalist had dared to criticize Croatia's new-found nationalism and all the cultural rebranding which followed it, and although I didn't have sufficient knowledge to be able to read her with objectivity, some of her words chimed in with what I'd seen and heard.

In particular, she accused the Croatian media of 'fostering the myth' of Croatia as the victim, when Croats had in fact committed similarly heinous crimes. She recorded how the nation's vice-president urged citizens to write letters to overseas friends 'telling the truth about Croatia', and thus beat the Serbs in the battle for better PR. She likened the rebranding process to Croats sitting in a cinema watching an official version of their lives being played out on the screen, and not being able to separate truth from fiction. She described how, during the difficult years of the early 1990s, 'every day new maps of Yugoslavia surfaced in the media with differently coloured patches, everyone experienced some colour and patch as threatening'. And how, suddenly, citizens of the city found that, because their father or mother had come from Belgrade thirty, forty or even fifty years before, they were no longer welcome.

Of the ranks of 536 officially registered writers, a few – including Ugresic – were recorded as 'unapproved' for not toeing the official line. In 1992 she wrote an article for a German newspaper about the ideological cleansing of the Croatian arts scene, and found herself the target of 'frenzied attacks' by her compatriots. They proclaimed her a liar, a traitor, a public enemy and a witch. 'The author,' wrote Ugresic, 'consumed by fire in her own homeland, left to continue her life in exile.' She now lives in the Netherlands.

I didn't need any map to tell me when we were finally approaching the Serbian border. The station buildings were pebbledashed with bullet-holes and many of the houses had no roofs. For many years this stretch of the railway had also been a casualty of war, and the train moved tentatively forward, as if expecting sabotage. At an uncheery place called Sid a curt group of Serbian immigration officers came aboard and ordered two of us off the train, myself and a middle-aged Austrian woman who smelled of spring onions. We were the only two foreigners on board.

'Visa,' commanded the officer who took our passports, pointing down the platform.

In the visa office – a grand name for a girl with a cash register and a book of postage stamps – the Austrian woman made a scene.

'Fifty-five euros,' said the visa girl.

'Impossible,' said the Austrian, thrusting a couple of banknotes across the counter. 'Six. It is six.'

The visa girl shook her head. 'Fifty-five euros,' she repeated doggedly, turning to me.

The Austrian woman turned, too. Her breath stank of alcohol.

'It's a trick, don't pay,' she shouted in guttural German. 'She's a liar, I was here last week and it was six. She only wants our money. Don't pay.'

The visa girl may have been sullen, but she didn't look like a criminal. She wearily picked up her book of stamps and slid them across the counter towards us, then pointed with a pen to the printed price: euros 55. This was sufficient evidence for me. Already aware that the whole train was waiting just for the two of us, and not prepared to see my luggage advance to Belgrade without me, I opened my wallet and counted out the required amount.

It was a ludicrous price to pay for a destination which no one wanted to visit, and it appeared to confirm every bad story I'd already been told about Serbia. But by the time I'd related this episode to two members of the Belgrade Tourist Organization, four hours later, I had already begun to radically revise my opinion of the Serbs.

The first sight of Belgrade had been of a knuckle-duster of concrete and stone rising out of the forested Pannonian plain. Closer inspection revealed a shanty-town infill of refugees and Romany families living in houses made out of old wooden pallets and packing cases, but with satellite dishes nevertheless. From the window I could see what looked like the most sustainable flea market in Europe, where refugees were sitting in the dust behind small heaps of military uniforms, dressing-gowns, teddy bears and hardcore pornography, all of it recycled several times before. This homeless population had added tens of thousands to Belgrade's official size.

The train rumbled for the last time across the Sava, now a closer relative of Newcastle's Tyne than the fresh and vigorous waterfall I'd first seen in Slovenia. Then I was in Belgrade station, its tarmac blistered once too often, possibly by passing bombs. In 1928 the Simplon-Orient Express had arrived here at 15.48 and departed again at 16.05, so Agatha would have had only seventeen minutes in the Serb capital. I fully intended to stay a lot longer, but then I had an audience with the Prince.

Arriving in a city which has had two decades of negative publicity is an unsettling travel experience. Serbs have long since been cast, even by Hollywood, as a nation of hitmen and homicidal maniacs, and the freest of thinkers might take a step backwards when a Serb comes knocking on their front door. After all the warnings from the Croats and the Slovenes I'd expected to be scalped almost as soon as I set foot on the blistered tarmac, but no one approached me as I carried my red Sunningdale suitcase towards the taxi rank. To have pulled it along behind me on its dainty little wheels would have been to attract far too much attention. I could visualize the epitaph on my headstone: 'Gigolo in Sunningdale, cannon-fodder in Belgrade.'

The first taxi driver confirmed my fears by asking for far too much, but the one I then hailed on the street was delightful. He good-humouredly pointed out the radioactive building next to my hotel (the stone came from Chernobyl), and described in detail how the local mechanics recycled second-hand car tyres from the West by gouging out their tread with chisels. 'This is the junkyard of Europe,' he said, and he said it without a trace of bitterness. As I paid the fare he told me that I would have no trouble in his city, because I 'looked like a Serb'. To this day, I'm not sure whether I should have taken this as a compliment.

In the Hyatt, a diligent public relations manager put in a call to the tourism people to alert them to the arrival of a foreign writer, and an hour or so later a car arrived outside the hotel to take me up to a reception at the Diplomatic Club. I didn't know whether such treatment would make me more like cannon-fodder, or less.

The Club was a large colonial-type bungalow up a leafy hill, with a couple of tennis courts at the back. The reception was an annual event hosted by the city tourism organization, and involved a few leaflets, a speech, a free beer each, and a self-conscious dance team of hairdressers in fluorescent leotards. Its aim was to try to get diplomats and their families – in the absence of any real tourists – to take a better, more leisurely look at the city to which they had been posted. Hopefully they might then tell their contacts in the outside world that Belgrade wasn't so dreadful after all. As a piece of marketing it was naïve, forlorn, and deeply under-funded, and it largely fell on deaf ears.

I had two conversations with other guests. The first turned out to be the daughter of the Libyan ambassador, a plump, olive-skinned girl of around fifteen or sixteen who was deeply unhappy with life in general and Belgrade in particular.

'I hate it here. It is hateful the way they look at me, the bloody Serbs,' she said, before sliding away to the far end of the tennis courts for a sulk.

On the other side of me a handsome, snappily-dressed man in his late twenties grunted.

'Not a happy bunny,' I murmured.

'There's a simple explanation,' he said. 'Look at her colour. That hair, that skin, for us that means gypsy. A gypsy girl getting in and out of a chauffeur-driven limousine, now that's something to look at. A lot of people in Belgrade are struggling to find anything to eat. Of course they're going to be curious about a stinking rich gypsy.'

He gave me his card. Goran Stanojevic, property rentals. I considered a diplomatic club an unlikely place to meet a lettings agent, and I said so.

'Why not? I may not get an official invitation, but these are my customers, so I must come. I know them all, and where they live.' He was calm and matter-of-fact.

'You do a lot of business with diplomats?'

'Diplomats, NGO staff, IMF, everyone. You can make a bad mistake in property in Belgrade if you don't come through me. A very bad mistake.'

I didn't like the sound of this. 'So how is the property business?'

'Bad, very bad. We need another war.'

I looked at him sharply. 'You can't mean that.'

'Absolutely. Two, three years ago this room would have been so busy you couldn't move. Diplomats, United Nations advisers, aid workers. International re-construction people with re-construction loans, you name them, they were here. And they had budgets, big budgets. Today, Serbia is old news. Now there's 9/11, Afghanistan and Iraq, we're not important any more. Everyone's left or leaving and all the money is going elsewhere. That's why we need another war. To bring back the budgets.'

'Who against?'

'Dunno. Someone will pop up. They always do.'

But surely everyone regretted the assassination of Prime Minister Djindjic? It was recent news.

'We've seen too much death to get upset by another one. He'll get a street named after him so we don't forget him, but he was stupid, he didn't look after the basic details. It served him right. He should have taken more care. And it is better for us, because he was the premier league, so the international community kept raising the goalposts before it'd give us more money. With him out of the way we're on to the second team, for sure. That means the tasks will be made easier, the money will flow. A good result.'

'For the cynical.'

Goran shrugged. 'How long have you been in Serbia? Hours only? Then you will learn. Nothing is straightforward. There is no black and white. Everything here is grey.'

I must have made a long face.

'But don't worry,' he said, grinning and clapping me on the shoulder, 'we have some wonderful girls. You can have a very, very good time.'

Once the crowd thinned I cornered the suit who'd made the speech and an energetic blonde in shiny gold who'd been the chief organizer. I queried them about my border crossing at Sid, and about the visa price. 'How can you expect to encourage international tourism with a cost like that?'

The suit looked glum. 'It is not us who started it. We put these charges on you in response to the charges you put on us. Nobody wants to.'

He retreated. The girl, Jasna, waited until he was out of earshot.

'He didn't know the visa was going up. The government doesn't ask our opinion. We are not important.' She pulled a long strand from her mop of blonde ringlets and started to chew at it, in what I later came to recognize as a characteristic gesture. 'I had to put this reception together with no money. Everything you saw here, I had to beg for it. I know it wasn't very good, and I know some people will make fun of it, but what are we going to do? We are the tourism department. We have to try to promote tourism, however futile it seems to be.'

I was lost for words in the face of this outpouring, and it must have showed.

'I'm sorry,' said Jasna, brightening and putting a hand on my arm. 'It's been a long day. So how are you?'

*

I didn't see Goran or Jasna again for a couple of days. Both had volunteered to show me something of their city, but first I wanted to see it for myself.

My starting point was the Hyatt Hotel, a glittery oasis of glass and steel among New Belgrade's marching rows of housing blocks, festooned with their webs of washing-lines. It was hard to find a bigger contrast. The Hyatt was the best address in town, every bit of hardware highly polished and every member of staff extremely attentive. Its bathrooms were in marble and chrome, its restaurants served sea bass, Thai curry and freshly made pasta, and its clientele were the horn-rimmed, red-braced international banker and the polish-domed, bookish international lawyer. They had come to meet the shaggy, over-dressed, over-cheerful local baron, who swaggered like a cowboy as he strode through the lobby, ostentatiously smoking a fat cigar. Meanwhile the city's deeply fashionable women gathered in the hotel's elegant tea parlour to chatter and nibble at pâtisserie, having just been chauffeured past rows of New Belgraders who were waiting outside their blocks for a tram, some of them wearing no socks.

These women were so highly polished and presented that they must have read the surprising opening paragraph of the *Welcome to Belgrade* magazine I found in my room. Its first entry was under the heading, 'Population', and read thus: 'Belgrade is a city of about two million inhabitants. Fortunately, more than half of them are beautiful, clever and unpredictable women.' Even Bangkok doesn't overtly promote its women as a tourist attraction like this.

The more traditional city sights are in downtown Belgrade, on a Serbian Ayers Rock which rises above the meeting point of the Danube and the Sava rivers. That strategic location, combined with the Serb persona as the boy in the playground who's always ready for a scrap, has made this the most biffed-about capital city in Europe. In 3,000 years it has been destroyed forty-five times in 115 battles, and in the last 100 years it has been bombed on five occasions, in 1914, 1915, 1941, 1944 and 1999. So I wasn't expecting to come across much in the way of quaint wooden houses.

From the Hyatt the centre lay across the Sava, here lined with floating ironmongery, some of it with funnels. The closest crossing was the Bridge of Friendship, a rusty box-girder construction which quivered nervously whenever a tram embarked across it. Underneath it was a paddlesteamer so dilapidated that Conrad would even have refused to take it up the Congo.

To me, climbing up through streets which were dusty with drilling between apartments peppered with open balconies, the architecture seemed a mix of lugubrious Vienna, monumentalist Warsaw and orientalist Istanbul. The square outside the station smelled of grilled lamb and oranges and had a cinema showing pornographic films, with graphic images of stars filling each other's orifices stuck to the doorposts with tape. Around the corner the Hotel Beograd radiated the smell of unwashed male, and a little up the hill stood the ruins of the former military headquarters, a blind giant with all its guts still hanging out and its brains fried by smart bombs.

The main boulevards ran along the top of the ridge towards the giant skullcap of St Sava's, the largest Orthodox church in the world, started in 1905 and still unfinished in what the Slovenes would no doubt condemn as a classic case of Serbian indolence. None of it was particularly aesthetically pleasing, but at least it was its own place, and not aspiring to be a Vienna or a Warsaw or an Istanbul. Two decades of isolation had here preserved a welcome slice of Eastern Europe in a world in which the concept of 'Eastern European' has all but evaporated. The restaurants served bean soup and cabbage and mince, and hadn't yet been over-run by McDonalds and ubiquitous pizzerias. The boulevards were lined by ponderous, unfamiliar department stores punctuated by banks, their main doors guarded by heavies in suits. The more fashionable stuff was hidden away in new shopping malls embedded within the older walls, presumably filling giant holes created by clusters of bombs. There the boutiques had Italian-sounding designer names you haven't quite heard of, like Vanito, Navigare and Marino, at prices which would make even Italians blanch.

In photographs it all looked pretty crap, but Belgrade's dour walls were being slapped by waves of energy, something that a photographer cannot capture. Downtown had an undirected exuberance akin to Berlin after the fall of the Wall. Those who could afford to wear the designer gear – and it was a staggeringly high priority in a city where the average wage is £150 a month – were spending their evenings out in Republic Square or patrolling the pedestrianized Knez Mihailova street, looking for action. Waves of high-stepping girls with wonderful figures moved between the trinket-sellers, the popcorn stands, the pavement artists and the musicians. Everyone was on the phone or eating ice creams, browsing bookshop windows with titles by familiar-sounding authors like Stivan Hoking, Dzejmi Oliver and Nik Hornbi. The better-off were sitting out in a couple of elegant cafés, while others stood watching a road movie of what looked like Belgrade suburbs played on a loop on a giant screen.

For most people, that excitable passeggiata down Knez

Mihailova ended in the peaceful, much-loved fortress park of Kalemegdan, Belgrade's high green forelock which flops over the confluence of the Sava and the Danube. Kalemegdan is the home of the only really old stonework which remains in Belgrade. Here stand the carefully restored ruins of 500 years of Turkish and Austrian occupation, in fragments of walls, gatehouses, ditches and embankments, although these days the park is a place for making love, not war. The moats are filled with tennis and basketball courts and bits of antique military hardware are grouped around the military museum, which contains enough weaponry to rearm the whole of Serbia. Old men play chess under the trees, Romany women sell lace to passers-by, buskers play in the ancient gates and lovers sprawl across the battlements. If you get lucky on the Knez Mihailova and manage to peel one of those high-stepping girls away from her friends, then this is where you start to tangle your tongues.

After all the dire warnings I'd expected Belgrade to be the Balkan Wild West, but most people were far too engrossed in making love to spare a thought for mugging a foreigner – or maybe I looked too much like a Serb. And after the bookishness of Ljubljana and the angst of Zagreb, it was rather a relief to be surrounded by baser instincts. This city was at least wearing its heart on its sleeve, and not trying to reinvent itself by erasing fifty years of history.

Goran the estate agent was particularly frank about local life, and although I found his self-assuredness rather less appealing, I appreciated his brutal honesty. When we met up again in a tavern in Skadarlija, the cobbled Bohemian quarter, he talked exclusively about those two Belgrade obsessions – making love and war.

'The bombing made us all a bit crazy. My whole

generation, twenty-five through thirty-five, had our lives messed up. We missed our teenage years. So now we're shagging. Shagging, shagging, shagging.'

He explained how the odds were stacked fantastically in the favour of men. Sixty per cent girls to forty per cent boys.

'How come?'

Goran grinned and ran his fingers through his hair, conscious as ever of his appearance. 'Too much shagging from behind. Makes girl babies.'

'Seriously.'

'Seriously, people believe that. Then there's the war, killed off some of the men. And it's a fact that more girls are born in periods of peace and boys in times of war. If you do a tour of our primary schools now you'll barely find a girl in some of the classes. But for us, in our generation, it's bloody fantastic.'

Goran's view was that, after many years of oppression and suppression, the Serbs were finally using the peace to make hay, and making hay he most certainly was. He'd lost count of the number of sexual partners he'd had, and couldn't pass a week without at least one new conquest.

'If I get desperate there are seven or eight old ones I can call on at any time.'

It was, he admitted, an addiction. He wasn't interested in the relationship beyond, only the sex, and a girl who wouldn't go all the way on the first date was just a waste of effort.

'The girls know that. I'm high status. I earn good money. I'm good looking. They know what they have to do. Anybody who doesn't do what I do is a fool. It's a tricky world, Belgrade, and you have to be single-minded. To be a king of the jungle you have to learn to swing from branch to branch, one silly mistake and hey, you're down on the jungle floor with everyone else. It sounds hard-headed, but the girls know the rules.'

'Sounds like they're your rules.'

'So who's really using who here? Why are they going with me? For me, myself, I? Or because I've got money and a car? Let me tell you something. Last year I sent text messages to a dozen women telling them I was erasing them from my phone's memory because I didn't want to see them any more. Within a matter of weeks eighty per cent of them had got in touch and I'd fucked them again. Why did they do that? Why? I'm not so arrogant as to think I'm a great lay. I do my three minutes and that's enough for me. So who's fucking around with who? If you ask me it's them pulling the strings, and I'm the one doing the dance.'

Goran frowned into his beer. 'And then, when they've got you, they give you all that talk about love . . . until, that is, someone better comes along. What's that line from *Arabian Nights*? "Women's love is as long as the hairs on a chicken's egg." Pah, not even that.'

There was something about Goran that reminded me of an American veteran of the Vietnam war I'd come across twenty-five years ago living on a beach in Thailand. His favourite conversational subjects had been the benefits to his body of a diet of fresh fruit and under-age girls. From Goran's age, I estimated it was likely that he too had been in uniform.

'Were you in the army?'

A clap of thunder interrupted his reply. A storm had been making a great play of rolling around the skies all evening, crashing and banging, but it was all sound and no fury and had only succeeded in making the city shiny and greasy. Typical Serb, the Slovenes would have said.

'Enlisted at nineteen,' said Goran, when the noise had

died down. 'Saw babies nailed to a wall. I was wounded in Srebrenica by a Muslim sniper. He didn't want to kill me, just wound me so that my friends would come to my rescue, so he shot me in the stomach. So I could shout and cry.' He was completely matter of fact about it. 'That's the way he got my best friend, that sniper. He was married, Boyan, to a lovely girl and they had a little boy. I send them money every month. The boy is twelve now, old enough to write me grateful letters, but I don't want to meet him, ever. Ever.' This he said through gritted teeth. 'Anyway, after Srebrenica I got cancer from depleted uranium, and spent five years in and out of hospital. That's when I decided what the hell, I'm going to have a good time, and started fucking the nurses.'

He took another long swig at his juice; he didn't touch alcohol because he didn't like losing his self-control. 'You can't blame us for seeming confused. We don't know what our values are. One year you are a hero for fighting for your country, and the next you're a criminal. I mean, I didn't even know I was a Serb until the war, I thought I was a Yugoslavian. And what did we do wrong? I don't know. What America is doing now – striking out overseas to protect its people – is exactly what we were doing, then. So that makes America a war criminal, too.'

I didn't want a political argument, so I asked him what he thought I should see in Belgrade. Goran shrugged. 'You want to meet people, not look at buildings. Buildings will only tell you about bits of the past. Personally, I only notice the girls. You want to meet some?'

'I do in fact have a date,' I said. And I explained about Jasna from the tourism office. Since the reception at the Diplomatic Club I'd had two or three telephone conversations with her which I could only describe as unusually flirty. Goran listened with interest as I described her.

'Go for it. Why not,' he said. 'She certainly will. Let me tell you something – she's past it as far as this market is concerned. From what you say she's not a stunner and she's probably approaching thirty. You can't make good soup with old chickens.'

'That's cruel!'

'But no less true. And you, a foreigner – you could be her way out. Her ticket to ride. She'll definitely do it with you.'

I had a couple of meetings to complete before going out with Jasna that evening. Oxfam's Serbian headquarters confirmed what Goran had said; they'd drastically down-sized their operation, training up locals to take over and sending expats elsewhere, and were likely to have little or no presence at all in a year or so's time. The UNHCR said much the same. What had once been the largest refugee operation in the world, with 2 million displaced people in the region, was old news, and a slimmed-down office was back focusing on processing the Afghans and Iraqis who washed up in Serbia while making a break for the West. The big budgets had gone East.

When she bounced into the hotel shortly after 8 p.m., Jasna was decidedly unglamorously dressed in jeans and a fleece. I realized I hadn't seen anyone so casually pre-sented since arriving in Belgrade. Here was someone who certainly didn't play the game according to Goran's rules, and I admired her for her independence of mind. On the phone, she'd talked about taking me to a friend's party, but she'd evidently changed her plans.

'I didn't think the party would be so good. I'm going to take you to Zemun instead.'

Ten minutes later we were installed on a terrace over-looking the river in what was the original Celtic settlement before Belgrade, drinking a silky Montenegrin wine.

'So who else was coming to Belgrade on your train?'

I told her about the Austrian woman who'd made a scene.

'Ah.'

'What do you mean, ah? Do you know her?'

There was a collision of ringlets as Jasna shook her head. 'But I think I know why she was here. New boobs. You can get them done cheaply in Serbia.'

For a while I was conscious of watching her as we talked, trying to place her in Goran's world. She was bright, cheerful and witty, with a straight-lipped smile that dimpled her cheeks. Her mobile phone warbled frequently, and the conversations that ensued would always be full of laughter. She clearly had many, many friends and was the person others looked to because she made things happen. I could see why the tourism office had entrusted her with the task of organizing the reception, even though it was not in her job description. But I got the impression that while others were drawn to her by her energy and her eccentricity, she was the one who, at the end of the evening, would be left on her own. Eccentricity didn't help in a buyer's market.

She told me how she lived on the seventh floor of one of the marching blocks of New Belgrade with her father and her sister, who was a primary school teacher.

'My mother died when I was very young. Granny came to live with us for two years while father adjusted, but that was a long time ago now. These days he does everything. Cooking, washing, ironing. He's a very funny man, my dad. We love him lots, my sister and I.'

We talked for a while of writing, of how the journalist system worked in the UK, and she revealed that she too was a published writer of short stories. From her bag she hauled a bound notebook full of scraps of paper.

'Poetry, too,' she said. 'Some of it in English.'

'Why on earth in English?'

'Poets are always trying to say things a different way. And a lot of my poetry is influenced by Pablo Neruda. You know Neruda?'

Now I was on the defensive. She probably knew more about English poetry than I did.

'So is this what you do at weekends? Write poetry?'

'My dad and I watch fishing programmes on the Discovery Channel. In English.' She giggled.

'Can I ask why?'

'Because it's incredibly peaceful. Stress-free. And because the presenters are so enthusiastic. It's ridiculous really. And then I spend a lot of time on the Internet,' she added. 'Finding poetry. Having a look at the world outside.'

'I suppose you don't travel much.'

'Travel? The Serbs? Who will have us? We're in prison here. Our original jailer is locked up in the Hague, but still nobody has been able to find the key to let us free.'

'Have you not been abroad, then?'

'I went to Poland on a choir tour once. They were all drunk, the Poles.'

Mention of choir led us into a discussion of the war years. It turned out she'd been rehearsing in the choir in St Sava's, the giant unfinished cathedral, when the NATO bombing began.

'We all piled into one car to get back over the bridge into New Belgrade, but everyone was trying to get out of the city. The bridges were packed, the traffic hardly moved. We were terrified. We didn't know whether the bridges were going to be the target. One last big flash and that would be us. Ash. You know what upset me most? Not the idea that I would die, but that my dad, who'd dedicated his life to us, would lose a daughter as well as his wife.'

Jasna wasn't as good at mastering her emotions as Goran, and now she was chewing her hair again.

'After that I was just angry. They came night after night. Why were they doing it to us, for God's sake? What had we done to them? We were defenceless.'

'I thought a Stealth bomber was brought down?'

Jasna's ringlets bobbed merrily. 'That was such a good moment, you cannot believe. An old Russian missile launcher did it. Wonderful. For a while everyone had the bumper sticker, you know, "Oops, sorry, we didn't realize it was invisible." A very good moment.'

'Your block wasn't hit?'

'No. And in a way the bombing was like a firework display. All the electricity went off. We'd sit on the balcony and watch, or else we'd have these big barbecue parties, because without electricity the freezer contents were going to waste and the cooker wouldn't work. So we went to open spaces and made fires and everyone grilled all their meat on the embers. Nobody went to work. It would have been fun, I suppose, if it hadn't also been very dangerous.'

She paused again to look out over the dark sheet of the boatless Danube.

'It is very strange at night, a whole city without light. Very peaceful. I think I'll remember it for ever. You learn how powerful moonlight is. I used to look at the moon for hours. I remember one particular night when there was no moon, it was all just shadows and voices. That day there'd been a small fairground between our block and the next, a fairground with a roundabout which had a giant princess on top. It was very dark, but the fairground people were still there. They started the generator for a moment to check something, and the princess lit up and started to rotate. That really burnt into my memory, the sudden appearance out of the darkness of war of that turning, smiling, princess.'

The next day I saw Jasna again, this time in a more official capacity as a tourist guide. She had with her the tourism department's official car, and its official driver, whom she called Johnny Bravo. If Goran was a lurve machine, Johnny Bravo was a pair of testicles on wheels. For him, stationary traffic was a personal challenge, and whenever he saw a gap in the distance large enough to accommodate his chassis he'd sweep out of the queue and head for it, thumping the steering-wheel with glee and reciting his favourite English mantra, 'Chicks, babes, girls.' Jasna assured me he'd not had an accident in the five months he'd been in the job, but nevertheless she refused to sit in the front with him. When she was out of earshot he was quick to tell me that, in an office of twenty-two women, he'd already slept with five. I suspect that that included her.

With the squeal of rubber and the smell of hot brakes we scorched around Belgrade, ticking off the oldest house, the cathedral, the diplomatic quarter, the government offices, the new railway station (started in 1975 and still not finished – typical Serb), and a couple of fairly piffling and decaying museums. As I walked round them, trying to make appreciative noises, I realized I was wasting my time, looking at the wrong things. As tourists we are programmed to hunt the essence of places through their art, their history and architecture, but that's because we practically never find ourselves in the likes of Belgrade. Sure, there was art here, but it was not in the museums, it was in the frenzied behaviour of the likes of Johnny Bravo; there was architecture, too, but it was not in the Austrian stucco but in the buildings with their guts hanging out. History was still in the air, not on the walls.

The only place where I found the recent past emerging in plastic form was the Museum of Contemporary Art, an ambitious building on the banks of the Sava. Among several installations making reference to war was a video projection of a boxer lashing out at words written in blood: 'Don't tell me who I am, don't tell me what I need. Don't tell me what I feel.' Next to it was another which showed the Windows Media Player start-up screen, bearing the stark message 'Catastrophic Failure'. I'm not sure whether this was intended, or whether the machine had actually gone dreadfully wrong, but there was a huge irony in using such strong language to describe the breakdown of what is after all just a bit of software, in a region which had spilt so much blood.

I'd been in Serbia for a few days when the word came through that Crown Prince Alexander II finally had room in his diary. Alexander is the latest of the Karageorges, the dynasty which had led the Serb uprising against the hated Turks and gone on to rule the between-the-wars kingdom of the Serbs, Croats and Slovenes.

The family originally took the throne in 1903 after the sticky demise of Alexander and Draga Obrenovitch, assassinated by a group of army officers. The Obrenovitches had met a blackly comic end. The officers had entered the royal palace at night, cutting the electricity and plunging the place into darkness. The royals, in their bedroom, had heard all the banging and swearing downstairs as the would-be assassins had bumped into all the furniture, and had had plenty of time to hide in a secret cupboard in their bedroom. It took the officers two hours to find them, and then only after a tip-off from palace staff. They'd stabbed and shot Alexander several times, and when he clearly wasn't dead they'd tried hurling him from the balcony – but he clung on to the railings, so his fingers had to be cut off too.

Ruling Serbia is a tough assignment and the Karageorges hadn't had an easy time of it, either. Alexander's grandfather, also called Alexander, was assassinated by the Croat Ustashe on a visit to France, and his father Petar fled to England during World War II. Alexander himself was born in Suite 212 in Claridges in London, although a pot of Serbian earth was placed under the bed so that it could be safely said he was born on Serbian soil. For the first forty-five years of his life the likelihood of him ever returning to Serbia seemed slim, so after a traditionally aristocratic education at Gordonstoun and Sandhurst he spent sixteen years in the British army before entering the business world. But then the political climate began to change in Yugoslavia, and suddenly there was a real possibility of exchanging his house in Kensington for the family palace in Belgrade.

Croatia and Slovenia, for their part, were not interested in any return of a scion of the old order, especially one who spoke little Serbo-Croat. In Croatia I'd been told a scurrilous anti-Serb story of how HRH Alexander had been regaled with so much drink at the banquet given in honour of his return that he'd no longer been able to control his sphincters. But I didn't think I could ask him about that.

On the appointed afternoon the taxi dropped me at the gates of the Royal Palace, a distant Byzantine-style château just visible through the trees. A soldier in the sentry post spelled out my name several times over the radio, and then a people-carrier with two heavies in suits came sweeping down the drive. They delivered me into the hands of the Crown Prince's press officer in the converted

stable block, who in turn passed me on to the chief inter-
preter, an urbane gentleman in a sports jacket several
sizes too large for him. He filled in time by telling me the
(short) history of the palace, preluding anything he
thought particularly insightful with an intensely irritating
false chuckle or two.

The actual interview took place in a classically lavish
palace room which had also been regularly used by
Milosevic. The floor was polished parquet covered in blue
silk carpets, the furniture richly brocaded baroque, and on
the walls were paintings by Poussin and others of a similar
school. French windows gave out on to a terrace and
beyond the stone balustrades I could see a wooded vale. A
couple of maids in the sort of doilied uniform you only see
in French farces delivered plates of *amuse-bouches* to the
table, and then the doors were closed so that they could
be opened with ceremony, as the Crown Prince made his
entrance. A king without a throne.

He was a plump, genial man, immaculately dressed in a
suit that had to be Savile Row, and his speaking voice was
Sandhurst with a Geneva undertow. He smiled pleasantly
as I explained my Agatha mission, but the smile never
extended to his eyes.

'I must say I too like trains,' he commented when I'd
finished. 'I had my honeymoon on the VSOE.'

For a while we talked of how he'd come to return to
Serbia.

'Things started changing in 1989, after the collapse of
the Berlin Wall. At the time I really believed there'd be
continuity for the communist system, that Yugoslavia
would continue being the buffer state between East and
West, but calls came in, faxes came in, from people who
wanted to bring democracy to Yugoslavia. Then terrible
things started happening. Ethnic cleansing, killing,

refugees, and I realized I had a new job, to bring peace and help people to get on. The dream of coming back became more real, but I had to get round a cunning dictatorship. Milosevic ran a pretty astute negative regime. Unfortunately the West got into bed with him, and the whole area paid a terrible price.

'I first came here in October 2000, after the regime had been overthrown by the people. Then I came back in December, and that's when the subject of us returning to live here came up. The government and I worked to establish a method, which culminated in July 2001, when we moved in here. They've been a busy two years, a complete change in our lives. We came here not to take, but to give, and I've thrown away my political hat. I came back to be a unifying factor. We need to put our differences aside for the greater good.'

The Crown Prince went on to describe how he and his wife had been travelling the country, hosting receptions and dinners for foreign industrial organizations and heading off overseas on trade missions, always in tandem with representatives from the relevant government ministry. Economic progress had, he said, been slow. It was tough trying to get anyone to focus on Serbia with everything else going on in the world. 'It seems that it is easier to pay for war than it is for peace, but we desperately need help. We still have five per cent of the world's refugees, 200,000 from Bosnia and 300,000 from Croatia. That's a lot for a small country, a tremendous burden. I'm very much against declaring them citizens of this country when in fact they've every right to be citizens in their own homelands.'

On the question of the conflict, he was in no doubt about the mistaken nature of the NATO bombing. 'I don't think you go and bomb a nation like that. It only served to unify the people behind the regime. But times are changed now, and we are friends with everyone. There are some areas which still have to be resolved, namely Kosovo and Bosnia, but I firmly believe that there will be no more war. A few incidents, maybe, but we're not killing each other, that's finished. We've paid a terrible price. Now our problem is as much about public relations, we're not too gifted at that. We need to explain our position. To do some lobbying. It requires tremendous art, but it would be money well spent.'

'And what about some tourism?' I was thinking of the visa price again.

'There's plenty of potential. We've a long stretch of the Danube, and several spas. We've also got a very fine ski resort which I frequent with my family. We have a major problem there in that the most important run has those horrible, er, bomblet things . . .'

'Cluster bombs?'

'Cluster bombs. It's very dangerous.'

'And what about your social life? Is there an aristocracy?'

'We've made lots of friends. Religious figures, intellectuals, politicians of all sides, ambassadors, we've had them all for dinner. And then one meets royals at weddings and funerals. We'll be over in Britain for the fiftieth anniversary of the Queen's coronation. Along with a lot of the other royals of Europe.' He made it sound like a small world.

It was a good moment to ask a final question about his personal ambition.

'So are you expecting to become King?'

Alexander wouldn't be pushed. 'There is an interest in constitutional monarchy,' he said, carefully.

'And do you expect to die peacefully in your bed?' I mentioned the fate of the Obrenovitches.

'I don't see a problem. It is more dangerous walking in some western cities. Today I was walking in a crowd, as I often do. They're a very emotional people and they want to hold me, sometimes a bit too enthusiastically. My only real danger is of being bruised.'

Afterwards, one of the Crown Prince's massive body-guards was instructed to take me back to the Hyatt in a black armour-plated Audi. He had that brutal self-assurance of someone who could break a neck with his bare hands. His silence made me uncomfortable.

'Were you with the Crown Prince on his walkabout this morning?'

He nodded.

'No problems?'

He shook his head.

'Does HRH speak much Serbian? Enough to talk to people?'

The bodyguard shrugged. 'Getting better. But some-times it's good he doesn't understand. Because of the rude words shouted from the back.'

I met Goran one more time in the nightclub in the base of the Hyatt. He appeared, as he had said he would, with at least half-a-dozen girls, all of whom seemed delicate, pretty and not in the least bit cheap and easy. But when I congratulated him on the quality and quantity, he scowled.

'Their heads are empty. They just want to talk. To talk about everything, the past, the future, their hopes. I don't care about the past, the future, I want to have fun, have a good time then go to bed.' For one normally so full of certainty, he seemed quite depressed.

'You know, I don't think you even like women,' I said.

'I don't understand them. I know the rules, but I don't

understand the game. I'm going to Timisoara this week-end to shag a few Romanian prostitutes. At least there it's a straightforward transaction.'

I said something about how women had brought a whole shed-load of new perspectives into my life, and I didn't see why it should be any different in Belgrade. 'Perhaps all the pressure to get a man gives them tunnel vision,' I ventured. 'They're so focused on looking good that there's no space or time for more individuality.'

'Ah. You mean the difficult ones. I can't be bothered with the difficult ones.' He grinned wolfishly. 'How're you getting on with your difficult one? What's her name?'

'Jasna.'

'So – have you fucked her yet?'

I hadn't.

Jasna had called me that morning and asked whether I was missing her. We were scheduled for one last drink, but I was beginning to have cold feet. Although no relation-ship actually existed between us, we seemed to have crossed some significant line and it was only a matter of time. We'd already had a second, rather intense, evening out in a floating restaurant on the Danube, over a barbecue of grilled fish. That day her doctor had told her that she had sand in her kidneys, and she was momentarily so vulnerable that I wanted to put my arms around her. But as soon as I started to express any sympathy, she brightened immediately and the danger retreated.

'I don't want to talk about it,' she said.

'What do you want to talk about?'

She smiled her lean, champagne-sipping smile. 'Do you think I've got a big nose?'

I shook my head. Mind you, she didn't have a small one either.

'Bleah. That's a pity. Because a big nose means you can smoke a cigar in the shower.'

In the end I'd called her and cancelled our last encounter. We'd got to know each other too well, too quickly, to remain platonic. On the phone neither of us really knew what to say, so I'd thanked her for being such a good companion and diligent guide. 'And tell me that I am pretty and that I will get married some day,' she'd said, forlornly. I could tell that she was chewing her hair.

A couple of days after I crossed into Bulgaria I found a small icon of St Nicholas, whom Serbs venerate as the patron saint of safe voyages, slipped into the pages of my notebook. As I felt its touch in my palm I thought of her. That compelling young poetry-writing ringleted Serb sitting cross-legged on the sofa in her block in New Belgrade, dreaming of Pablo Neruda and watching big men pursue tiny fish on satellite TV.

TSAR BORIS AND THE BLACK SEA

I needed a break after Belgrade, and Sofia wasn't it. The Balkans had been an intense experience and I found I couldn't face tackling another city. I knew it as soon as I stepped off the train and joined the dusty shadows mooching through the giant communist mausoleum that was Sofia station. The station was ringed with people in kiosks, peering out through glass grilles patched with cracked sellotape, like railway priests waiting to hear fare-dodgers' confessions.

But this wasn't typical Sofia. Beyond the station limits the city had had a makeover. Fifty years of history had been hastily papered over, and in its place rose what seemed to my eyes, after Belgrade, a pallid Vegas, full of casinos, western brand names and executives in suits. Sofia had wholeheartedly embraced capitalism and turned its back completely on Eastern Europeanism almost as if it had never existed. Lots of new, shiny regional head-quarters (which would originally have chosen Belgrade as a more strategic location) had settled on the Bulgarian capital. Meanwhile many of the former monuments of

East European culture had been left to rot, the mausoleum of a railway station among them; in a destination where the concepts of entrepreneurship and privatization hold sway, nationalized industries like railways have bad karma.

I had a vague plan for Bulgaria that involved a bit of a diversion from the Agatha-quest, and when a shopkeeper ripped me off outrageously over a soft drink within an hour of setting foot in the city I put that plan into action. There were no Agatha connections to keep me here – beyond the fact that Bulgarian secondary schools study her novels as set texts – so I set off to trace the route of the very first Orient Express.

Back in October 1883, when Georges Nagelmackers' Wagons-Lits service was originally announced in the pages of *The Times*, the projected journey time was seventy-five hours, and the theory was that there'd be no change of trains all the way to Constantinople. In fact Nagelmackers could have been hauled over the coals for misrepresentation, because he knew very well when he wrote that announcement that the last sections of the railway had yet to be completed. Accordingly he was taking a huge public relations gamble when he invited several dignitaries and important journalists on his inaugural run. If they were expecting luxury all the way through to Turkey, they were in for a surprise.

The group included Nagelmackers himself, the French minister of finance, Turkey's first secretary, Belgium's minister of public works, and six journalists, three French, two German and one Dutch. A large crowd of interested onlookers also gathered at Gare de l'Est, where Nagelmackers cleverly dashed their expectations with an old engine and a couple of scruffy wagons, and then restored them by backing in the real Orient Express, a gleaming construction of teak and glass, splendidly windowed and brilliantly lit with gas lamps. 'As well appointed and comfortable as any luxury flat in Paris,' wrote Edmond About, one of the French journalists.

The train followed the pre-war routing via Austria, Hungary and Romania, and for the first two-thirds of the trip everything had gone swimmingly. The coaches were half as long again as anything previously seen on the railways, and included a mail-carrying wagon for luggage. The ornate dining-car, hung with crystal and gilt chandeliers typical of Parisian salons, had a smoking room for the gentlemen, with leather *fauteuils* and footstools, and a ladies' retiring-room with a *chaise-longue* and Louis XV chairs. Edmond About painstakingly described the dining-car tables with their snow-white tablecloths and gleaming cutlery and wine glasses, and the Burgundian chef with a black beard like a Scotsman's sporran. The chef turned out to be a flamboyant, emotional character, prone to breaking into song, and he made a big impression on those pioneer travellers. His very first dinner menu was ten courses long and was served by waiters in powdered wigs. About also wrote admiringly of the new experience of shaving in comfort while travelling at 50 m.p.h., no doubt an important consideration in the years of cut-throat razors.

Vienna brought new excitement when the all-male passenger list was spiced with the arrival of the wife and sister-in-law of the Austrian minister of roads. 'Two delightful sisters,' wrote About. Also joining was a Hungarian band, and as the train crossed the Hungarian plains each of the younger male members of the party took it in turns to dance with each of the Austrian sisters. By the time the band struck up with the Marseillaise even the Burgundian chef joined the party. Leaping out of his kitchen, waving a frying pan in one hand and clutching an egg-beater to his huge chest, he proceeded to sing the French national anthem at the top of his voice.

When they reached the Romanian border town of Giurgiu, however, the triumphal procession came to a premature end. Ahead lay the Danube, as yet uncrossed by any railway bridge. So the party were forced to leave the sanctuary of their luxury train and disembark into the tumbledown riverside shanty-town. There their baggage was seized by a swarm of peasants with mangy dogs, and they boarded a ferry to cross the river to the Bulgarian town of Ruse, assuming they'd be catching an onward train to Constantinople.

In Ruse they had a second disappointment. The direct rail link to Constantinople had another six years until completion, and so they were forced to join a local train for the Black Sea town of Varna, which was Bulgaria's only rail route at that time. From there the plan was to catch a ship to complete the final leg of the journey by sea.

Conditions were suddenly a long way from what the illustrious group had become accustomed to. The Burgundian chef had remained with his travelling kitchen to prepare for the journey back, so instead the passengers had to make do with plates of chewy grilled partridge and Turkish pastries improvised at a station *en route*. Nagelmackers had instructed one of his crew to bring as many bottles of brandy and wine as he could carry, to keep the whole party on message. It was hugely different from what the VIPs had been led to expect, but it certainly gave the journalists plenty to write about.

At Varna they were piled into little rowing boats, 'each manned by a villainous-looking Bulgarian with an enormous moustache and a fanatical gleam in the eye' for the transfer out to the *Espero*, a Trieste-based Lloyd-Austriaco vessel full of sweating humanity, on which they completed their journey. After nine days' rest in Constantinople they turned around and made the return trip, arriving back in Paris to a hero's welcome. Two of the journalists, Edmond About and the wonderfully-named Henri Stefan Opper de Blowitz, wrote books about the experience.

Ruse today may be Bulgaria's fifth largest city, but a great sleepiness seemed to have descended upon it the afternoon I arrived. The magnificent ploshtad Svoboda, the central square, was busy enough with strolling lovers and even a melancholy dancing bear, but you'd only to walk fifty yards or so in either direction and the boarding-up began. It felt like a hibernating animal at the onset of winter, limiting the blood supply to its outer limbs and curling up around its warm heart.

In ploshtad Svoboda there was plenty of fine floral stucco and *Jugendstil* wrought iron, but the opera house was dark and all the museums were closed. Even the Danube, officially classified as a wild river for most of its length, was broad, sullen and disinterested. The long pleasure gardens along the riverbank were deserted apart from a couple of tramps sleeping on the benches and a handful of men in their underpants, fishing. In the distance rose the chimneys of Giurgiu's chemical factories, long the source of cross-border disputes and acid rain.

I was down on the riverside looking for the Railway Museum. It had, I'd heard, some eccentric old rolling stock from those early days, and it occupied the former riverside station from where those pioneer passengers had embarked unwillingly for Varna. Unfortunately it didn't appear on any of the tourist literature for the town, so for a while I followed a rusty old track along the water until it came to a sudden stop in what turned out to be a hospital compound. A taxi was waiting outside the hospital entrance. The driver looked puzzled as I tried to explain what I wanted in a mixture of English and German, but he nodded, so I climbed aboard, forgetting that a nod of the head means 'no' in Bulgaria.

Twenty minutes later, after several local inquiries, the taxi driver was warming to his unwelcome task, although we still hadn't found a language in common. We were back on a quiet lane by the river lined with parked cars with a pair of men in each, doing something or other which required peace and quiet and which probably wasn't listening to the cricket. At the end of the lane stood what was plainly an old Victorian railway station from an English country town, with a station garden full of old rusty hulls of steam engines. The driver and I grunted at each other in satisfaction, but we were premature. The entrances were locked, and there wasn't even a sign which said museum.

At this point, if I'd arrived on foot, I'd have given up and retreated, but by now the taxi driver was fully engaged on my quest. He prowled around the station, trying doorhandles, until one opened, revealing a set of stairs up which he disappeared. A couple of minutes later he returned with a beefy middle-aged woman with skin like gorgonzola who addressed me in French. Yes, she said, she could open up, and no, she didn't get many visitors. In fact I was the first this week.

Now that a channel of communication was open, the taxi driver made a suggestion which the lady translated. 'He asks if you want him to stay?'

'Please.' I didn't particularly want to walk back past the line of car-bound cricket-lovers, lest I got invited in for a maiden over.

The museum curator (for such she was) seemed

delighted to have a visitor, particularly once I admitted to being British. It was the British who had built both the station and the Ruse to Varna line, she said, and it had been Bulgaria's first. She explained how for a while in the 1880s this little station had been put on the international map as travellers from western and central Europe passed through *en route* to Constantinople, in the wake of that first trainload of VIPs. In the compound she found me one of eight locomotives purpose-built for the route by Sharp, Stewart and Atlas of Manchester in 1866. It was in surprisingly good order, while many of the more recent locomotives were flaking and crumbling. In fact some were so far gone that one injudicious tap on the funny bone would have reduced them into giant pyramids of rust.

Most of the coaches were better protected from the elements under the station awning. Here was the Turkish Sultan's coach from 1889, a basic jazzed-up two-axle cattle wagon with velvet seats. He'd used it, said the curator, to tour his kingdom when Bulgaria was still part of the Ottoman empire. Like Serbia, Bulgaria had been subjected to a long and gruelling period of Ottoman rule, during which the Turks had insisted that church floors had to be built below ground level to ensure they were lower than the mosques.

Next to the Sultan's wagon was a coach built for King Boris III, the Bulgarian monarch who had been famously obsessed by trains in general and the Orient Express in particular. In his memoirs Britain's King Edward VIII describes how, during a state visit to Bulgaria, he had been largely ignored by Boris and his brother because they were arguing about who would drive the train home. Boris's father Ferdinand had been a train enthusiast, but it was his son who used to run riot on the Orient Express, demanding to be allowed to ride on the footplate. One of the *chefs de train* had even had to whack the young Prince on the bottom with his slipper for continued misbehaviour.

After Ferdinand's abdication (he chose the wrong side in World War I), Boris, now King, would use his royal prerogative to insist on actually taking over the controls of the Simplon-Orient as soon as it crossed into Bulgaria, waiting until it was over the border and pulling the communication cord, then strolling along the track to the locomotive. Unfortunately he had a penchant for speed, and his demand for more and more steam pressure from a fire that was stoked hotter and hotter eventually led to the spontaneous combustion of the official driver's clothing. The unfortunate man leapt from the train and was killed; the King brought the train safely into the next station, but after that the government of Bulgaria insisted that he must forgo the temptation to be both an engine driver and a monarch. Later he was to die mysteriously during World War II, a week after being summoned to meet Hitler – and two weeks after having secretly contacted the Allies.

Not unsurprisingly Boris's personal coach, built in 1911, recreates the décor and style of the best of the Orient Express. It has a reception room, a restaurant and a kitchen complete with an ice cupboard. The curtains are velvet, the wall covered in marquetry of walnut and oak, the floor is padded leather, and above the windows is the King's own crest, set in mother-of-pearl inlays. Radiators surround the walls, and there's a lever to control the heat. And next door to his extravaganza stands his father's, built in 1894, in similar, albeit less lavish, style.

The museum curator hovered expectantly as I wandered through these little monuments to railway obsession, opening the velvet curtains so I could see better. When I declared myself satisfied with what I had seen, she invited me up into her office so she could look up the full details of the manufacture of all the British locomotives from her wall of reference works about Bulgarian trains. I slavishly copied everything down, even though it was too much the full anorak for me. Branimir the taxi driver had come up with us, and over an insipid cup of Bulgarian instant coffee the conversation moved from my journey in pursuit of Agatha Christie (whom she had read, but he had not) to how he had come to Ruse in search of excitement once his children had left home, after twenty-five years as a potato farmer.

Two hours later I was on a train myself, heading down that pioneer route towards Varna. Branimir had delivered me to Ruse's main station, a high-pillared deeply serious building which looked like the headquarters of a bank. I can't read Cyrillic, so I'd had to verify the train times with an information desk woman in a toilet attendant's smock, who'd pasted all the schedules into her puzzle books so that she could both look up departures and do spot-the-ball simultaneously. Then I'd sat on the station bench, drinking my Pipi Bubble, next to three old gents divvying up a pungent garlic sausage with a pocket knife. Together we watched the trains come and go with the wheel-tappers counting them down, and the boiler-suited station staff sauntering in and out of doors marked variously *salle d'attente*, *mouvement*, and *kommandant*.

My express, when it came, was hauled by a Skoda, reminding me of all those now-passé Skoda jokes ('What do you call a Skoda with a sun roof? A skip,' 'What's the difference between a Skoda and a Jehovah's Witness? You can shut the door on a Jehovah's Witness'). But, in line with the new Skoda world order, this machine hummed along capably and within minutes of shaking off Ruse we were in rolling grasslands thick with weeds and wild-flowers, broken by the occasional outcrop of trees. Compared to the visual drama of Slovenia and Croatia there was something fuzzy and pubic about this landscape. With insufficient mechanization to put things in order, it had few straight lines. Mostly it was empty of all life except for what looked like a distant beetle struggling across a counterpane, which turned out to be a tractor doing its best to keep a handbrake on nature. Aside from a couple of gypsy-like encampments with tents of sticks and polythene, and a man with a scythe working his way right to the horizon, there was no one out on the land to nurture it and keep it under control.

At the start of the fifty years of communism the one million Bulgarian smallholdings had become 920 giant collective farms, and the majority of the former small-holders had decamped into the cities to become factory workers. Those fifty years had been enough to erase the love of the soil from former farming families, and today only 45 per cent of Bulgaria's arable land is actually cultivated. Even fruit and vegetable gardens on the out-skirts of villages, naturally thick with melon patches and vines, were overgrown. Bulgarians had lost interest in their countryside. They'd all done a Branimir, and gone to live in cities.

An hour or so down the line it began to rain, the first serious rain of my journey. It fell in thick wet curtains, revealing the outside world only in glimpses. Once, emerging from an embankment, the train ambushed a horse and cart with a foal trotting alongside. The foal bolted at the noise and the mare reared up to follow, the farmer hauling hard at the reins and cursing as his load of sweetcorn scattered across the track behind him. Another time we swirled past a mist-shrouded cowherd dressed in a blue nylon Pacamac who looked fleetingly in at the window. Perhaps he too was dreaming of driving a taxi in Ruse, and perhaps there was someone onboard who looked longingly back, wanting to exchange a mess of an urban existence for the simplicity of a dozen cows who loved him deeply, and never expected to have, tomorrow, anything different to what they had today.

The express wasn't busy, but the seat covers were clammy with the sweat of previous passengers. Initially I was seated opposite a rough-shaven young man in a green tracksuit who studied me with some intensity and then fell asleep in the staring position, so I never quite knew whether I was being watched or not. He was eventually driven out by a dumpy old lady who had a serious loquacity problem combined with an in-built radar which warned her whenever a potential listener stepped within hearing distance. That listener didn't need to respond or even give eye contact; just being spotted on her radar was enough to trigger the flow. I speak no Bulgarian but I could identify the word Varna, which cropped up often. So what was she talking about? Fifty facts you always wanted to know about Varna? Stories from the Varna of my youth? Varna through the ages? Varna on 50 stotinki a day?

It was a relief when, half-way through the journey, the compartment was invaded by four street musicians, excited and dripping with rain. They were muscular, energetic, fit-looking men in their mid-forties, and no doubt their performances would have been very robust. More importantly, though, there was something about their presence that intimidated the dumpy monologuist into immediate silence.

Looking at the tanned, tight-skinned and smiling faces,

I supposed that they were probably Romany – many street musicians of Eastern Europe are – but I couldn't be sure. Their hair was swept flat with hair oil, they wore black waistcoasts and they filled the compartment with the smell of goat's cheese. The drummer heaved his drum up on to the luggage rack, but the accordion player and the clarinettist nursed their instruments on their knees. Their feet were tapping from the moment they sat down, and every now and then that suppressed rhythm would hit the surface and one or other of them would break moment-arily into the skirl of a tune, which would then be passed briefly around the compartment, like a musical parcel.

One of the band, the clarinettist and senior partner, spoke sufficient German to establish where I was from and where I was going. He himself had, he said, travelled once to Frankfurt, but with another band, and he knew the names Birmingham and Newcastle, although not for the usual footballing reasons.

'I know English music,' he announced. Then, holding his clarinet up to the others for a moment's silence, he launched into 'Que sera, sera'.

The rain stopped and the view cleared as we drew near to Varna, but what it revealed was not a pretty sight. For half a century Bulgaria had been a country of heavy industry, mostly iron, steel, petrochemicals, fertilizers and machinery. It was particularly famous for its forklift trucks. But 85 per cent of its market had been Warsaw Pact countries, and the whole shebang collapsed with the Berlin Wall. Industries which were so heavily state-controlled and subsidized were never going to appeal to venture capitalists from the West, come to pick over the bones, so now they stood there, the empty skeletons of manufacturing, monstrous, dangerous and full of weeds. Lake Varna, with its big-ship access to the Black Sea, had been an ideal venue for such industry, and its shore was lined with gantries, cranes, industrial carcasses and piles of unwanted output. For a while we rattled past what must have been hundreds of miles of steel piping, made in an era when productivity was more important than product. In those days if you were a Warsaw Pact country and it was your turn to take 25,000 miles of Bulgaria's top-quality one-metre diameter piping, then you took it without a murmur of dissent. You were doing it not because you needed any of it, but for the sake of the workers, for the sake of the greater good, and because it was your turn. The fact that, one day, those hundreds of miles of giant tubing and the immense installation that made them would become useless souvenirs of economic mismanagement didn't enter anyone's head.

And so the train jogged along a shore littered with abandoned machinery and the wrecks of rusting coasters. The air smelled eggy and sulphurous and each disused factory sat at the epicentre of a nest of decaying detritus, amid drifting smoke and dust. Whole areas were dis-coloured grey, greyish blue, brown, and rusty red. Every couple of miles there'd be a freight yard full of old box vans, flat-bed trucks and even an old steam engine covered in moss. A few tracks were still in use by tanker wagons blackened with oil and crucible-shaped wagons bleached a whitish blue by some acrid chemical.

It wasn't always easy to tell whether a factory was abandoned or not, but a power station, one of the biggest of the dinosaurs on the shore and one of the closest to the city, was still showing some vital signs. In the middle of the giant wrangle of metal and dirty brick was a boiler-suited man hoeing a neat little vegetable patch. Obviously someone who liked plenty of lead in his greens.

*

In Varna, it didn't take long to establish that I was too late in the season for the summer hydrofoil service to Istanbul, and therefore couldn't completely emulate the journey of the pioneer Orient Expressers on their boat of sweating humanity. So I settled down for a bit of R & R. I needed a break. The city itself, Bulgaria's second largest, was a pleasant enough resort, with wide boulevards and parkland running down to where the Black Sea rippled and shimmered. It had a popular shoreline of beaches and techno bars, but the memory of all those nearby power stations was too fresh in my mind to encourage lingering. Instead I took the bus out to Golden Sands.

The gated enclave of Zlatni Pyasatsi, better known to the rest of the world as Golden Sands, was the first Bulgarian resort on the Black Sea. It was started back in the late 1950s, carved into a large area of densely forested shore that was so snake-infested at the time that lorryloads of hedgehogs had to be shipped in from Albania to get rid of them before the tree-fellers would agree to start work. Originally intended as an earthly Eden for members of the politburo, it had eventually become the playground for Czechs, East Germans, Poles and Hungarians, as it was one of very few places in the Eastern Bloc with a guaranteed supply of both sun and sand.

Today it is a mass-market destination for those western Europeans for whom the price is crucial to the decision to travel. Package holidays here are among the cheapest on the planet, albeit still not cheap enough for Bulgarians themselves, who on average earn a paltry £80 a month, and thus cannot afford to stay in their own resort. And beer sells at the equivalent of 50 pence a pint.

Golden Sands's three-mile beach is of fine sand, planted in regimental rows of different coloured umbrellas and sun loungers and punctuated at regular intervals with lifeguards and massage stations. The warmish, clear-water sea has light surf and half the salinity of the Mediterranean. Behind the beach runs a promenade lined with restaurants and pool-bar complexes with water-slides, some of which stage synchronized swimming shows after dark to get the punters in. Those complexes are surrounded by portrait artists, archery and shooting galleries, mechanical bucking bison, pools with bumper boats, stalls where you paint your own ceramics and photographer's studios that will shoot you in vintage clothes. Overall there's a fairground jauntiness about the place, which doesn't pretend to be anything other than it is: a paradise of artificial entertainment.

The hotels are a touch brutal to look at and offer all sorts of non-traditional hotel services such as eye tests, dentistry and cosmetic surgery at far cheaper prices than you'd get them in the West. My room had an empty fridge ready to receive all the cut-price beer that the management assumed I'd be buying, and the bar was busy with middle-aged Russian bottle-blondes with the sort of translucent skin that looks better when the sun has set. For much of the day they'd sit around on the terrace swatting wasps and washing flaky pastry down with bucketloads of dis-gusting coffee, and in the evenings they'd teeter off in search of nightlife in unfeasibly tight leopardskin trousers, usually with a few handfuls of cellulite brimming over the edges.

At dusk, Golden Sands started pulsing with live music. Almost every restaurant of any size had a band belting out Elvis, Abba or Meatloaf, and doing it pretty well. For a couple of nights I ate at the Golden Dreams grill restaurant, where the meals so exactly replicated the pictures on the menu that there must have been an art director checking each one before it left the kitchen. I

chose the venue because of its leather-trousered song-
stress, a cross between Bonnie Tyler and Cruella de Vil.
She could turn her hand to everything from Techno to
Puccini, but her talent and energy were tragically wasted
on a dining-room full of half-cut foreigners, who were
only there for the beer.

In addition to the Russians, Golden Sands was busy
with overweight Germans, a fair number of young
Scandinavians, and several planeloads of Israelis who flew
in just for the casinos, as this was the closest non-Muslim
(and therefore non-threatening) nation to Israel which
permitted gambling. It made a curious mix.

There were plenty of salt-of-the-earth Brits, too. It had
been a while since I'd been within range of my own
nationality, and I found myself drawn like an eaves-
dropper to anyone I heard speaking English. Not that they
were always that easy to understand. Most had the sort of
regional, tribal accents that took me a moment or two to
interpret and which must have been completely impenetrable to the Bulgars. These were people who'd
worked hard all year, saved hard, and now they were off
on their 'olidays, full of bonhomie. Typical of the bunch
were Steve and Pete, two beer-gutted bachelors in T-shirts
emblazoned 'Tap on Tour' whom I met at a bar by the
beach.

'Tap-dancers, eh,' I said, eyeing the T-shirts. Judging by
the bodies they barely concealed, it looked very unlikely.

Steve looked at Pete and Pete looked back at Steve. 'Not
us, mate. That's short for the Brewery Tap, that is.'

'In the Wirral,' chimed in Steve.

'Tap on Tour. There's eleven of us. Come here every
year. Regular, like.'

'Why Bulgaria?'

'Have you seen the price of a pint? For most of us,

down the Brewery Tap most nights, coming here is cheaper than staying at home.'

It was Steve and Pete who'd introduced me to Stephane, a tall, laconic thirty-six-year-old ex-town-planning officer from Brighton whom they'd been to see in Varna. The Brewery Tap boozers were interested in buying a cheap villa on the Black Sea to reduce their drinking overheads even further, and Stephane, as they put it, was their 'main man'.

I don't think I've ever met a more understated estate agent than the long-fingered and distinguished Stephane Lambert, and the prospect of being Steve and Pete's main man didn't appear to fill him with enthusiasm. It turned out that he had drifted almost accidentally into the property business, and he still had a slight air of wondering what on earth he was doing there.

Once he'd dispatched Steve and Pete to look at a villa, we sat talking on the balcony of his office in Varna and he related how he'd arrived in the country some years earlier, as a volunteer on a UN-sponsored project called Beautiful Bulgaria. He'd spent his first couple of years in Ruse, where he had become a celebrity almost overnight as the English messiah who was bringing money and creating jobs. Beautiful Bulgaria's thrust was to employ the unemployed rather than to spread work through the usual crony system which dominates the new Bulgarian economy, and that made it very popular on the street. It also had a sizeable budget.

'A lot of people wanted to be our friends. A lot. I only had to sneeze and I'd get into the news. We'd get invited to everything, to open exhibitions and judge beauty competitions. Couple of years back I was voted Man of the Year. They even asked me to be mayor.' He said it completely without pride.

'So why move into the property business?'

'You can only spend so long being a volunteer. It gets to you in the end; it's partly the disorganization and partly the lack of thanks. It was invaluable experience, though, because all the reconstruction work made us lots of contacts with architects, builders and engineers. On weekends we'd disappear off into the country, and I realized that a lot of country villages are basically abandoned, which seemed a criminal waste.'

I agreed that the Bulgarians didn't seem too interested in rural living.

'I bought a couple of houses,' Stephane continued. 'At a couple of thousand pounds each, it was not exactly going to break the bank. Then a TV programme called *A Place in the Sun* asked us to help with some local arrangements in return for a credit, and when the programme was broadcast we were inundated with e-mails. By that time I'd fallen in love with a woman and with the country, but I'd had enough of Beautiful Bulgaria. So it seemed a good moment to set up in business.'

'There's money to be made?'

'In the coastal stuff, yes. Most of our customers are very ordinary people who are fed up with Britain, for whatever reason. A lot are from the north, and they've not got a big budget. Their main interest is recently built coastal villas, the sort of stuff you can get in Spain for five times the price. And with Bulgaria about to join the EU, it's a good investment.'

'Not your personal interest?'

He shook his head. 'I prefer the inland areas. In fact we've recently bought a whole village. I'll show you, if you want.'

A couple of days later I checked out of my hotel in Golden Sands and headed into the swirling hills to rendezvous with Stephane in his adopted home of Veliko Turnovo, the Bulgarian equivalent of a hilltop town in the Dordogne. We drove out on empty, forested roads to his Sera Livada, which turned out to be an abandoned settlement of just twelve houses, many of which were barely more than ruins covered in vines, nettles and overgrown fruit trees. Most were half-timbered and clay-tiled, with living accommodation upstairs and livestock accommodation below. Nobody lived here any longer; no dogs howled from behind the village gates, there were no chickens rootling around the well and even the handful of properties that did have roofs were likely to need rebuilding from the ground up.

'It looks like a lot of work,' I commented as we clambered around the rubble. It took a lot of imagination to visualize a colony of Brits living here.

'I'm in no hurry. Skilled labour comes pretty cheap. I could create a small eco village resort, or I might just sell them on individually as they are. Depends.'

'What do the locals think?' It seemed a bit cheeky to me, buying whole slices of someone else's heritage.

'Bulgarians are not interested in old houses. This place was abandoned. Most of the families who owned these properties were delighted when we tracked them down. They never thought they'd ever get anything for them.'

Back in Veliko Turnovo that evening I met up with Stephane again, this time in the company of a shaven-headed Bulgarian called Nikolai and a lethargic tousle-haired Englishman called Mark who was drinking Red Bull like there was no tomorrow. It seemed to be having no tangible impact on his energy levels.

'We were at school together,' explained Stephane, introducing his friend. 'Mark's sold his house in England and is now having an extended holiday in Bulgaria.'

'Been here long?' I asked.

Mark grinned unhappily. 'Couple of years.'

That was quite an extended holiday.

In a moment when both Englishmen were away getting more drinks at the bar, I asked Nikolai what Mark actually did during the day.

'He sleeps. And waits for Stephane to come home. God knows what he's going to do when Stephane marries and has kids.'

With a couple of pints of beer inside him Stephane was even more frank about the property business.

'Clients can be surprisingly rude, and they don't seem to be able to make allowances for the fact that this is Bulgaria,' he complained. 'I guess people are used to treating estate agents badly.'

Nikolai echoed the Englishman's words about the locals welcoming house-buying foreigners.

'The country needs the money. Country people especially. We're bumping along the bottom here and we need all the help we can get. Capitalism doesn't come easily to most of us because by and large people are content provided their neighbour isn't doing better than they are. There's a Bulgarian joke about the devil in Hell keeping all the various nationalities in different pots. The only pot without a lid is the Bulgarian one. Why? Because if any Bulgarian tries to climb out, the others will be sure to pull him back down. So the lid isn't necessary.'

'Communism and Bulgaria were a natural combination,' chipped in Mark, hopefully.

'It wasn't our choice,' contradicted Nikolai. 'It was Russia's decision. Ever since Russia stepped in to save us from the Turks we've followed them around like a grateful dog. So when they chose communism, we chose it too.

We didn't pass Go, we didn't collect £200, and now we're forty years behind.'

'You can't really fault a system which provided free welfare and education and work and food for everyone, no matter what their origin,' said Stephane, backing up his friend. 'Unfortunately, such a system is not a natural fit with human nature. The human being is more prepared to do work when it is for his own good, and be idle when he is in the pay of the state. On Beautiful Bulgaria we provided paid work and free transport for the long-term unemployed, but still they'd try to sell all the materials to passers-by. It drove me up the wall.'

We all agreed, with regret, that progress only comes through personal gratification, and that the good of the whole is not sufficient motivation for the industry of the individual. It was a pity that so many man-years had had to be wasted to arrive at those rather depressing conclusions.

And then conversation turned to lighter matters; whether weightlifting – at which Bulgaria excels – would ever make it as an international spectator sport.

TRAVEL, THE CURE FOR ALL IGNORANCE

The long history of the Orient Express contains plenty of examples of idiosyncratic behaviour, from the case of the Italian financier who seemed to run his whole business from the train, to the Austrian archduchess who travelled frequently to Paris to have her poodles trimmed, and insisted that they be fed *wiener schnitzel* fried in butter three times daily while on board. There were VIPs who brought their own chefs, and others who declined to eat the dining-car's food but instead had trays delivered from hotels along the route whenever the train stopped.

Arms dealer Basil Zacharoff, who always carried a cigarette case with cigarettes wrapped in high-denomination banknotes in case of emergency, would arrange to have prostitutes slipped on board, but only red-headed ones. Then one day his compartment became the refuge of a fragile Spanish duchess called Maria who was being assaulted by her unstable husband, and he fell in love. (He was later to give Maria the Casino at Monte Carlo as a wedding present.) Equally well-heeled was Calouste Gulbenkian, the businessman who originally developed the oilfields of Iraq and who later became known as Mister Five Percent. Gulbenkian slipped on to the train in 1896 to evade the massacre of Armenians in Constantinople, dressed in rags and carrying his baby son Nubar in a rolled-up carpet. Tradition has it that he then sold the carpet to a fellow passenger for a substantial sum.

One of the most exotic of the regulars was the Maharajah of Cooch Behar, who travelled with seven of his wives. They were dressed, Indian-style, in tight, navel-exposing tops which scandalized Parisian society, and they would board at Gare de Lyon from a private platform which was specially screened off from public view. On the train, he would commandeer a whole sleeper and dining-car for his exclusive use, fill them with divans and swansdown cushions, and keep the curtains closed for the duration of the journey, fuelling all sorts of speculation about what he was up to in there. Nobody would accept the explanation that all that extra bedding was just for protection against the unaccustomed cold. Unfortunately one winter the train's heating system failed completely while passing through Bulgaria. His scantily clad harem had already borrowed all the extra on-board rugs, but they were still suffering, so the Maharajah had to send the train crew out on to the station platforms to offer cash to the locals in exchange for their rough shepherd's tunics. Which must have made his wives look interesting.

Overall, though, the most famous cold moment in the train's history, immortalized by Agatha Christie in *Murder on the Orient Express*, was in the depths of the particularly severe winter of 1929, when the train disappeared into a snowdrift just over the Turkish border and wasn't discovered for nine days. At the time Turkey was still very exotic and communications were haphazard, so all sorts of accounts of what happened started to fly around. At first it was thought that all on board had perished, and then there were reports of fighting with wolves. Even the more recent railway historians are inclined towards the fanciful – but then it is an extraordinary story.

Evidently the train leaving Paris on 29 January had around eighty passengers on board, a mixed bag of businessmen and diplomats, as well as two Jesuit priests who read their Bibles even during mealtimes and a nervous unaccompanied Austrian woman called Fraulein von Werner. She was one of the twenty who were booked to go all the way, along with Turkish opium smuggler 'Slim' Souf, the private secretary to the British Ambassador in Turkey and a King's Messenger with his diplomatic bag chained to his wrist.

Snow was lying all around as the train crossed central Europe, and the weather reports from up ahead were bad. At Venice the Wagons-Lits office received a telegram to the effect that the temperature had dropped to –35° in Romania, but assumed it was a misprint. The *chef de train* had been sufficiently anxious about the conditions to call Paris from the station in Budapest, but was told by his superiors to press on. By the time the train had crossed Bulgaria the snowflakes were as large as goosefeathers and a stationmaster on the Turkish border warned them that the track ahead hadn't been snowploughed. Still the Express continued, now slowed to a crawl, until a large drift stopped it altogether by the Thracian village of Cherkes Keui, a place where it had been ambushed by bandits many years before. The passengers called for it to reverse, but it was already stuck fast.

It snowed for three days, burying some of the coaches completely in a nine-foot drift. On board, both passengers and crew were seriously concerned for their survival. Only murky daylight penetrated through into their highly decorated igloo, wine was rationed by the glass, and meals were cut back to one per day. Eventually the locomotive ran out of fuel for the steam heating and people retired to their bunks to stay warm. After four days without sign of rescue, the *chef de train* called a meeting; a tunnel would have to be dug through the snow, he said, both in order to search for provisions and to try to get a message through to the outside world that they were still alive. So the able-bodied got out there and dug, although 'Slim' Souf refused to leave his cabin 'on medical grounds'. It took them two days to break through to daylight.

With houses now visible, the train crew constructed a makeshift sled and the *chef de cuisine* and two others set off to get provisions, full of hope. When they arrived at the village, their reception was far more hostile than they'd anticipated. The villagers were concerned for their own well-being in such freak weather conditions and were very distrusting of the strangers who'd suddenly appeared in their midst, and they only agreed to part with a single chicken in return for the *chef de cuisine*'s spare change.

Back on board conditions were getting worse. It had all become too much for Fraulein von Werner, who tried to cut her wrist with a broken mirror. So next day the posse went back to the village, this time with a substantial amount of money collected from the passengers. 'I have come not to haggle, but to buy,' announced the *chef de train*. The villagers, appreciating the desperation of these foreigners and sensing a once-in-a-lifetime opportunity, ignored their own needs and sold their logs, chickens, eggs and even sheep, for ridiculous prices. It was sufficient to keep the passengers alive for a further three days, when a convoy of six sleighs of Turkish soldiers finally reached them with the news that a breakdown train was on its way.

The train was eventually freed after ten days stuck in the snow, and arrived in Istanbul eleven days late. For Agatha, who specialized in placing her murders in isolated communities from which no one can come or go, it made a gift of a setting for a story.

My own journey along the Thracian stretch of track was enjoyably uneventful, and not in the least bit cold. The Sofia to Istanbul sleeper was made up of coaches the colour of dried blood, originally the property of Mitropa, the German-speaking world's sleeper network. Mitropa actually started with Wagons-Lits coaches which had been stranded in Germany and Austria during the wars, and its service filled a gap left by the Orient Express when the latter was re-routed and rebranded Simplon-Orient to avoid Germanic countries. The vintage of this particular coach was hard to ascertain, but it had curtains, sheets, wide berths, a wall of imitation leather to which a woollen blanket had been attached to soften the impact of rolling around in bed, and a cabin attendant who sold beer and soft drinks and had a stove for making fresh coffee. It was the most comfortable of my non-Orient Express trains so far, and it would have been a fine way to travel were it not for the pfaffing officialdom at the Bulgo-Turkish border, which took ninety minutes to wade through at two o'clock in the morning.

It was a good approach to Istanbul, too. After slaloming through a pleasant, dimpled land like a well-oiled ball-bearing running through a Thracian pinball machine, the train hit the coast, broaching small boatyards, street markets and a school playground, too tired after its long journey to bother to find a way around the edge. Eventually, after interminable suburbs, we punched through a hole in the old city wall and were among looming, drunken wooden houses, a few bits of Byzantine masonry and the gently steaming domes of a hamman. The Bosphorus appeared on the right hand side, sullen, grey and gleaming like mercury, and then there was the elegant Sirkeci station, which still had its Orient Express restaurant with gleaming silverware, lantern roofs and stained glass windows, although the surrounding gardens which had once descended in terraces to the shore had long since been consumed by roads.

After all the distractions and diversions of the Balkans, I was back in Agatha Christie heartland again. This was her first big stopover on her 1928 journey, and she would have overnighted in Istanbul many a time on subsequent trips to and from the Middle East. On that first trip she stayed in the seafront Hotel Tokatlian, which no longer exists, but on further occasions she sometimes chose the Pera Palas, the hotel built by Wagons-Lits in 1892 for the specific purpose of providing accommodation of a suitable standard for its train passengers. In fact in its early days of operation a special palanquin was provided to transfer VIPs directly from Sirkeci station, across the neck of the Golden Horn and up Beyoglu hill to the hotel, a service which was included in the room price of 80 piastres a night.

From the outside the Pera Palas doesn't look like anything special, crowded as it is between the American Embassy and a new Sofitel, but it has been the address of choice of crowned heads and spies, and has made regular appearances in books by Graham Greene, Jan Morris, Dennis Wheatley and Paul Theroux. Writing in the 1920s, American author John dos Passos decribes an espionage murder in the foyer, where an envoy from Azerbaijan in a frock coat and a black astrakhan cap is shot by a bearded

Armenian, and blood spreads out on the mosaic floor. Fifty years later, in *The Great Railway Bazaar*, Theroux writes of a 'décor of decayed sumptuousness, an acre of mellow carpet, black panelling, and rococo carving on the walls and ceilings, where cupids patiently smile and flake'.

The Pera Palas of today is little changed from either of those accounts. It feels more like a museum than a hotel. The dark wood reception desk is staffed by the sort of old-fashioned gentleman you might find in an ancient barbershop. The foyer has tessellated stone floors, mirrors, high ceilings and heavy wooden furniture dressed in purple damask that could easily absorb bloodstains. The white paint on the walls has long ago turned elegantly to cream, the crimson curtains to a dusky red. The chandeliers don't quite glitter any more, and the plaster reliefs on the ceilings have dulled from gold to brass. Behind the foyer is the Agatha Christie Ballroom in an internal courtyard with a tall gallery of mashrabia-carved windows rising to leaded domes. Beyond that is the dining-room that used to serve Orient Express customers with a starter of sardines, followed by a choice of rump steak or macaroni cheese, and finished off with a soufflé, always Agatha's favourite. The 'Oriental Dishes' section of the menu was habitually left blank, although something could no doubt be produced in the unlikely event of a customer asking for it.

The thick net curtains which softened every window suggest that this was once a place whose customers didn't particularly want to look out, and nor did they welcome others looking in. The satisfaction lay in being safely inside, in a Nagelmackers cocoon, away from all those unpredictable foreigners. In all, a hotel for those who believed that a necessary feature of travel was a good lie down in a darkened room before tea, prior to a gin, steak and soufflé. It felt admirably authentic, but a touch drab, and it was suffering badly from a lack of custom in the run up to the Iraq war. Even the air tasted old.

The hotel is particularly proud of its birdcage lift, which rises in stately fashion up through the red-carpeted stair-well in a sheath of wrought iron and polished brass. This is supposedly the oldest hotel lift in the world, and it is operated by a whippersnapper of a bellboy who asks, whenever guests step aboard, whether they would like to see the rooms occupied by Kemal Ataturk or Agatha Christie, presumably in return for a handsome tip. In its time this lift has carried quite a cross-section of glitterati, and most of the first-floor rooms had plaques recording regular residents. Kings Zog of Albania, Petar of Serbia and Nicholas of Montenegro made up a Balkan corner along with Marshall Tito, and along the passage from Ataturk's pad were the rooms of Mata Hari and Greta Garbo. Who knocked on whose door first, one wondered.

I had managed to secure Agatha's room, number 411, and was not altogether surprised to find it a far more modest affair than the others, on a side of the hotel that didn't have a particularly interesting view. Whether she actually stayed in Room 411 is debatable, but she was never profligate with her money, and it would have been out of character for her to have taken the best suite in the house. In the room were two brass bedsteads, an antique writing desk, and a locked glass case with a selection of her books. All of it was undoubtedly imported for the purposes of marketing, but it felt authentic nonetheless. Sitting where she had supposedly sat I began to feel surrounded again, not by the unbearable lightness of being, but by the astonishing ubiquity of Christie. All the way along my route she'd been practically a household name, and even in Istanbul the local bookshops had a fair selection of titles like *Hercule Poirot iz üzerinde*, which I guessed meant that he was indisposed. Her name even came up, quite unprompted, in a conversation with an American businessman about the Pera Palas's short-comings over a rather chewy breakfast in the hotel dining-room, where the coffee urn had been replenished with coffee-flavoured tar. His conclusion had been 'If it was good enough for Agatha, it's good enough for me.'

Several of the floor tiles in my room were disconcertingly loose, but it wasn't the hotel's fault. This must be one of the few hotel rooms in the world where the guests deliberately dismantle bits of the floor.

The designation of Room 411 as hers was largely the work of a glossy American psychic and self-publicist called Tamara Rand. Rand had been signed up in 1979 by Warner Bros, who were keen to promote a film about Agatha's missing ten days, with the ostensible aim of trying to make contact with the dead writer and solve the mystery of that disappearance once and for all. Without leaving Hollywood, Rand duly went into a trance in which she saw Agatha on a train (presumably the Simplon-Orient Express), placing a secret diary in her handbag. She later put the same diary in a wooden box and locked it. Rand next saw her in an Istanbul street, approaching a building with 'huge wooden double doors, and I saw a name Pera Palas. It was obviously a hotel.' The trance followed her as she rode upstairs in the lift to Room 411, prised up a floor tile, placed the key to the wooden box under it, and put the tile back.

All of this detail was duly transmitted to Istanbul, and a party of journalists and a representative of Warner Bros arrived at the Pera Palas, searched the room and found a key – although given that no one knew the whereabouts (or even the existence) of the supposed wooden box, it was a fairly useless discovery. The hotel manager recognized its publicity value, however, and consigned it quickly to a bank for safe-keeping. When Warner Bros asked to obtain the key he asked for an outrageous $2 million to release it. Shortly after the whole flimsy episode, Tamara Rand's PR company from Beverley Hills wrote to the manager reminding him of the 'profitability of all the recent press attention', and went on to propose that 'we could assist you in organising a press junket (*sic*) to Istanbul to accompany Miss Rand on her quest. We could, dependent on how much accommodation and expenses you can provide, determine the most appropriate journalists to invite.' The manager politely declined.

In her 1928 trip Agatha had spent two nights and a day in the city, partly in the company of a Dutch mining engineer she'd met on the train who'd appointed himself her guide and who had taken her out to dinner both evenings. At the end of the second evening he'd lingered in the hotel foyer, sized her up, brought up the idea of becoming her suitor and then in the same breath dismissed it. It would not have been wise, he said. 'No, not wise,' she'd agreed, describing him later as a 'nice man' to whom she owed a pleasant day of sight-seeing in Constantinople, but no more. It's an episode she breezes over in her autobiography without much comment, but it must have had a morale-boosting significance as her first potentially romantic encounter since the break-up with Archie.

My second night in the hotel had a romantic flavour to it, too. It was tango evening in the Agatha Christie Ballroom, and I watched from the upstairs gallery as intense and handsome couples in evening wear scythed across the parquet floor below, high-kicking, tossing their heads and holding everything in. They looked as if they were auditioning for *Hercule Poirot Has a Hernia*.

'Why don't you go down?' said the duty manager, finding me peering through the mashrabia.

'It's not easy, when you're alone,' I said, lamely.

'You will quickly find someone,' he said.

But I went back upstairs and finished off *Man in a Brown Suit*, and then left it on the desk of Room 411 for future Agatha fans.

I lingered for a few days in Istanbul. It may have multiplied in size several times since Agatha's day, adopted a mantle of westernization and become a favoured tourism destination, but it still danced to a different tune. By day I leaned over the bridges with the forest of rod and line fishermen who were steadily filling their buckets and glass jars with sardine-sized fish, and doing it with a professionalism that suggested that it had to be a source of income. At night I joined the rivers of people drifting up Istiklal Caddesi to Taksim Square, under the wheeling, indistinct ghosts of seagulls, glowing radioactive orange in the dark sky. The main streets could have been Paris – the Arab quarter – while the side streets were lined with cafés where backgammon was being played with uncommon savagery and sweaty nightclubs where men were dancing with other men without a moment's self-consciousness. After the introspective Balkans, this felt like a self-confident, mature culture, but then people here have grown up, grown old, retired and died in a society which has been fundamentally unchanged since the day they were born. Few residents of Balkan countries can say that.

Agatha described Istanbul as a maddening city, since when you are in it you can never see it. And it is true, it's a giant doodle of a place, all spangles of water and shoulders of land. You never quite know which way you are looking, because each view has the same basic ingredients: one-third heavy, sullen sky, one-third land honeycombed with concrete, and one-third choppy water with boats snuffling around the edges. Each piece of land has a mosque or two on the skyline like a pair of terrapins which had long since crawled out of the water only to find their return path blocked by a warren of warehouses and shops. So now they call to each other in anguish, five times a day.

It's only when you take to the water that you begin to appreciate what a ridiculous place it was to build a city, right on a major shipping lane. The Bosphorus divides Istanbul, separating Asia from Europe. The windows of the city ferries regularly fill with giant walls of moving metal as another giant bulk carrier makes its way from the Med to the Black Sea, via downtown.

Getting to know the ferry system is like getting to know an extended family. Some of the boats are short, fat and pompous uncles, others long, elegant and languid aunts. Some have jauntily tipped-back smokestacks, blowing hard as they struggle to keep to their schedules, and others are sleek, upright and humming efficiently. But most have the same family characteristics of blunt noses and fat bottoms, funnels like mustard pots, decking furred by thousands of feet a day, and granular complexions produced by many decades of rust and repainting. Together they put together a slow dance, like the drunks on the dance floor at the end of a long night, each weaving hypnotically to its own internal tune, and keening, 'Eminönü, Eminönü, Eminönü . . .' 'Karaköy, Karaköy, Karaköy . . .' Every now and then one of them makes a particularly natty, frothy pirouette and emits a celebratory single note, a sort of musical raspberry, to make sure everyone takes notice. No doubt that raspberry is perfectly in harmony with whatever song is going on inside its engine room, but it makes little musical sense to anyone else.

The perambulating ferries bring Istanbul a certain peace of mind. There is no room on the land for anything as frivolous as parkland in this city while there are still drill-bits to be rented out and hubcaps to be sold, so if you want a quiet moment to pick your nose, read the paper or hold hands with your loved one then a ferry is the place to do it. Sit up on deck, watch the stern kiss the wharves, feel the uncompromising grip of the hawsers and hail a waistcoated waiter rollicking past with a tray bearing curved little glasses of sweet, minty tea.

Once on the water you could also get a glimpse of other, more distant, worlds. Out on the Bosphorus I saw the same UND ro-ro ship I'd seen in Trieste all those weeks before, and which had probably done the trip at least two or three times by water to my paltry once across the land. Then there was a tall ship from Varna, its spars muffled with sails, which would have made an interesting voyage if only I'd known about it. And next door to that was a pair of once-white Russian rust-buckets from Odessa, with that romantic mixture of cabin accommodation and deck cranes that suggested a mixed voyage around harbours called Sebastopol and Novorossiysk full of Cossack fishermen and decommissioned nuclear submarines.

All this marine exotica reminded me of an account of my father's – who'd have liked to travel much more if God hadn't made him a GP and bestowed on him an over-whelming sense of duty – of joining a liner here. The ship had been heading out from the Black Sea to the Mediterranean, and he'd found himself surrounded by wealthy Russians who dressed their children in sailor suits and spoke to each other in French. If I hadn't had an itinerary planned I'd have been tempted to knock on the doors of a few shipping agents to try to do the same. Instead, I had to be satisfied with taking a little chugger up the Golden Horn, its deck planking so scuffed and fibrous that it was as spongy as a carpet.

Despite the grandiose name the Golden Horn turned out to be a backwater filled with a thick minestrone of algae and baby jellyfish. Its stops were like small country railway stations, where the pontoon-master tore himself away momentarily from planting lavender and geraniums out in old plastic paintpots to take the mooring ropes in his gardening gloves. The names of those stops were posted on a wooden ladder-board on the ferry's flank, like psalms to be sung in church. The engine room did the singing, its thrown-back hatches filling the air with revving descants as we approached every stop.

In the end I used a ferry, as Agatha must have done, to take my leave of Europe, crossing the Bosphorus to disembark at Hydarapasa, the railway station for all points East. Outside the Pera Palas I'd said a fond farewell to the shoeshine boy who'd quickly learned that, even if my shoes didn't need his attention, a good quip could produce an easy tip. He was always offering to procure me something or someone entirely inappropriate to his tender years, and was gathering material for his dissertation on why Russian girls made the best belly-dancers.

'A million lira if you can tell me who Agatha Christie was,' had been my parting shot that morning.

For once, his face clouded over.

'I don't know, mister. Have you lost him?'

Of all the railway stations in all the world, Hydarapasa must have one of the most dramatic settings. In her autobiography Agatha likens it to a lunatic asylum heaving with travellers, and describes how she was shepherded through the Customs process by Thomas Cook's local representative, whose way of attracting the officers' attention was to jump on to a bench and wave a pound note, shouting, 'Over here'. She omits to mention how the station rises, like a proud neo-German *schloss* complete with turreted corners, directly from the quayside, where it is surrounded on three sides by water.

The station was built in 1906 by the Anatolia Baghdad Corporation, a subsidiary of the German-owned Chemin de Fer Ottoman d'Anatolie (CFOA) which ran most of the Turkish rail network at the time, as well as much of the port. The current Turkish rail authority, the TCDD, still does. The rail-ferries plug in on the left flank after their short journey across the Bosphorus, and ranged around the station's base are handfuls of tugs, as if ready to tow the whole edifice out to sea in the event of attack. Mind you, they'd have their work cut out, because the architect used 1,140 tons of iron and 19,000 cubic metres of hardwood, and the result is a landmark by which ship's captains learn to navigate. Its location, on 1,100 twenty-one-metre piles driven down into the soft shore, has nearly been its undoing, because some years ago a tanker hit the breakwater and the heat from the resultant fire melted the lead in the stained glass windows.

Inside, in the booking office hallway, the pillars are covered with frescoes of phoenixes and the high ceilings with floral rosettes. The clerks sit behind a screen of etched windows under an arch of coloured glass, with customers threading towards them between railings of polished brass. The station restaurant is walled with faïence tiles and supervised by a damp-stained portrait of Kemal Ataturk. Everything is orderly and peaceful, and only the regular waves of passengers disembarking from the ferries by the front steps hint at the crowds witnessed by Agatha, eighty years before.

My train took at least an hour to shake itself free of the tentacles of Istanbul, into fields where farm labourers, their heads swaddled against the intensity of the sun, were lined up in readiness for the final of the 100-metre weeding. For a while we seemed to be in some sort of manufacturing corridor along the edge of the Sea of Marmara, with factories, piles of slag and mountains of scrap on one side, and containers, packing cases, cranes and wharfs on the other. It was like a more modern, functioning version of the shores of Bulgaria's Lake Varna, but here the Turks were really getting stuck in. Add this to the effort they expended on their fields and the hours they spent in their shops, and it was easy to see how the Ottoman Empire had managed to spread so far. These people put 110 per cent effort into everything. The work-horses of Europe.

After three hours of heading east the time came to branch south, off the Istanbul–Ankara route. The supercilious electric locomotive refused point blank to leave the main line and was replaced by a complaining diesel, which chewed its way up through a blizzard of orange groves into a narrow, steep, forested valley with a mountain stream and flash-flood gullies that were dry and full of weeds. The valley smelled of sage and thyme and, judging by the quantity of birdsong, it was also a welcome retreat from the heat of the day. For a while the train chased its tail around the top end of the valley searching for an exit, and then the trees fell away and we emerged into a high, scrubby grassland, yellowed by the sun. The Anatolian plateau.

It was like emerging into parts of the Scottish Highlands, wide, open and lonely with the same big sky and intensity of light. Only here the occasional patch of mist was not drizzle but dust blown along by the wind or kicked up by the wheels of a car. In places the wind had driven off the topsoil completely, leaving only bare standing waves of limestone and outcrops of rock weathered into disturbing shapes that would have been the stuff of nightmares for anyone out wandering alone at dusk. Some of these rock formations were so substantial that the locomotive was forced to sidestep them and seek another way through.

You know you're in for a long journey when passengers spread towels over their knees and start to prepare the ingredients for a salad. A bear of a man with a blunt face and a grizzled, close-cropped beard leaned across the aisle towards me with an apple, a cucumber and a very sharp knife; no bags of crisps or Mars bars on these trains.

'Eat. It's a long journey.' And he said it in a way that would brook no disagreement. 'Where are you going, my friend?'

'Konya,' I said, slicing into the cucumber. The city had a reputation for being devoutly Muslim and deeply conservative, but it was also the train's last stop before plunging on deep into the night, and I didn't want to cross Turkey in the dark.

'To see the dervishes?'

'Uh-huh.' I had indeed planned to visit Konya's Mevlana Museum, if just because the whirling dervishes had so epitomized the complete exoticism of life beyond Europe for early travellers.

'And you? Where are you going?'

'Konya too. I have a house there.'

He introduced himself.

'Alp Aslan. Or you can call me Half-Past Ten.'

I thought I must have misheard.

Alp Aslan chuckled heavily. 'Many years ago, when I was a student, I worked in a sugar beet factory in your Wisbech. All the others there, the English people, they couldn't get my name right. Alp Aslan, it means mountain lion, but it's difficult, yes? So one day one of the office girls, she gives me a new name. Half-Past Ten.'

For some people this might have been an offensive example of British xenophobia, but not for Alp Aslan. 'Funny, eh, Half-Past Ten.' He crunched into his cucumber.

A couple of stops further I suggested we adjourn to the dining-car for a post-salad glass of tea, via the platform, to save lurching down long corridors. We'd only just descended when the whistle went and the train began to move. I had visions of being stranded minus my luggage in the middle of the Anatolian plateau, but Alp Aslan had shifted very quickly for one of such large size, and we made it safely on to the running board.

'That's better,' he said, clambering in. 'I always find it good to move the legs on a long journey.'

My lunch donor turned out to be a former electrical engineer who'd spent his last ten years working in Saudi Arabia on the restoration of holy sites. He'd also assisted Turkish Muslims who wanted to make the haj pilgrimage to Mecca, many of whom would stay in his house. Now back home, he divided his time between his faith, his friends, his love of travel and watching anything with Michael Palin in it on TV ('a very nice man'). He had the serenity of someone who'd seen the world and was now happy to have returned home, where he could share that experience with others and to listen to theirs, but he hadn't enjoyed Saudi.

'Something goes wrong when people of little education suddenly have too much money. The Arabs treated us, fellow Muslims, like slaves.' He was waving his teaspoon emphatically. 'That state will not last, it is too cruel, there's not enough personal freedom. How did you find the Bulgarians?'

And so, in a buffet car divided into two – the grubbier end for young beer drinkers and a more civilized, table-clothed end for the rest – I described my journey thus far, and how I had been disappointed to find how quickly Eastern European culture had evaporated in the face of Western consumerism.

'Ah, there are people who are hungry in the soul,' said Alp Aslan, when I'd finished. For him everything always had a spiritual dimension. 'In Saudi I used to organize the accommodation for visiting engineers. One week we had a Belgian man, I showed him the house, OK, I showed him where we eat, OK no problem. The next week we had a Hungarian, I showed him the same thing. "No," he says. "My contract says five star hotel, it says I must have special orange juice" ... we had a whole week of problems with him, special this, special that. That man, he was hungry in the soul.'

'So how did you end up in the UK?' A young Turk turning up at a Wisbech sugar beet factory sounded like an interesting journey.

He told me how, when he was a student, he'd assembled an old Citroen 2CV out of scrapyard remains, and set off for western Europe at a time when young western travellers were all coming in the opposite direction.

'I suppose they were hippies. I used to share the road with them, but I never stayed where they stayed. They weren't very clean, and I like to be clean. Our village people were delighted to see them, "Come stay in my house". But these people are like ants, where one goes others follow, especially when it is free, and eventually the

village gets fed up and tells them to go away. Then the
hippies start to say bad things about us. Then we get
Midnight Express.'

He points out the fields of withering stalks rolling past
the train windows.

'This is opium. For medicine. All owned by the state.
But hashish, there used to be plenty. These days we are
very strict, not like then.'

I agreed that the Midnight Express hadn't been a very
distinguished successor to the Orient Express.

'Inshallah, that route has gone.'

The whole Midnight Express phenomenon was an
interesting consequence of border re-drawing. After
Turkey had been on the losing side in World War II, the
redesignation of its territories had given Greece a part of
Thrace which was still crossed by the original main line
from Istanbul to Edirne and thence into Bulgaria. Border
guards would come aboard for the duration of any
Turkish train's transit through this now-foreign enclave to
make sure no one got off, but it wasn't an easy task and
they were not particularly diligent. In the 1960s
and 1970s a slow night train – the so-called Midnight
Express – became very popular among Western hippies
who were awaiting trial in Turkey for drugs offences;
they'd buy a ticket to Edirne and then slip off the train
while it was dawdling through Greece. There they'd
masquerade as innocent tourists who'd lost their passports, and find their way home. Eventually a new track
was laid and the loophole removed, but not before the
Alan Parker film of the same name, with its harsh
portrayal of life in Turkish jails, had greatly offended the
Turkish population. You could see why the traditionalist
Turks had wanted to batten down the hatches, and keep
all foreigners away: Turkey had opened itself up to the

West, and the result had been a baptismal flood of hippies swiftly followed by an international reputation for prison brutality and corruption.

'It wasn't an easy introduction to the tourism business,' I suggested.

'No, no. Tourism has been helpful to our country,' Alp Aslan replied. 'Any industry has its disadvantages. Many years ago I met an American hippie in a perfect enclosed bay with a freshwater spring near Alanya. It was like a swimming-pool, and it was all for him. I remember him saying that it would not last, that purity, and I disagreed, because we have a law about building within a certain distance of the coast. Well, I went back there a couple of years ago. You can't get near the water because of the ring of hotels.'

'Sad.'

'Sad, yes, but it is progress too. More people come to Turkey, so more people understand Turkey. Now we have friends far away, where before we only had hippies. Before tourism everybody was suspicious of everybody else.'

Our attention was drawn suddenly to the window as a military train rumbled past, loaded down with armoured cars and tanks, in a disturbing portent of what was to come, further East.

Alp Aslan scratched his beard. 'You have travelled. I have travelled. We understand each other. But President Bush? Has he travelled? What is that expression – travel broadens the mind? I wonder if he would still be demonizing the Islamic world if he'd come here on his holidays.'

'President Bush, the backpacker? Now there's an interesting idea.' We both laughed, and then moved the conversation on, aware that we were skating over thin ice on a discussion that could be horribly dangerous. We didn't know each other well enough for that.

The train had arrived very late, after a long tedious trek across a plateau so flat and dark that the lights of a village on the horizon could easily have been a clutch of fishing boats out at sea. Once in Konya, Alp Aslan had installed me in a good hotel, taking it upon himself to approach the reception desk and agree a room rate that seemed remarkably low. When I expressed surprise, he'd patted his beard.

'It's this. In Konya, this means a lot.'

I liked Alp Aslan enormously but I can't say I warmed to his city. The Hittites had christened it 'Kuwanna' 4,000 years ago, but its heyday had come 3,000 years later with the rise of the Seljuk Empire. Konya had been designated the capital of the Seljuk sultanate of Rum, which incorporated most of Anatolia, but instead of the romantic caravan stop stuffed with masterpieces of Seljuk architecture I'd expected, I found myself walking around a modern, clean, well-organized place full of wide boulevards and fountains. There were no colourful shanty-towns, fortresses or tumbledown old quarters, but only uncompromising housing blocks rising in waves right to the edge of the steppe. The altruistic town planners had created an efficient housing cooperative which meant that, in return for four years' rental – the sort of savings level that most people could attain – you could have your own flat constructed. There was no need for anyone to live in poor accommodation.

This was Thatcherite housing policy with an Islamic foundation, and making everyone a property owner had certainly proved the key to civic pride. The residents of Konya were plainly leading good, holy lives, totally free of impure thoughts, of the threat of street crime, and of the temptations of alcohol (the city was effectively dry). In the tea gardens at the centre of town, among trellises of roses under a spreading chestnut tree, well-behaved courting couples made bottles of soda last for ever.

But not everyone was sin-free in this stairway to heaven. Alp Aslan had told me that, despite the evident prosperity, there was an embarrassing financial difficulty developing behind the scenes. Dozens of holding companies had set up in Konya for the benefit of those Turks working overseas who distrusted the bankers of Istanbul. These overseas workers wished to make investments with their 'green' Islamic capital which were more in line with their religious beliefs. In order to avoid the taxation systems a lot of this 'Anatolian Capital' was entering the country in cash, in suitcases, destined for those holding companies. There was no name more trustworthy in Turkey than Konya, and most of the companies based in the city were completely legitimate and were quickly becoming a giant force in domestic economics. But a few less honest operators had chosen to base themselves here too, littering their sales literature with 'God Permittings', and some of the investors were waking up to find they'd effectively been throwing their money away. The city fathers were naturally very keen to weed out anyone who was trading on Konya's good name.

I wasn't due to meet Alp Aslan again until lunch, so I spent the morning in the Mevlana Lodge, with its polished wood floor and cream-painted naves hung with lanterns of all shapes and colours. It was effectively a giant tomb, with half the floor area covered with sarcophagi draped in embroidered velvets. Each headstone was crowned with a turban, as if the dervish in question could one day rise through the floor to whirl again, straight into his hat.

Sultan Mevlana, a deeply thoughtful and forgiving Sufi mystic who'd chopped off no one's head, devised whirling as a way of achieving meditative ecstasy and ultimate union with God. His tomb was in its own apse richly painted in reds, greens and gold, with whorls, florals and Quranic calligraphy around a single window of white and green leaded glass. Opposite it stood a huge copper bowl for collecting April rainwater, which was meant to have curative powers. If our April rainwater had curative powers then we'd all live to 100, we have so much of it.

But there were no whirling dervishes, new or resurrected, anywhere to be seen and no dervish shows just down the road. Over the centuries since the Sultan's death in 1273 the dervish lodges had spread, and become increasingly entrenched with increasingly intransigent views. Kemal Ataturk had eventually banned them back in 1925, considering them an obstacle to the advancement of the Turkish nation. Today you can only see whirling in Konya once a year, at a special, and supposedly non-religious, Mevlana festival.

I met up with Alp Aslan again in a small restaurant in the old town, where he was so well known we had to shake all the staff by the hand. Over soup and grilled meat he told me he'd retired early, partly through ill health – heart bypass and kidney stones – and partly because he'd made more than enough money in Saudi. So he'd decided to rest; why work, when you don't have to?

'Now I make myself available to societies.'

'Religious ones?'

He nodded. 'To tell young people about my experience of the world. I tell them that the most important thing is to be fulfilled in what they choose to do.'

'So what,' I wondered, 'do these societies make of what America is choosing to do?'

Alp Aslan leaned back and surveyed me, as if contemplating whether to give it to me with both barrels, or just one. But when he spoke, it was with a surprisingly conciliatory tone.

'Iraq will probably be a better place without Saddam Hussein, but the war must not go on for too long. Might is only right for a limited time, look at Genghis Khan. Justice, that is the important thing. If the US treats Iraq with justice, then I don't think there'll be any backlash from here. But if America shows itself to be greedy, then it'll be a problem. A real problem.'

From there we moved quite naturally on to the topic of Israel. 'There, you see,' explained Alp Aslan, 'comes the problem of justice. There is no justice, not for the people of Palestine. For them, Israel sets the parameters and inflicts the penalties. Imagine if a foreign power claimed the heart of London, and you could do nothing because it had a big, powerful bully of a friend. Well.' He sighed heavily. For once words failed him. 'I have Jewish friends, but we can't talk about it. It is such an injustice, and it is deeply felt elsewhere in the world. Deeply felt.'

After lunch, we dropped in on Alp Aslan's social circle. This took us first to a shoe shop, where we shook the hands of another man with a grizzled beard like his, and then to a paint shop, where half a dozen men of all ages were sitting around on stools, waiting for something to happen. Here chairs were brought and mint tea was ordered from a seventy-five-year-old man who'd been brewing tea, professionally, from the same little booth for the last sixty years.

'I come here every couple of days, to this paint shop,' said Alp Aslan. 'We drink tea and talk about God, the world and people we know. These are very good people, and they have time to talk in the paint business. So now, what shall we talk about? Your book? Is it going well?'

I said something about not being too concerned about the actual material – there was no shortage of that – but not feeling confident about the style. The words and the paragraphs. 'It has got to be well written.'

'Nonsense,' roared Alp Aslan. 'It is the content, the feeling is what matters, what you have gone out and found out from the world. Travel – it is the cure for all ignorance. What you have got is far more important than what others might assemble from their dictionaries at home, however well they put it together. Big words, pah.'

'It is a genius to communicate a lot with a little,' added the grizzle-bearded shoe-shop owner, who'd now joined us.

Alp Aslan nodded approvingly. 'Look at Hemingway, so easy to read, and yet some people take one thing from it, some people another. You don't need big words, that only impresses the people who write in the newspapers, and they are the ones who just stay home.'

I must say I hadn't expected to have such a wise and thoughtful discussion of my profession with a handful of devout Muslims in the backstreets of Turkey's most religious city, among tubs of emulsion.

When the time came to go, Alp Aslan borrowed the shoe-shop owner's twenty-five-year-old VW Golf to take me to the station. There I had to dissuade him from buying a present for my wife on the grounds that it would be many weeks before she received it, and I didn't want to lug it around Iraq.

As we waited for the train, on the very platform where Colonel Arbuthnot and Mary Debenham had stretched their legs in *Murder on the Orient Express*, we came at last to a discussion about God. It was inevitable; we'd pretty much discussed everything else.

'How can you not believe?' he said, when I confessed to being an atheist. 'You have a heart; what makes it beat?'

'But science can explain that.'

'Science just shows us in even more detail just how wonderful creation is. The other day I was watching a programme on the Discovery Channel about a lizard which, when it is threatened, combines two different gases out of its rear end to create an explosion. Do you not find that incredible?'

I agreed that it was.

'So, science cannot do that. Science cannot bury a TV in the ground and expect a TV tree to grow. It is missing that final thing, that spark of life, that miracle of creation. Take an egg, a simple chicken's egg. It is just white and yellow and nothing else. And yet from this white and yellow comes a creature with feathers, blood, claws and a beak. Isn't that wonderful? This is something far, far more wonderful than anything a human being will ever be able to do through science.'

The blare of a horn announced the imminent arrival of my train.

'No,' continued Alp Aslan, summing up. 'Of the existence of God there is no doubt. The question remains of choosing the right way of worshipping him. And usually that is just a matter of birth. You were born a Christian, I was born a Muslim. Our faiths share a lot. A lot of the Bible is in the Koran, most people don't realize how much. But I cannot accept this idea of presenting God and his son as a man, it is belittling. The power of God is far, far greater than that.'

And then the train was there, and we were shaking each other repeatedly by the hand. I was trying to find words that might express how good it had been to meet him, and how good he had been to me, but Alp Aslan brushed them aside.

'So that's what you should do next,' he said, laying a hand on my shoulder and propelling me towards the door. 'Do a travel book in search of the miracle of creation. Go looking for God.'

HUBBLE-BUBBLE ON THE TOROS EKSPRESI

In her 1928 journey Agatha Christie experienced a life-enhancing moment of great beauty on the descent of the Taurus Express from Konya to Adana.

The Express was on its second evening out of Istanbul, plunging down through the Taurus mountains on the far side of the Anatolian plateau, when it stopped and everyone piled out to admire the sunset. The place was called the Cilician Gates, she wrote in her autobiography; she was to stop there again on many subsequent journeys, sometimes in the early morning and sometimes in the middle of the night, but she would always remember that glorious sunset moment of her first trip. She even made mention of it in *Murder on the Orient Express*, having the wistful Mary Debenham gaze through the Gates and murmur, 'How beautiful.'

I caught the rattly old day train from Konya to Adana for the express purpose of seeing those Cilician Gates by daylight, so that I too could get a glimpse of what had moved Agatha so. It was an optimistic plan, because my pre-journey research had found no scheduled stop called

The Ctesiphon Arch, built in AD 400 south of present-day Baghdad,
gets star billing in this 1930s poster for the 'Magic Carpet to the East'.

MRS. AGATHA CHRISTIE.
Author of "The Seven Dials Mystery."

Agatha Christie (*above*) in her early thirties, around the time of her divorce from Archie (*above, right*), flying hero and catalyst of the author's disappearance, which made front-page news (*right*) in 1926.

£100 FREE CROSS-WORD COMPETITION: SEE PA

Daily Mirror

THE DAILY PICTURE NEWSPAPER WITH THE LARGEST NET SALE

No. 7,199   TUESDAY, DECEMBER 7, 1926   [24 PAGES]

MYSTERY OF WOMAN NOVELIST'S DISAPPEARA

EARL'S DAUGHTER TAKES THE AIR IN

SEASON 1927-28

The Magic Heart of the East

TOURS
TO
MESOPOTAMIA
(IRAQ)

Under the Management of
THOS. COOK & SON, LTD.

Thomas Cook based his new Mesopotamian tours (*above*) on the luxurious international trains (*above, right*). In 1929 a freak snowfall buried the eastbound Express (*right*) by the Turkish border with Bulgaria; its nine-day isolation was the inspiration for *Murder on the Orient Express*.

L'ILLUSTRATION

Slovenia turned out to be fertile Agatha-hunting country … (*right*).

Splendid ticket window (*above*) at Istanbul's Hydarapasa station. The author (*right*) with Alp Aslan, in the paint-shop salon in Konya.

Train-driver Bedur (*left*) shepherds the one-coach express from the Syrian border to the glorious station (*below*) at Aleppo, a medieval trading crossroads dominated by the knuckled fist of its Citadel (*bottom, left*).

Damascus' Hejaz station (*right*), very much the end of the line.

THIS PAGE: Agatha and Max survey a potential dig site in 1935.

OPPOSITE PAGE: Haider in the souq at Chifil (*top*). Tracks in the desert (*centre*), the remains of an archaeologist's light railway at Uruk. The original dig house at Nimrud still stands (*bottom*).

Iraqis were delighted to be photographed with an Englishman, despite the imminence of war.

The site of the supposed Garden of Eden, a flyblown place where the Tigris and the Euphrates meet.

anything remotely like the Cilician Gates. There was nothing of that name on the map and the railway staff had no idea what I was talking about when I tried to explain what I wanted. So I sat myself on the side of the carriage that should eventually have a view out over the Cilician (now Çukurova) plain and kept my nose pressed hopefully against the window as the old local started to squeal downwards off the Anatolian plateau, into a succession of tunnels and hand-carved embankments. I was hoping for a magical moment where the train driver, approaching a pair of Ozymandias-like Byzantine pillars which framed some tremendous view, would depart spontaneously from his script to allow us to refresh our souls with the uplifting power of nature, but no such moment came. The train ground interminably on, slow, uncomfortable and getting steadily hotter as we descended. There was a fair bit of brutal mountain scenery, all of it misty, and we stopped at every other lamppost, but not one of them bore the legend 'Cilician Gates'.

My nose was well out of joint by the time we finally reached Adana, a hot, uninteresting commercial capital on Turkey's most uninspiring stretch of Eastern Mediterranean coastline. The city was full of school students wearing tartan, all of whom seemed to find the sight of a sweaty foreigner more unusual than a street full of teenage clan McTurks. It took me ages to find a hotel anywhere near the station – one which apparently doubled up as a student boarding-house to make up for the lack of passing trade.

It seems that few foreigners ever came this way, because a humourless, hard-faced man with a handbag and a piercing stare was waiting for me in the foyer when I came down on my way to find something to eat. Perhaps he was the students' guardian, summoned to verify that I hadn't swanned into town to check that nothing unsuitable was being worn under the kilt. He grilled me, in German, with all the normal questions: who was I, what was I doing, where was I going – his eyes running right through me as if he was the skewer and I was the chewy bit of kebab. Annoyed with him, and even more annoyed with myself for blushing under the interrogation, I stammered and apologized for not speaking German very well. 'I can see that,' he said.

Even more depressing, over in the mustard-yellow station, was the complete lack of information about the once-weekly rail connection across the Syrian border to Aleppo. The familiar name 'Taurus Express' was on the departure list, but its destination was not Damascus, but the eastern Turkish town of Gazantiep, which wasn't even particularly close to the border.

The man behind the ticket desk and I were lacking a common language, but he did seem to agree that an Istanbul to Damascus train would indeed be passing through at 5 a.m. the following morning. However, he would neither sell me a ticket nor tell me whether I needed to make a reservation, which I found fairly odd behaviour for a ticket clerk, so I began to wonder whether he was just humouring me in the hope that I might go away. I drifted off, unconvinced, and fearing that I was on the lip of the first major upset of the journey; the non-existence of a pair of mythical gates was a disappointment, but the non-existence of a whole train was seriously bad news. Particularly if it meant another week kicking my heels in Adana. In my worst moments, I even contemplated catching a bus.

Perhaps I should have been warned by Agatha's comments on this stage of her own journey. Apart from the uplifting moment at the Gates, she'd only mentioned the increasing tastelessness of the food and a bad attack of bed bugs. The bugs had emerged from the old-fashioned railway carriages and feasted on the juicier travellers on the train, inducing headaches and fever. Her own bites had become so inflamed that she'd had to slit the sleeves of her blouse and coat to release the pressure. Her temperature had reached 102 degrees and only abated once she'd reached Aleppo.

On paper, the Taurus Express has a long pedigree. In the late 1920s the Compagnie Internationale des Wagons Lits was busily extending its empire further east with a through train planned to go all the way from Istanbul to Aleppo, where it was to split, and one section would eventually continue on to Baghdad and another to Tehran. In its most glorious years between the wars the Taurus was thus a continuation of the Orient Express, and in similar luxury, although Agatha's 1928 journey was a touch too early for it to be in its prime.

The line itself had a rather controversial birth. It had been pioneered by the Germans, who hoped to carve out more of a niche for themselves in the Near East, to the alarm of the British, who feared that it might eventually provide unwelcome overland access to their interests in the Indian subcontinent. Mindful of British opposition, the German engineers avoided the easier coastal route, which would have been within range of any Royal Navy battleships lurking in the Eastern Mediterranean, and instead struggled up into the Anamus mountains using thirteen tunnels, finally leaving Turkey by a very inaccessible back door.

It was a wise move. The First World War broke out before the line was completed, but by 1917 the work was far enough advanced for the Germans to begin to move military hardware up through the tunnels and around towards Africa, well out of reach of Navy guns. The project was finally completed just before the Armistice in 1918, whereupon the French army moved in to occupy both Cilicia and Syria. By the time Agatha came through in 1928 they'd handed control of the Turkish part of the railways over to the Turkish Nationalists, while the Syrian end of operations had been reborn under the French mandate as the Chemins de Fer Syriens (CFS), a name it still carries today.

Between the wars, with the Middle East finally struggling free of colonial influences and the likes of Jordan, Syria, Lebanon, Iran and Iraq setting up as independent nation states, the route of the Taurus Express became loaded with political significance. Gentleman spies like Robert Baden Powell travelled through, pretending to go butterfly-hunting burdened with preserving jars and nets on poles, but in reality sketching Turkish forts and marine installations. There's an apocryphal story from British Intelligence of an attempt, in the 1930s, to recruit a waiter on the train into the service, only to discover that he was in fact a major in the Turkish army who was already in the employ of four other countries beside his own.

It was the modern reincarnation of this train that I hunkered down to wait for, before dawn the following morning in Adana station. I'd had a sleepless night, listening to locomotives crashing around in the goods yard. Each time I heard a yowl I imagined my Aleppo train passing through, early – and the thought of missing it, and of being marooned in over-tartaned Adana for another week until the next one, brought me out in a cold sweat. I felt as if I'd reached the cliff on the edge of the known world, with the familiar beginning to crumble away under my feet and the distant shore of

Aleppo still too far away in the mist to be safely reached. For a while in the pre-dawn my only other companions on the platform were a pair of ancient ex-servicemen, wearing their medals and sitting companionably together in silence, having reached the age when they'd no further need for either sleep or conversation. I'd no idea which war those medals would have been won in, but the Turks had usually been allies of the Germans, so I kept my distance.

Our silent triumvirate was only finally broken by the arrival of a man on a moped balancing a tray of sesame breads on his handlebars, who proceeded to open up the platform kiosk. Dawn was breaking. The Express would be, he said, a couple of hours late; it usually was.

When the train eventually unwound itself into the station, it seemed to confirm my worst fears. It was indeed the Toros Ekspresi, but its destination boards carried no mention of Syria. So where was my train to Aleppo? Had I really missed it, in the early morning? Please not, please! A couple of train guards looked blankly at me when I inquired, but it was my sesame bread friend, now doing a brisk trade with all the disembarking passengers, who pointed down towards the end of the platform. 'Halab,' he said.

Sure enough, the very last carriage in the train was a different livery to all the others. It was a sleeping-car, and I noted with enormous relief that it carried the logo CFS, Chemins de Fer Syriens. That luxurious, strategically significant, thrice-weekly express from Istanbul to Aleppo and Damascus had been reduced to this – one twenty-year-old ex-German coach, once a week, tacked on the end of a Turkish train.

The sleeping-car attendant, dressed in a tracksuit, was leaning off the back step busily selling sacks of sugar at bargain prices to the platform staff, using a mixture of English and Arabic. He looked me up and down in some surprise when I made it clear I wished to come aboard. Did I have a ticket?

'I don't,' I said, 'but I have money,' and I patted an encouraging-looking bulge in my pocket which was actually a ball of tissues. The attendant's grin was brown and chipped; money he liked, especially money that came into his hands in the corridor of his coach, with no paperwork required. So he let me on and unlocked a clean compartment with a couple of bunks, fresh linen, curtains and a sink.

'Good?' he said.

'Good,' I echoed. Actually, after the anxieties of overnight and the potential death by slow strangulation of another week in Adana, it was more than good – it was wonderful. It got even better when he shuffled back along the corridor moments later with a strong cup of Turkish coffee flavoured with cardamom.

The sleeping-car turned out to be a little bastion of Syria attached to a long streak of Turkey. There were only six passengers on board, all of whom had started at Istanbul, eighteen hours before. The attendant kept the doors which communicated with the rest of the Express securely locked, and even the Turkish railway officials had to come round via the platform. It was a Syria-on-wheels, a double-bogeyed diplomatic bag, and I began to understand why the railway officials at Adana had known so little about it and not been able to sell me a ticket. To have someone join mid-way through the journey was a rare event indeed.

With no seats, only beds, the six passengers were all out in the corridor, talking, smoking and watching Turkey crawl by, and the arrival of a newcomer was a moment of

218

unexpected excitement in a long, languorous trip. A middle-aged Romanian couple were heading for Damascus to spend a week with a cousin in the Romanian embassy. Two rather brutal-looking young Syrian businessmen were on their way home from Istanbul, where they said they'd been selling Aleppo-made *nargileh*, hubble-bubble water pipes. In the cabin next to mine were a young Lebanese couple, Sharif and Farida, who were just returning from their honeymoon in Istanbul. He was a rather bookish-looking tax accountant who spoke good English and even better French. She was shy, doe-eyed and had a sort of undefinable glow about her, the glow that somebody should quite rightly and romantically have on their honeymoon. On the occasions I retreated to my room I could hear her singing softly to herself on the other side of the thin wall. She reminded me of the water-carrying village girl who mesmerizes Mowgli at the end of Disney's version of the *Jungle Book*.

The Cilician plain bumped slowly past, a flat fertile landscape of cotton fields, each with its handful of Turkish women bent double, inching forwards like coloured beetles using their feelers to find the safest way across an ochre carpet. Whole tribes of Turkish women spend most of their lifetimes like this, in the quarter-past-six position, with a baby tucked under one arm, a sack under the other, but still with both hands available for picking cotton.

Just outside Adana we rattled along the perimeter fence of the huge airbase at Incirlik, from where US warplanes were taking off to patrol Iraq's northern no-fly zone.

'Look,' said the hubble-bubble boss, with something approaching a sneer. 'America.'

And it was true, the scene on the other side of the fence was like a slice of the suburban mid-west, with bungalows on lawns, letterboxes on posts, gas-guzzling pick-ups on driveways and children's toys parked neatly round the back; evidently Americans can't exist overseas without bringing their homeland with them. And when, a handful of miles later we passed under the unmistakable silhouette of a twelfth-century Crusader castle, perched on a rocky outcrop, it occurred to me that both were symbols of the same thing: the West attempting to demonstrate to the East, through military muscle, that it knows best.

By now I'd greased the palm of the cabin attendant with several million Turkish lira, and he was well enough disposed to invite me to join him in his pantry to smoke a bit of hubble-bubble and maybe play a bit of poker.

'For money?' I asked, fearing he'd got me down as a soft touch for a few million more.

'No, no, no!' he protested. 'Never, no money. Islam says – cards OK, money, no!'

In the end the cards were forgotten. Everyone but the Romanians packed into the pantry, and I produced a photograph of my wife and kids, and then my passport, which was passed around and carefully studied. Sharif, the bookish Lebanese newly-wed, deciphered the immigration stamps for all the names of the countries I'd visited, translating them into Arabic. The others nodded sagely as he read them out, murmuring approvingly at the mention of the Islamic ones. Why, when I'd been to all these countries, asked someone, had I not been to France or Spain, when they were so close to my home? So I explained how, being British, I had licence to travel at liberty to all the countries of Europe without even having to ask permission. I'd never appreciated, until I saw their expressions of wonder, what a privilege that was. Whenever they travelled anywhere they were either suspected of being terrorists or of wanting to stay for ever.

The water-pipe came round. It tasted of apple, and it had a pleasantly narcotic effect which was hard not to enjoy. But when I offered the mouthpiece on to my neighbour, the strong-armed Mr Hubble, he recoiled, took the pipe out of my hands, bent the mouthpiece back on its hose and made to offer it across the room.

'So,' he growled.

'What was wrong with the way I did it?' I wanted to know.

'You like my penis?' piped up Hubble's sidekick Mr Bubble, demonstrating a surprising vocabulary for someone who up to that point had said nothing in English at all. This was the only thing he said to me on the whole trip, and I assume it was an explanation, not an offer.

After that the pipe was handed around with a great deal of smiling and exaggerated care, and conversation rumbled on. Mr Hubble, who had a macho swagger that I didn't like, used the train once a month, he said, because he did good business in Istanbul.

'Do you speak Turkish?' I asked.

He shook his head. 'I speak calculator,' he said, and mimed punching a little keypad. 'What do you think President Bashar Assad?'

'To be honest I don't know much about him.'

Mr Hubble frowned. Then he made a gesture towards me that probably would have started a fist-fight in many European countries. A gesture that I think was intended to express virility. 'A strong leader,' he growled. 'Very important in Araby, a strong leader.'

The train slowed to tractor speed as we climbed up into the Anamus mountains, the diesel toiling loudly away up in front, hauling us into steep, purple-veined valleys. Flat-roofed box houses with trellised wigs of vines were wedged against the hillsides on piles of stones, overlooking small systems of terraces divided by avenues of mountain fir, eucalyptus and slender cypress. Butterflies were dancing in the shade.

'Beautiful,' said Sharif, and it was hard not to agree. He'd overheard the exchange I'd had with Mr Hubble about Bashar, and now he'd come to tell me, *sotto voce*, about Lebanon, where democracy worked and where everyone was free to say and think what they wanted, without fear of angering the state. I think he, too, thought Mr Hubble was not quite what he said he was.

From there, the conversation steered around to social mores. It turned out Farida was his first cousin. They'd known each other since childhood, had been an item since their teens and engaged for five years, while he worked his way through all his accountancy exams. During this time she had stayed at home, waiting for the big moment to arrive.

'So, with Lebanon being very free,' I asked, 'were you allowed to . . . er, share a bedroom?'

For a moment Sharif didn't seem to have cottoned on. 'Oh no,' he said, with a look almost of horror. 'Not in Lebanon.'

I felt I was beginning to understand Farida's morning-after eyes. In those five years she'd have been sitting at home, waiting for married life to begin and wondering what sex could possibly be like, whether she might learn to enjoy it, and fearful that some new lustful animal would be hiding within the man she loved, waiting for the moment to emerge. And now, finally, that moment had come and it had been all right – more than that, it had been pleasurable. The relief, the satisfaction and the joy were written across her face. Her train had finally come in; love, and sex, had arrived, and it had been carrying no unwelcome surprises.

The Syrian coach was finally separated from the back of the Toros Ekspresi at Fevzipasa, a station which was little more than a set of sidings in the hills. There it was re-attached to the head of a long string of trucks. I groaned; these were the sort of trucks that you never actually see moving, the sort that are part of the landscape, not of the transport system, and which remain perpetually in sidings. Being attached to them was like putting down an anchor.

Fortunately I was wrong. These trucks turned out to be rare examples of the movers of the species, and after a short pause we jogged onward across high plains, towing this long, squealing tail behind us.

By this time the ruddy lowland soil had turned a thunderous lava black, interrupted by lozenges of green where the young sweetcorn and tobacco had started showing through. The only sign of life was the occasional wandering donkey, one of which brought the whole train shuddering to a halt by standing obstinately on the track.

As we approached the Turkish border, Mr Hubble renewed his deodorant and changed his shirt. He seemed to be anticipating a sweaty moment or two, although it wasn't clear what he had to be anxious about. Hopefully it was nothing more than a bit of innocent contraband, but it could be a lot worse, given that it was not far from here, near Gaziantep, that Turkish police had recently made international headlines by stopping a Turkish taxi with a consignment of uranium hidden under the seat. Everyone assumed it was destined for Iraq, but it had been pretty close to the Syrian border at the time.

We crawled into the Turkish border station of Islahiye and stopped next to a small mountain of sacks and boxes. The passengers decanted from the train and a couple of immigration officials in the stationmaster's office examined every passport suspiciously. With just one passenger train a week in each direction, this was their big moment, and they were intent on taking their time over the unfamiliar paperwork.

In the end there was no need to hurry. The driver let the diesel's engine splutter and die and we sat in the shade of a tree and watched several men argue with the guard over the various sacks and boxes. It was, it seemed, a matter of setting the appropriate levels of baksheesh to get them across the border – and even when that was sorted, each box and sack needed to be manhandled into vacant compartments in the sleeping-car, because the freight wagons were all customs-sealed. This process was so long-winded that the sleeping-car attendant had enough time to make two trips to some local supermarket in a taxi, re-appearing laden with large plastic storage boxes which filled the sleeping-car's corridor. I couldn't help feeling, as I stepped over these boxes when the time came to finally clamber back aboard, that they were indirectly related to my presence, and that without my very generous 'ticket money' he wouldn't have had the wherewithal for last-minute shopping in Turkey.

Ten minutes later the wire fences and ditches of the border itself finally hove into view. This was a serious crossing, with manned watchtowers and foxholes, machine-guns at the ready, and as we came abreast of it the Syrians on board started to chant 'Turkey . . . Turkey . . . Turkey, SYRIA!', slapping each other on the back as we moved across. It could have been just patriotism, but it felt more like relief at having got away.

The first Syrian checkpost, Meydan Ikbis, was an empty place parked on a barren high plain a couple of hundred metres or so inside the fence. Here we all went through the same procedure again, taking our passports into the station building, while a handful of boys ferreted through the sleeping-car to disinter all the sacks and boxes that had been loaded on the Turkish side. The Turkish diesel rumbled off back to its homeland and was replaced by a far more decrepit Syrian one, a long-snouted museum piece, its midriff covered in webs of oil. The sleeping-car was finally disconnected from the goods wagons, and our international express, by now reduced to just one coach, was ready to go.

Except it wasn't. The Romanians had not emerged from the immigration office, and it was evident from the sound-effects from within that all was not well. Borders are tense places, and after a long period in an airless office with men in uniform whose language she couldn't speak, Mrs Romania had dissolved into tears, while several uni-formed officers were sitting around looking embarrassed. There was, apparently, a visa problem, and one which the Romanians were hoping to resolve by contacting their cousin in Damascus by telephone. Meanwhile the train wouldn't be going anywhere.

An hour later, with the sun now declining in the sky, Mr Romania emerged, grim-faced, to remove their luggage from the train. The cousin in Damascus hadn't been found. We were free to proceed, but they had to go back across the border.

During that long intermission in the sidings I'd had a chance to speak with the driver of the Syrian diesel, who'd already been waiting for six hours for the train to arrive, and was equally prepared for six more. Bedur was a lean, lantern-jawed Kurd with a relaxed, easy manner which suggested he felt in no way impressed by, or inferior to, foreigners. He looked more like a man of the mountains than of the railways, and he should really have been dressed in a sashed *galibiyya* and a turban rather than the pale blue uniform of the CFS.

Seven passengers counted as a busy train, he said. They'd recently had a one-passenger arrival which the Turkish side had incorrectly reported as being completely empty, so no diesel had been sent up from Aleppo to bring it down. The sleeping-car had simply been left, locked, in the sidings until the lone passenger, a Turkish commercial traveller, had managed to raise relatives in Turkey with his mobile phone. They in turn had called Turkish railways, who'd called Syrian railways, who'd summoned Bedur and sent him off up into the mountains to rescue the stranded Turk. 'You think this train is late? Now he, he was *really* late.'

At Bedur's invitation I swapped the relative comfort of the sleeping-car for the chance to ride up front on the three-hour journey to Aleppo. There was little luxury in being up in the diesel, a 1,800 horsepower General Electric made in Chicago, thirty years before. From inside, it felt like a great vibrating lump of agricultural iron-mongery, and there was no sense of any huge surge of power when it accelerated. Bedur and his co-driver Ahmed sat sideways on, like a pair of telephone operators sitting at antique consoles, and I squeezed between them, with Bedur fussing about whether I might get my trousers dirty with patches of oil.

The line pitched, climbed, dived and carved its way through the hills, and our speed never exceeded forty kilometres an hour.

'Laid by the Germans a hundred years ago,' Bedur shouted. 'If we try to go any faster the diesel will dance.'

Sure enough, on a steady straight, the speedometer needle crept upwards and the locomotive began to bounce from side to side, with alarming clunks from beneath the floor.

'Not good for the coaches,' said Bedur, throttling back. Not good for the tracks, either.

By now the sun was nearly gone, and the soil had changed colour from black to the deep red of very lean meat. Rows of bluey-green olive trees marched, military style, across the landscape to meet us, wave upon wave of them, climbing the hillsides and descending the valleys and repeating for ever. Occasionally there'd be a smudge of smoke where the workers had gathered clippings and prunings which they were using to brew sweet tea. Even from the driver's cab the land smelt fresh and good.

Bedur looked across his homeland approvingly. 'Kurds, all Kurds,' he said. He pointed out the direction of his own, distant, village.

An hour after leaving the border it was dark and the locomotive had become a myopic metal dinosaur prowling down through the hills towards its nest, preceded by its spear of light. From the driver's cab that headlight picked out the kinks in the rails, and what had looked perfectly safe by daylight looked pretty rickety by night.

Bedur hooted and flashed at anything that moved. There were, he admitted, no signals on this line, nor any barriers on the road crossings, but neither were there many cars on the roads or trains on the track: one local passenger train in each direction per day, and perhaps three or four freight trains. The signalling system was entirely in the hands of the stationmasters, who handed him signed chits of green paper when it was clear to proceed, which it invariably was. Word-of-mouth systems like this only work when the railway network employs a staggering 14,000 people, as Syrian railways does, even though there are basically just half a dozen working lines and the principal route (Damascus to Aleppo) has just two passenger trains a day. On routes where the trains travelled faster, said Bedur, every road crossing would have someone to stop the traffic, but here on this line they were largely unmanned, and they made me nervous. Sure, Bedur would slow, hoot and flash, but there'd always be some driver who'd risk it and lumber across at the last minute. There was an air of inevitability about it – surely the car would stall, and we'd plough through it in slow motion, as in the movies. But it never happened, and Bedur said it never had, for him at least. He'd been driving for twenty-five years without an accident, even though there'd been occasions when he'd worked a twenty-eight-hour day, taking a freight train from Damascus to Deir ez-Zur, and then hauling a passenger train back.

'But surely,' I began, recalling a conversation I'd had with a train driver in India who'd had twenty-five people kill themselves by lying down on the track in front of his locomotive, 'surely there are suicides?'

Bedur grunted in acknowledgement and splayed the fingers of one hand. 'In twenty-five years I have five. Four kill themselves. One an old man . . . walking in front. Not suicide. Deaf, didn't hear.'

With an hour still to go to Aleppo we stopped for a couple of minutes in a station for Ahmed, the co-driver, to refill the kettle. Up until that point he had kept us supplied with constant cups of tea, bullied into it by Bedur, who'd announce 'Chai, Ahmed' every twenty minutes or so. As far as I could see his only other role was to log our arrival at every station and to look backwards on suitable curves to make sure our one coach was following in orderly fashion, but perhaps Bedur would have let him do more if I hadn't been there.

The stationmaster approached while Ahmed was filling the kettle, and Bedur leaned out to greet him.

'Est-ce que vous parlez français?' he said.

The stationmaster's response was fluent. 'Mais oui. Do you have someone else who speaks French?'

I said I did, and we had a brief exchange through the cab window, the stationmaster and I, the gist of which was that people were nice and that I was pleased to be in Syria. Then Ahmed was back and Bedur keen to go.

'That makes him happy,' said Bedur as we pulled away from the station. 'He doesn't get much opportunity to speak French, stuck out here.'

It was a culturally surreal little moment in the middle of the Kurdish hills.

We finally arrived in Aleppo, which once upon a time had been the self-important terminus for the Taurus Express, seven hours late. Bedur crawled through the dense suburbs, suddenly surprisingly tense, but it was only once we were safely in the station, *ilhamdu lillah*, giving thanks to God, that he explained why.

'Palestinian refugees,' he said, 'lots of them, living by the tracks. Another driver killed a child playing on the tracks. Since then we have stone throwing and they try to derail the trains.' This, then, was truly the Middle East.

Back in the sleeping-car to collect my luggage, I caught a glimpse of the rear views of Hubble and Bubble disappearing hurriedly towards the exit. Sharif and Farida, the only passengers who'd intended to continue on to Damascus, had also had enough.

'We're going to find a hotel,' said Sharif. 'We'll complete the journey back to Lebanon by bus. It's faster and more convenient.'

That meant that, with Hubble and Bubble gone, the Romanians still holed up back at the border, and myself and the Lebanese departing, the one-coach, once-weekly

Istanbul to Damascus international express was left to do the final seven-hour leg of its journey completely empty, apart from the cabin car attendant and all his smuggled plastic boxes.

How things had changed since Agatha's day.

RETURN TO THE BARON

It is a great relief for any traveller to arrive in a city which
he already knows, especially after a long and difficult
journey across unfamiliar territory. Aleppo will always be
deeply foreign to me, but the fact that I could remember
how to get from the station to the Baron Hotel – a
pleasant walk through the central park – meant I could
safely ignore the importuning taxi drivers.

That pleasurable sensation of stepping back into the
familiar is something that Agatha recorded in her
archaeological memoir *Come Tell Me How You Live*,
exulting in her return to the civilized world of Aleppo
after some weeks out on the dig at Chagar Bazar, in
eastern Syria. 'Alep! Shops! A bath! My hair shampooed!
Friends to see!' she wrote. I didn't personally feel a
desperate need for a bath or a shampoo, but there was
someone I particularly wanted to see.

Aleppo station was just as I remembered it, with a clock
made by Garnier of Paris next to the office of the *chef de
gare*. In the days when this was the terminus for the
Taurus Express the liveried coaches of the Wagons-Lits

company were regularly in the station with their uniformed attendants, as if Aleppo was a mere hop and a skip from the French Riviera. It was also the station in which *Murder on the Orient Express* had its beginning, with Poirot clambering aboard the Taurus – then comprising a dining-car, a sleeping-car and two local coaches – for Istanbul, having just completed some unspecified mysterious business in Asia Minor. On that occasion there were even fewer passengers than there had been on my train: just Mary Debenham, Colonel Arbuthnot, and Poirot himself, who was seen off from Aleppo by a tongue-tied French Lieutenant on a cold and frosty morning.

The station still carries a sense of self-importance. Huge brass lanterns hang from a ceiling that alternates carved dark oak beams and red plaster, like a giant backgammon board. Sunlight streams in through high mullioned windows and moves in patches across a marble floor which is kept highly polished by regular patrols of staff. There are no more French Lieutenants, but a surprisingly modest (by local standards) bust of ex-President Assad stands in one corner, and in the other the information booth is staffed by pretty girls with dark ringlets and tight jeans, signifying that this is not, yet, one of the more repressive regimes of the Middle East.

Over the centuries Aleppo has ridden out the invasions which have tugged Syria this way and that, resulting in an almost impossibly complex web of history that only an archaeologist can really begin to comprehend. From the earliest times this land was recorded as being under the control of Akkadians from Mesopotamia (now Iraq), who were eventually expelled by the Egyptian king Thutmose, seeking to expand his empire north. Hittites from central Turkey then moved south, pushing back the

Egyptians under Tutankhamun, and allowing Phoenician traders to settle in the coastal ports. From the thirteenth century BC various principalities in what is now Jordan and Lebanon whittled away at Hittite power, but none of them were able to resist the might of the Assyrian empire, which once again invaded from Mesopotamia. By 732 BC all of Syria was under the command of Sargon II, who sounds like a character from *Lord of the Rings*.

It is from these Assyrians that Syria took its name, although most of the visible history still extant in the countryside dates from subsequent eras, from around 300 BC to AD 600, during periods of Roman and Byzantine rule.

By this time Islam was spreading fast through the Arab population of the Middle East, and it swiftly became an irresistible military force. Jerusalem fell in AD 638 and soon Syria became the hub of a Muslim revolution which stretched right across to Spain in the west and down to India in the east. The new Umayyad dynasty established itself in Damascus, building mosques and palaces, and starting a long power-struggle with the Abbasids from Baghdad.

It was into this context that the Crusaders arrived, responding to a plea from Pope Urban II for the recapture of the Church of the Holy Sepulchre in Jerusalem. Using tactics that verged on the barbaric, they successfully took Jerusalem in 1099, but they simply didn't have the numerical presence to do much more than look down upon their conquered lands from castles like Krak des Chevaliers. It was Salah ad-Din (Saladin to most of us), a general born in the same Iraqi village, Tikrit, as Saddam Hussein, who rocked the Crusaders back and forced them to sign an agreement which brought some measure of stability to the region, before his successors the Mamluks finally chased them away. By the sixteenth century Syria was occupied by the Ottomans, and it prospered until the early nineteenth century under Turkish rule. During that time Aleppo became a vital trade centre between east and west, an important souq for the surrounding desert, and a key stopover on the pilgrimage route to Mecca.

During World War I, though, the land was once again the scene of fierce fighting, this time between the British, based in Suez, and the Turks who were seeking to capitalize on their allegiance with Germany by making territorial gains into Africa. This was Lawrence of Arabia's big moment, and with the help of courageous Arab nationalists he harried the Germans and the Turks, blowing up trains and ambushing troops in the desert.

Once the war was over those Arab nationalists started to set up Greater Syria, an area which included Palestine and Lebanon. Unfortunately for them, however, their courage was to be poorly rewarded, because the victors may have relied on their help during the fighting, but they were too arrogant to recognize their sovereignty in the peace that followed. Instead the League of Nations awarded the French the Mandate controlling the Greater Syria region, and the nationalist King was sent into exile. (At the same time the British were awarded what was then Mesopotamia, later to become Iraq.) In the years that followed France ceded a certain amount of autonomy to local officials, but full independence and the establishment of the nation we recognize as Syria didn't come until 1946, and by then French culture had become deeply ingrained in Syrian society.

That influence is immediately apparent when you walk out of Aleppo's railway station. The boulevards of balconied six-storey apartments could be straight out of Haussman's Paris, and you can sit yourself down at a pavement café and order an espresso from a moustachioed waiter in a white tunic with a Gauloise tucked behind his ear. The people – particularly the businesslike Armenians in their suits – are stylish in an old-fashioned European way, like a crowd of Parisian janitors out walking in their Sunday best. In this city you can buy European bread, lacy underwear, beautifully wrapped oriental pâtisserie, and have a deed of oath drawn up in French, Arabic, Armenian or Russian. The central park, with its tree-lined gravel walkways, statues of poets, fountains and knee-high clipped hedges, was modelled on the Jardins de Luxembourg, and there are lovers on the park benches, although you'll not see them do anything more than hold hands.

The sexual temperature rises higher in the evenings, when young men gather in the commercial district of town around giant, lurid cinema posters of gun-toting musclemen and girls in bikinis. This part of the world favours the sort of B movie that never makes it on to the big screen in the West, but even in Syria these movies are incomplete, having been judiciously censored to reduce the bikinis to a fleeting glimpse. In sex, though, anticipation is everything, and the atmosphere on the street outside the cinemas is one of greatly inflamed excitement, and one which itinerant traders make the most of by peddling anti-impotence oil. Most of their customers are teenagers with no sexual experience at all but who don't want to be found wanting when the big day comes. Perhaps they'll save enough to be able to afford one of the Russian prostitutes who have set up shop in town, in a spirit of free trade following the downfall of communism.

For me, walking back through the door of the Baron after a three-year absence was like shrugging on a forgotten jacket retrieved from the back of the wardrobe; it was long since out of style, with frayed cuffs and leather patches on the elbows, but it was a comfortable fit, and you had to acknowledge that it had been well made. The hotel receptionist, a bosomy mature lady with that rather knowing smile of a matron in a public school who'd seen it all before, allocated me a room. But I realized, after climbing the pitted stone staircase past original Orient Express posters and crossing a wide hall of tessellated tiles, that it was on the renovated wing. It had been re-equipped in a style which might have worked well enough in package tourism, where punters need to see pictures of exactly what they're going to get before they leave home, but in the Baron the old and the new were like chalk and cheese.

After a bit of renegotiation I took a room two doors along from Agatha's, which had always been 203. This was more like it: several wall tiles were missing in the bathroom and many more were covered in a dirty skin of limescale. The lightbulb was naked, loose bits of wiring were tacked to the plaster and there was a radiator attached to the wall at head height. The bedroom had the obligatory hatstand, the old-fashioned bakelite phone, a giant bruise of uncertain origin on the wall and a bed that had a definite list to starboard, threatening to pitch any light sleeper out on to the floor. This was the Baron I remembered.

Back in 1928, when the Middle East was still very new territory for any form of tourism, the Baron was the only Aleppo hotel which Thomas Cook would recommend. Its style was reassuringly familiar in a land which was scarily exotic, and for which most travellers were deeply un-prepared. Just how unprepared is indicated by the 1928 edition of the Thomas Cook Handbook, which advises customers packing for Syria that 'There is nothing better for travelling than a suit of Scottish tweed, supplemented by an ulster or other warm overcoat and a good waterproof.' The author had probably never ventured further east than Ramsgate.

Agatha had stayed at the Baron frequently with Max, and the couple had become close friends with Coco Masloumian, who was the son of the hotel's founder. Back in those days, the street outside would have been a quiet lane, but today it is one of Aleppo's busiest arteries and traffic noise torments anyone trying to sleep in the front rooms. The terrace where Agatha apparently sat for long hours, writing, is at chin height to the traffic lights, and it is not an easy place to hear yourself think, let alone hold a conversation. As I arrived that evening I passed an elderly English couple steadfastly sitting out there, reading and writing postcards, much as Max and Agatha might have done, and equally formally dressed. I was prepared to bet that they were the occupants of Room 203 and that they had chosen the hotel, as I had, for its Agatha connections.

The young Max Mallowan's archaeological career was still in its infancy when he first passed through Aleppo with his famous wife. In those days the dig season was short – often just three or four months in late winter and early spring – and most archaeologists' wives were only too happy to stay behind in England. Living conditions out in the field were at best primitive, in accommodation under canvas or in rudimentary mud-brick houses with no running water. You had to be passionate about your subject, too, for there was nothing to do other than dig and talk about digging, a deeply competitive business at that time with many active sites all over Mesopotamia. Furthermore, the ambience on a dig was a bit like an army mess or a gentlemen's club, where archaeologists gave each other nicknames, smoked pipes, read learned journals and presumably also burped, farted and didn't wash very frequently, although that doesn't tend to get recorded in their memoirs. In addition, many of them were often slightly awkward or eccentric characters who were not particularly adept at social situations. The last thing they wanted on the dig was a woman.

But Agatha, having had one marriage fail on her, was determined not to become a dig widow as well as a golf widow, so she set out to carve herself a niche in expedition life among all the men, taking a role in cleaning and reassembling clay fragments, and later as dig photographer. In this she was to become remarkably successful – she loved the landscape, was unfazed by the deprivations and became very interested in the subject matter – but she had some initial opposition.

When she'd first met Max he'd been an assistant to Leonard Woolley at Ur. Leonard's wife, Katharine, was one of the rare wives who did accompany their husbands, but she was also a complex personality and her whims and wishes ruled the entire Ur dig. In 1928 Katharine had been perfectly happy with the idea of Agatha as a celebrity guest at Ur, but then she'd gone and married the young dig assistant. Thereafter it was made clear to Max that, while he was welcome to remain as a member of the team, he could not bring his new wife.

For the first year of their married life Max didn't have time to make new arrangements, so he was forced to spend that season back with the Woolleys at Ur, leaving Agatha and travelling to Iraq straight from where their honeymoon had ended in Greece. In Patras, he'd had to wrench himself away from his new wife's sick-bed – she'd had a bad case of food poisoning from eating fish – in order to get to Ur by the agreed date. It was his job to prepare the house for the Woolleys' imminent arrival, and Katharine had particularly insisted on a new bathroom. The Greek doctor who'd attended Agatha in Patras had been very surprised at the way in which newly-married British men behaved when their wives most needed them, disappearing off to the East like that. Accordingly, when the Woolleys didn't actually arrive at Ur until several days after the pre-ordained date, meaning that Max hadn't in fact needed to leave Agatha so abruptly and in such a state, he was as angry and frustrated as a mild-mannered man could be.

And so, for the 1931 season, he'd searched out an expedition where Agatha could travel with him, to a dig based at the self-same Nineveh I'd first heard mentioned by Mrs Masloumian, back in the prehistory of this book. Nineveh had once been a huge and mighty Assyrian capital on the banks of the Tigris, just across the river from the modern city of Mosul in northern Iraq. The dig leader was an epigraphist called Reginald Campbell Thompson (CT to his chums), who conformed neatly to the image of a careful Scot by being both stingy and believing in the necessary rigours of exercise. Before agreeing to accept the presence of the new Mrs Mallowan at the dig, he invited the couple to his English home on a wet weekend and took them on long, cross-country walks to see how she coped. When she showed resilience (Agatha had had plenty of experience of long wet walks on Dartmoor), he drew up a contract with a clause which stipulated: 'Mrs Mallowan will be a welcome guest at the expedition's house for the last month of the expedition; she paying her own expenses, travelling and otherwise, and one pound weekly for service, board and lodging to the expeditionary funds while in the house. The expedition shall not otherwise be responsible to her: she will not publish locally or elsewhere any account of things found, without reference to Dr Thompson.'

Max travelled out to Nineveh first and Agatha followed a month later, travelling to Aleppo on the Taurus Express and catching the onward train as far as Nisibin, which was as far as the Baghdad railway went at the time. Violent rain meant that she was three days late in arriving, but nevertheless Max was waiting for her on the station platform; three-day train delays were not unusual at that time of year.

After Ur, which is set in the vast and unrelentingly hot plains to the south of Baghdad, Nineveh was a delightful dig, with a view of mountains and none of the social tensions created by Katharine Woolley. The Mallowans had their own room in the expedition house, and Agatha got along well with Campbell Thompson's wife, Barbara, who was probably grateful for female company. The house was sparsely furnished, however, and early in her stay Agatha crossed the river to Mosul souq and bought herself a solid table on which she could place her typewriter, so that she could write *Lord Edgware Dies*. Campbell Thompson was astonished at such profligate expenditure when there were plenty of packing cases to rest on.

Any initial nervousness at whether she could truly share in her new husband's passion quickly evaporated. 'I enjoyed my first experience of living on a dig enormously,' Agatha wrote in her autobiography, describing herself and Max as 'bursting with happiness' at Nineveh. Every day she'd accompany him out to his own project, a pit which he eventually excavated to twenty-five metres deep, and she shared with him the excitement of the substantial pottery finds he made, quickly learning to identify pot sherds from all the different eras. An archaeological dig was, after all, not unlike the scene of a crime, with plenty of careful analysis and reconstruction to be done.

Even though she never put any particular priority on it, her own work progressed well, too. During the years 1930–36, with a dig season every winter, she produced eleven novels and four collections of short stories – double her habitual output – which in itself was indicative of a happy, productive state of mind.

It was Max's success with the Nineveh pottery that allowed him to raise sufficient sponsorship from the British Museum and the British School of Archaeology in Iraq to lead his first ever independent expedition, the following year, to Arpachiyah, a village a few miles northeast of Nineveh. This time Agatha was no longer just a latecoming observer, but travelled out with Max via Aleppo and played a significant role on the site, cleaning and piecing together the pottery and working in the makeshift darkroom to print the photographs. She also found time to write, getting *Murder on the Orient Express* under way.

Max struck archaeological paydirt at Arpachiyah in the form of a sprawling building possibly dating back to 5800 BC which had evidently burnt down, leaving a wealth of artefacts inside – pottery plates, stone vessels, polished obsidian and human figurines from the Halaf period. He found enough there to justify a second season, but a dispute at the end of the dig with the Iraq museum over the division of the finds, a dispute which got so serious that it eventually involved a correspondence with the League of Nations, meant that either he didn't want to return to Arpachiyah for a third season, or he wouldn't have been given permission to do so.

In any case the political climate was changing rapidly in what was becoming known as Iraq. In 1932, while the

Mallowans were still at Nineveh, the country had been released from the British Mandate and granted full independence as a nation-state. By the time of the Arpachiyah dig the fledgling military were already becoming involved in Iraqi politics, with a series of coups and counter-coups. With anti-British sentiment running high, it would probably not have been a good idea for the Mallowans to stay on.

Next season, therefore, saw them in Syria, moving closer still to Aleppo, and surveying a selection of tells or mounds for the next suitable locations. This part of their lives is particularly well documented by Agatha in *Come Tell Me How You Live*, with some engaging anecdotes of dig life. She describes, for example, how she'd prepare for departure in London by buying the 'sort of clothes worn by the wives of empire builders', together with one really soft down pillow, several fountain pens and no fewer than four wristwatches, because 'the desert is not kind to watches'.

To do their exploration the Mallowans bought an old Ford, which they christened the Queen Mary, in Beirut. The driver they hired turned out to be something of a Mr Toad, as Agatha describes. 'Aristide glides softly up behind an overladen donkey, with a man and woman trudging beside it, and lets out a terrific blast of his horn. The donkey stampedes, the woman screams and rushes after it, the man shakes his fist. Aristide roars with laughter.' When Agatha and Max chastise him, his response is indignant. 'Am I not driving a lorry? These miserable Bedouin must get out of my way.'

Even today the Syrian landscape around Aleppo is rich with tells, every one of them a potential archaeological treasure-trove. These are the icebergs of history, with a Roman crust on top and piles of far more interesting and ancient stuff far below the waterline; the art lies in guessing, from the eroded protruding tip, what might lie below, and how far down you'd have to go to get to it. The Mallowans walked around so many of these tells, usually in the same direction, that Agatha noticed her shoes were starting to wear on one side only. Max finally selected one promising-looking mound at a place called Chagar Bazar, and rented a house which had looked suitable by daylight, but which turned out to be already occupied by a healthy population of mice and cockroaches, neither of which had yet learned to be afraid of human beings.

The first Agatha knew about this infestation was when she was woken by the sensation of tiny feet on her skin. 'I am ashamed to say that at two a.m. I become hysterical. When morning comes, I declare, I am going into Kamichlie to wait for the train, and I am going straight back to Alep! And from Alep I shall go straight back to England!' Whereupon the beds were hauled out into the courtyard, and the night was completed under the stars. The next day a cat was brought, and within five days it had caught everything that moved, and she was no longer threatening to return home – especially now that the shy expedition architect had completed his first task, that of building her a lavatory. Agatha was sufficiently self-deprecating to appreciate that this was an unusual first base for a friendship between the dig's only woman and its most reticent man, but Robin Macartney, the architect of that lavatory, went on to become a close friend, and designed several jacket covers for her books.

Chagar Bazar became the setting for two seasons of happy dig life, and Agatha, now a very good photographer and rapidly becoming an expert on pottery, found herself relating easily to the small children and to the brightly dressed Kurdish women. To many of the Arab workers she dispensed medicine, more often than not to cure their constipation. One of her laxative powders was credited with helping a local woman to conceive male twins – the mechanics of that don't even bear thinking about – and her reputation as a medicine woman of great power and wisdom spread far and wide. The local sheikh, though, was harder to impress. 'I see your wife reads,' he said to Max on one of his visits, watching Agatha from a safe distance. 'Does she also write?'

There was something about the rhythm of the place and the simplicity of life in the desert that appealed immensely to the author. She described the life of the children as some sort of idyll, 'like in the fairy stories of old, wandering about over the hills herding cattle, sometimes sitting and singing.' She loved the gentle fertile country and its simple people, who knew how to laugh and how to enjoy life, who were idle and gay, and who had dignity, good manners, and a great sense of humour, and to whom death was not terrible.

There's a simple but evocative episode towards the end of *Come Tell Me How You Live*, when rumours of impending war in Europe were casting a shadow over the Mallowans' future in Syria. Agatha and Max were having a paddle and a picnic by a wadi when an old man came herding his goats over a hill of marigolds towards them. He sat down, and, after a period of silence, asked them where they came from. When they responded that they were English, he nodded his head.

'Is it the English this country belongs to now? I cannot remember. I know it is no longer the Turks.'

'No,' says Agatha. 'The Turks have not been here since the war.'

'A war?' The old man is puzzled.

'The war that was fought twenty years ago.'

The old man reflected for a while. He does not remember a war, but he does remember many unusual trains on the railway.

'That, then, was the war? We did not realize it was a war. It did not touch us here.'

As I read this passage from the book I found myself hoping that, on the journey that still lay ahead of me, I would find goatherds who hadn't been touched by war.

I hadn't returned to the Baron Hotel just for the sake of the peeling décor and the chance to sleep two doors along from Agatha's room. Or even for a second trip with Mr Walid and his Studebaker, although he was still prowling the corridors and was quick to offer me a half day to St Simeon at a reduced price, given that I was a repeat customer. I'd come for a second chance to meet the proprietor's ageing mother, with whom I'd taken tea three years before. My recollection of her was as a prickly character, but since then she'd also achieved considerable significance in my eyes as the only person on my journey, apart from Janez Cuček, who remembered actually meeting Agatha.

The only way to get in touch with her was via her son, Armen, a prospect which also made me slightly uncomfortable. After my last trip I'd written a newspaper piece which had been brutally honest about the hotel's fixtures and fittings. I'd even mentioned Mr Masloumian himself, likening him to a slightly pompous prep school headmaster. I knew a copy of the newspaper article had reached the hotel, but I didn't know how he'd reacted to it, or whether I might be on some kind of black list. Enemy of the Baron.

If I was, Mr Masloumian made no mention of it – or perhaps he didn't recognize my name. He was friendly enough when we met in the foyer, although he warned me about his mother's state of mind. She was in the restaurant having a late lunch, he said. She'd had a very tiring day and was rather inclined to mood swings. But she had consented to see me nevertheless.

Armen led me down through the sombre, empty dining-room to where his mother sat, eating vegetables and rice in the far corner by the window. She was as I remembered: handsome, alert and suspicious, with a tight perm and a frosty manner. I felt unwelcome and intrusive, but this was a rare chance of talking to someone who'd actually met Agatha on her travels, and I had to take it.

I started by narrating a bit of my difficult train journey from Turkey, explaining my purpose in being there, and asking her whether she'd ever travelled with the Taurus Express.

'I did try it once,' she said crisply. 'In the mid-1950s. I didn't enjoy it.'

'Oh?'

'I went to sleep with the window open and woke in the morning to find all my clothes covered in smuts from the engine. Then, at Ankara, the blessed thing broke down and we had to wait forever for a replacement.'

'And you never tried it again?'

'A couple of years later the service stopped.'

'Did you not come out by train in the first place?'

She shook her head. 'By ship,' she said, 'from Cyprus. In 1947.' She'd been a nurse, the daughter of a peripatetic lighthouse-keeper who'd had postings all over the UK, and she'd originally come out to Syria after responding to a newspaper advertisment placed by Aleppo's Al-Azizie maternity hospital. Still very much in operation.

'How old were you?' I asked, thinking that the city must have seemed impossibly exotic to a young Englishwoman.

She fixed me with a steely glare. 'What rude questions you're asking.' For a moment I feared she'd refuse to say anything further, but then she relented. 'Twenty-five.'

She agreed that the city had seemed wonderfully strange, 'like scenes from *Arabian Nights*', but it had also had a cultured, partly French-speaking expatriate society which had swept her up, and the Baron Hotel had been the epicentre of that social life. I could imagine all the eligible young men in town coming to pay court to the fresh, newly arrived English beauty – because there was no doubt she'd been beautiful. She'd probably had an exhilarating few months playing the field until she'd eventually fallen for the most powerful presence, the hotel's proprietor, the energetic, charming Coco Masloumian.

At that time the Baron was in its prime and Coco was already a good friend of the Mallowans. It was he who had invited them around to dinner, one night in 1954.

'Actually, he'd invited them to "drinks", but we already had friends coming around to dinner that night and Coco had always intended them to stay on,' recalled Mrs Masloumian.

'The Mallowans came punctually at 6 p.m., earlier than all the other guests, which wasn't terribly convenient because I had three small children at the time and my husband was still over in the hotel taking orders for pre-dinner drinks.' It had been an awkward first half-hour, during which she'd struggled to find common topics of conversation. 'I said something to her about my children, and you could tell she wasn't remotely interested. She had eyes which looked straight through you. And as she was teetotal you couldn't get her to relax by giving her a drink, either.'

Eventually the other friends appeared, and Mrs Masloumian had introduced Agatha and Max to them as 'Mr and Mrs Mallowan'.

'I didn't want to trade on the fact that Agatha Christie had come to dinner,' she said. 'But the result of that was that no one really paid her much attention. One of my friends even asked who that difficult woman was. Eventually, a guest arrived who knew her real identity, but not everyone believed it straight away. I remember over-hearing someone murmur, "If that's Agatha Christie then I'm Napoleon."'

Once the secret was out, though, the party warmed up, and by the time the evening ended everyone was seated at her feet, suggesting ideas for stories.

'For a long time afterwards we all used to go out and buy her books expecting to see some of those ideas turn up, but they never did. Of course the main real life character who did appear in print was her husband, who was the absolute Poirot. Not foreign or fat, of course, but otherwise spot on in all his mannerisms, very precise and fastidious.' She paused, and looked at me, expectantly.

'Did you get the impression that they were a happy couple?' I asked.

'They were well suited,' she said, cautiously. 'You know, interested in each other.'

'What would they have done during the day?'

'In those days there was society here,' Armen butted in, impatient to assume the reins of conversation from his mother. 'A different class of person, not these blessed so-called, er, rucksackers, who eat at the schwarma stalls. Agatha would have sat on the terrace writing one or other of her books, while Max would have gone to the archaeological sites in the neighbourhood, although they were not strictly his period, of course. In those days they weren't easy to reach. In fact there are only proper roads today because I told the director of antiquities that we must have them.' Mr Masloumian was lighting his pipe and getting into his stride. He started to tell me, possibly as a shot across my bows, how he had recently instructed his solicitor to sue a German guidebook publisher for suggesting that the Baron had closed down, when his mother interrupted him.

'I'm not surprised, with doorhandles that come off in your hand!'

This was obviously a sore point, and Armen didn't look best pleased.

'Mother, I told you, I'll see that it is sorted out.'

'You should have left them as they were. It was just change for the sake of change . . .' Mother and son started to snipe at each other like a married couple about the state of the hotel and the renovations. It couldn't have been easy for him, living in the shadow of his father, or for her, watching the Baron's inexorable decline after her husband's death. It was hard to tell what was the main force behind the decay – his inability to do the right thing, or her intransigence about having anything changed.

Aware that my presence was becoming less welcome by the minute, I rose.

'It's been very kind of you . . .' I started, but Mrs Masloumian reverted instantly to her Agatha story, and now she was more belligerent.

'I've had more than enough of the whole shooting match,' she said. 'I'm fed up with people I've never met saying I said this or I said that.'

She looked pointedly at me, and I tried to look sympathetic. I could see she was irritated at being sought out not for herself, but for having met Agatha Christie, and at being forced yet again to narrate an encounter which she personally had found unsatisfactory. And in a way I admired her for not dressing up that encounter as being more romantic or more entertaining than it had been, as many other people would have been tempted to do. It was an encounter between two women who had not been on each other's wavelength, and she hadn't tried to pretend anything else. An encounter which had formed just one tiny episode in her own exotic, exciting life story, which was possibly worth a book in itself. But nobody was interested in that.

'Thanks, thanks very much. It's been very interesting, very,' I offered, bowing my way backwards out of that sombre dining hall.

That evening, with the encounter with Mrs M under my belt, I retreated to the Baron's lofty bar. There, among the leather armchairs, I met the same Canadian I'd got drunk with three years before. Kevin was a chubby thirty-something with sensual lips which he tried to hide in an only partly successful beard. He worked as a construction engineer building grain silos, usually funded by overseas aid agencies. As such he regularly found himself putting the foundations in among what he called 'old stuff' under the ground, and I remembered him telling me how on one occasion he'd actually crawled down into a tomb full of bones. Needless to say that particular archaeological site now has a grain silo on top of it.

Once we'd got over the surprise of meeting again – I suspected he lurked here regularly for the chance of meeting unaccompanied travellers over a watery, brewed-in-the-bottle Al-Shark beer or two – he updated me on local changes.

'We don't get the big numbers of Ruskies we used to,' he said. 'Mind you, some of the hotels are still completely Russian. The number of prostitutes is increasing all the time, though. From the Ukraine, mostly.'

'I've not spotted any.'

'Then you've not been to any of the nightclubs.'

'Are they just dancing? Or do they go all the way?'

Kevin's bottle paused on the way to his lips. 'Search me. I've not been to any either.'

We talked briefly about my train journey, and he told me how every year a retired railway engineer from the former East Germany came over for a two-month working holiday, during which time he repaired all the broken-down locomotives which had been put aside for him by Syrian railways. Some of them were over half a century old.

And then we talked of Iraq, now looming large on my personal horizon.

'I've worked with plenty of Iraqis, and always found them absolutely charming,' was his opinion. 'They all think I'm American, of course, but it's never made them unfriendly. I have to say I feel very sorry for them. How're you crossing over?'

'By bus.'

'I haven't been near the border in a while but I'd be interested to see what's going across. Sanctions, and all that. I know there's a large, semi-legal trade in fuel oil, which the Iraqi refineries are giving away for free as an unwanted by-product. A lot of businesses over here rely on it.'

'Do the Iraqis think there's going to be a war?'

Kevin shook his head. 'Don't think the Syrians do either. How could there be, with so little pretext?'

'But what about all that oil?'

'No way. Even Big George wouldn't do anything so cynical. No, I tell you what,' he added, taking a big pull at his Al-Shark, 'I predict that water, not oil, will be the next big justification for war. The Syrian aquifers are going down at a rate of fifteen feet a year. That's serious for Syria, and it's even more serious for Iraq.'

'Where I suppose it doesn't rain very often.'

'You know what Mesopotamia means? It means "land between two rivers". The Tigris and the Euphrates. They both originate in the mountains of Turkey. Without those two rivers Iraq would not, could not exist.'

Kevin explained that while Iraq and Syria had signed bilateral agreements preserving the flow of the Euphrates, Turkey had yet to sign any agreements with any of its neighbours about any of its watercourses. On the contrary, it had initiated its own Central Anatolian Project, which included the construction of twenty dams on the Euphrates and the Tigris by the year 2020.

'Those dams will pull the plug on Iraq,' Kevin concluded. 'The poor buggers will die of thirst. They don't have any other source of water.'

We gazed into our cloudy Al-Sharks, looking for a solution.

'There's something immoral about one country depriving another of water,' I said. 'Surely water at least should be allowed to flow unhindered across borders?'

'It's worse than immoral,' he answered. 'It could bring about the end of the world. Do you know the Armageddon prophecy in the New Testament?'

I shook my head.

'The last great battle in the world will be at Armageddon,' he explained. 'And the kings of the East will only gather for that battle when the Euphrates dries up. Read all about it in Revelation chapter 16.'

It was a sobering thought to carry with me to the station. Goatherds may not notice a war, but the lack of water will hit them hard.

THREE DAYS IN DAMASCUS

In her journey of 1928 Agatha described travelling from Aleppo to Damascus on a train which 'never seemed to go more than five miles an hour' and which stopped at every trackside tent to pick up passengers. Today you can't make this journey during daylight hours, which is a pity because the track sweeps out into an arid landscape where nomadic Bedouin still herd their sheep. Syrian railways have conceded the daytime customers to the road, because the six-hour journey time by rail cannot compete with the private fleets of long-distance buses which cover the same distance in four hours on a boring dual carriageway. So instead CFS only runs sleeper trains, to allow passengers to arrive in the capital city feeling refreshed.

Personally, I don't think any journey without a view has much charisma, but it is hard to find fault with the Aleppo to Damascus sleeper. It's efficient, cheap and clean, and if Agatha had to travel on it today she'd have even less to say about it than she did then. For her, in the pre-dual carriageway era, this was the last leg of her journey which was feasible by train. The line all the way through to

Baghdad via Nisibin on the Turkish border still had a few years to go until completion, so the accepted way of doing the final part of the journey was still by robust taxi service across the desert.

In 1928 she'd had a room reserved for her at Damascus's Orient Palace Hotel, opposite the Hejaz railway station in the city centre.

The Hejaz station is a handsome building with Ottoman arches, an intricately panelled interior painted British Pullman umber and brown, and an upper gallery walled with tall and rather lurid stained glass windows. Agatha wouldn't have arrived here, however. The station was built in 1917, in readiness for an ambitious train service planned to ferry Muslim pilgrims down to Medina in Saudi Arabia, and thence overland for the short onward journey to Mecca. However, as with the Taurus railway, the route had only just been completed when World War I broke out, and it, and the Ottoman/German troop trains that started to use it, became the regular target of Lawrence of Arabia and the Arab Nationalists. Some remains of the trains that were derailed are supposedly still standing on the now-defunct line inside Saudi.

The route never recovered from this early hiccup in its career and today the Hejaz is a grand white elephant, its buildings filled with railway clerical staff filing their nails and gossiping in corners. Ninety-five per cent of Damascus's passenger trains arrive at a more modern, prosaic terminus out in the suburbs, while all the Hejaz station can offer is a once-weekly summer service to Amman in Jordan. Instead, a couple of antique coaches converted into a bar are moored to the platform, and inside they have a karaoke machine and secluded booths for lovers and drinkers. A short distance down the track stand a handful of old Swiss-made steam engines, a couple dating back to 1894, at least one of which – judging by the oil and grease on the gear and the ground – is still in working order.

The Orient Palace Hotel was built in the same flurry of optimism that created the Hejaz, but at least it is still very much in business. Just beyond reception is an opulent mirrored ballroom with a floor spangled with marble, lit by chandeliers and surrounded by velvet chairs, but there's little or no dancing here these days. A television blares in one corner of the otherwise deserted room, and through the glass doors you can look into the dining-room, where each table is prepared with a strict allocation of four bottles of Coca-Cola.

The reception staff shook their heads when I asked about a room; the Orient Palace was fully booked for a year ahead with pilgrims, religious tourists who'd flown in from Iran to visit the Umayyad mosque, which was an easy walk from the front door. Every night 2,500 of them squeezed into the Orient Palace's eighty rooms, and there was no space left even for the most fanatical disciples of Agatha Christie.

Damascus has huge resonance both for Christianity and for Islam. It lays claim – along with Aleppo – to being the longest continuously inhabited city in the world, being mentioned in cuneiform texts found in Egypt and in northern Syria dating back to the third millennium BC. St Paul was converted on the road to Damascus, and was later lowered in a basket from the town walls to escape the angry Jews – none of whom, of course, remain. Some of the villagers in the surrounding hills still speak Aramaic, the language of the Bible, and the head of John the Baptist is supposedly in a shrine in the heart of the Umayyad Mosque.

'To the nomad Arab wandering over shadeless miles,'

soliloquizes Cook's Handbook from the 1920s, 'there could be nothing sweeter in his ears than the sound of water in Damascus.' The modern city bears little resemblance to that romantic image, being largely composed of ochre and grey rectangles topped with the occasional set of egg-box domes rippling in the waves of heat. Those rectangles are pierced by minarets, like needles sticking out of a hand-stitched carpet. The only running water is a rivulet of filth in a concrete ditch through the centre, where any noise it might make is completely drowned out by car horns.

It's essentially a low-rise place flowing with yellow taxis, and if you look down from one of the taller hotels you can pick out little cameo scenes on the rooftops, among all the rusting satellite dishes and squeaking air-conditioning units; a couple of backpackers smoking a joint and a man in his pyjamas having a shave. To the north, a village suburb rises up the wall of the distant hills, and when its lights come on after dark it twinkles like a collection of stars that have fallen to the ground around the green rockets – the illuminated minarets – which shot them down.

At street level there's a big distinction between the new town, with its lookalike Pizza Hots and Varsaces, and the older city, where women in chadors flap along high-walled alleys like giggling crows. In the souq are Rasputin beards and student goatees, ginger hair and hooked noses, Calvin Kleins, haj caps and mullah turbans. Damascus is one of those places which has yet to succumb to the homogenization of the rest of the world and there are no McDonalds, chain stores or cashpoint machines. Agatha Christies, however, they have.

I chose a bookshop and walked in, to find myself in a narrow room as tall as an elevator shaft with tightly packed shelves right the way up to the ceiling. Everything was in Arabic and practically the only form of illustration on any dustjacket was calligraphic rather than pictorial, in accordance with Islamic beliefs. This, together with the long beards on the young men behind the counter, led me to conclude that I'd chosen a religious bookshop by mistake. I would have made my excuses and left but by now one of the young men was hovering expectantly in front of me, so I mentioned the words 'Agatha Christie' without much hope of success. I was wrong. He turned, gestured to a shelf half-way up the wall, and repeated 'Agatha Christie'. He then, of course, wanted to know which one I wanted, so I suggested some of the more familiar titles, none of which he seemed to recognize. Getting him to read out the Arabic titles didn't help either, so I tried to mime them. *Five Little Pigs* would have got me into trouble, so I tackled *Murder on the Orient Express*, it being the most relevant of her titles. It seemed logical at the time, but looking back on it now I'm glad nobody I knew saw me chuffing around that tiny bookshop, hooting and stabbing myself in the back, watched by three fundamentalists with scary beards.

In the end, sheepish and unsuccessful, I bought the furthest book on the left, with a cover illustration of a zombie chasing a young girl. This, apparently, was *Isla Misteriosa*, which is not a title which appears on any Christie bibiliography I have ever seen. Perhaps there's a publishing industry in Syria which has continued to churn out Christie-type crime stories. If the zombie on the cover was anything to go by, they've strayed a long way from the world of vicarages and tea.

Agatha spent three days in Damascus before setting off across the desert for Baghdad in what was effectively a large taxi run by a couple of enterprising New Zealanders who were unfazed by huge arid spaces. I had a couple of days before I too was due to set off for Baghdad, with a coachload of European 'tourists' whose motivation I had yet to learn. Our only common link was a man who had the right contacts with the Iraqi ministry to get us all a visa.

In truth, it was a nervy time to be going anywhere near Iraq, with daily reports of exchanges of fire in no-fly zones and US President Bush talking up his concept of regime change and pressurizing the United Nations to come up with a resolution that would justify invasion. Even Syria, a country which hadn't enjoyed good relations with Iraq, couldn't avoid feeling some sympathy for its neighbour, partly because it too had been branded by President Bush as part of the Axis of Evil. Personally I saw no sign of Evil and encountered no anti-Western sentiments in Damascus, although several of the shopfronts carried homemade signs encouraging locals to boycott American products.

How we would be received once we crossed into Iraq no one really knew, and I didn't really like to think about it until the time came. It'd be wrong to say that I wasn't anxious, but as the rhetoric from the West grew louder and more insistent, it became more and more urgent that we crossed the border as quickly as possible, before the sparks turned to flames.

Agatha, of course, had no such cause for concern. Back in 1928 these were all imperial lands. Syria was safely French and Iraq (aka Mesopotamia) was British-controlled, so for a couple of days she strolled around Damascus, killing time. In the souq she bought herself a chest of drawers inlaid with mother-of-pearl, ivory and silver, and ordered it to be freighted back to her home in

Devon; unfortunately, when it arrived six months later much of the interior had been reduced to sawdust by a voracious worm which had stowed away inside. She also tried a hamman or Turkish bath, which completely mystified her. The bath attendant had turned various taps and wheels to release boiling water across the stone floor, filling the air with steam and making it impossible to see anything. Then he'd left her, without telling her what to do next. Saunas were unheard of in those days.

For me the steam treatment sounded more appealing than the shopping and it would take my mind off the uncertainties of Iraq, so I spent my first morning over in the old city being pummelled, soaked and scrubbed.

Ritual bathing is an important part of Islamic life, and the twelfth-century Hamman Nur ad-Din is one of the oldest and grandest bath-houses in the Islamic world. The main hall, down a set of steps off the souq, is like the inner courtyard of a merchant's house in pink and grey marble, with daylight flooding in from a windowed dome up above. At the centre stands a fountain surrounded by potted plants, and on each side, in arched naves, are raised platforms with red-carpeted benches and floors of green baize. Above the benches runs a line of wooden pegs for clothes, a handful of mirrors in which bathers can comb their hair, and a couple of framed quotations of Quranic verse.

Placing myself in the hands of a succession of the Nur ad-Din's men in vests, I was soon naked but for a striped linen sarong. A large hairy buddha-figure in a loincloth steered me by the elbow into a steamy anteroom, sat me on the floor, and scrubbed me all over with what looked like an oven glove made of wire wool, before soaping me down with a mitt of split reeds. Once he'd decided I was pure enough to sweat a few buckets, I clattered across the floor in wooden clogs into the obscurity of the steam room, a place of unfathomable size with basins in the shape of lotus leaves. An arched roof patterned with studs of coloured glass gleamed dully down through the hot fog. It was impossible to make out where the steam emanated from, but it was so suffocating that it was hard to stand up straight. Occasionally other users would come stooping by, like fog-bound ships in mid Channel, tacking across a floor whose mosaics would have been perfect for snakes and ladders and hulloing each other like Pooh looking for Piglet in the Hundred Acre Wood.

I was sitting there, contemplating my past, present, future, and the droplet on the end of my nose, when a voice emerged from the mist to my left. 'Would you scrub my back?' it said. I looked around, but seeing no one I kept stumm, hoping the question had not been directed at me. But it was repeated, and this time it was followed out of the mist by a stocky, middle-aged man holding a camel-hair loofah. I wondered straight away whether I wasn't being picked up, and whether the back-scrubbing request wasn't hamman-speak for 'Oops, I dropped the soap,' but it would have been rude to say no, and in any case I was so slippery with soap and sweat that if anyone had tried to grapple me I would have just skidded off under the nearest urn.

This was how I got to meet Ayman Zeineddin, a forty-five-year-old Syrian property developer who had come to the hamman, he said, to wash away the frustrations of a bad day in court. I was naturally curious about the court bit, but before I'd even got into my scrubber's stride the Nur ad-Din's masseur, a giant man with the physiognomy of a Ukrainian wrestler, called me away for a pummelling.

It wasn't the last I saw of Ayman, though. Twenty minutes later, feeling blubber-boned and tingly, I passed back through the hands of the vested, each of whom replaced something wet with something dry, until the last stage where I had to wait momentarily for my locker key while the locker attendant sank his forehead into a pile of towels that faced Mecca. Then I was back up on a carpeted bench on the green baize platform, sipping a fragrant glass of tea, wrapped in a green towel turban, a white linen stole, a green and white sarong, and with a pink and cream rug across my knees. Ayman was already there, similarly wrapped, and we sat there gossiping, like a couple of old dears at the hairdresser.

He was vigorously optimistic, solid, squat and terrier-like, with a storm of nasal hair. He had learned his English from the BBC World Service, listening to it religiously every morning from 6 a.m. before heading out to his office.

'It's verrry good, your BBC, verrry good.'

It transpired that his main partners in the property business were Syrians who'd been working in Saudi Arabia. 'They come back with a lot of money, so they want to buy land. Usually to build something. So they come to me, I know where there is land to buy. The right price.'

'That sounds to me more like a property agent.'

Ayman wagged his finger. 'I am a good Muslim. Buying and selling for profit, yes, but borrowing, commission, usury no. No, no. The law of Riba.'

'Doesn't that mean you have to have a lot of capital? If you can't borrow?'

'You look in my office, in the drawers. Many, many Syrian pounds. Thick like this. Thick.' He held up his thumb and index finger as if holding a wad of banknotes.

'What about robbers?'

Ayman shook his head. 'We don't have many robbers in

Syria. Although the police are weak, religion is strong.'

As for that day's court appearance, it was a regular occurrence, he said.

'When you want to divide a plot of land, you must go to the court. In front of the judge I represent myself. It is usually straightforward if you know what you are doing, but to get that court time, that's the problem.' Ayman's expression soured. 'You must pay. Unofficial payments, you know what I mean.' He hung his head. 'This is when I don't like my people. Always this scrabble for money. Money, money, money. They know I've got it and they want some of what I have, just for doing their job. We may not have robbers, but we have many people like that.'

'You get people like that everywhere in the world.'

'That is why I am studying to become a lawyer,' Ayman continued. 'To gain respect. In this country it is very important to have a title to gain respect. Then they will not dare to ask me to pay them extra just for doing their job.'

I was curious where he had acquired all the capital to get a start in what was evidently a very cash-intensive business, so Ayman related how, many years before, a group of Syrian friends working in Saudi Arabia had persuaded him to abandon a university course in civil engineering.

'They had this idea for a car import business to Saudi. Luxury cars from Germany. But they didn't speak German or English, only Arabic, and they needed somebody to go to Germany to do the purchasing. So they asked me. Speak English, speak German.'

For ten years they'd done well, making a fortune by Syrian standards, but the relations with Germany had gradually soured. Ayman described the Germans as 'untrustworthy', but I suspect by that he meant they didn't trust him.

'So expensive!' he exclaimed. 'The hotels, the restaurants, everything so expensive! Many times I sleep overnight in city parks. In Stuttgart I sleep on the tables of my friend's restaurant.'

I could just imagine him turning up at glitzy car showrooms in the morning, slightly dishevelled, speaking heavily accented German, grinning and waving his wads of cash. God knows what the salesman had thought of him.

In the end it was the Japanese who'd scuppered the business from afar. In the mid-1980s they'd made a concerted assault on the luxury car market, and fitted their new top-of-the-range models with every extra imaginable. The German manufacturers, meanwhile, plodded along in their own uncompromising way, refusing to react to these Japanese initiatives, and they eventually lost all their Saudi market share – but they certainly didn't welcome this ebullient little Syrian who slept on park benches telling them where they'd gone wrong.

I liked Ayman very much. He had a good life, he assured me. He'd never married, but lived alone in the family house with two cats. A couple of evenings a week he'd go across to the Syrian restaurant in the Sheraton hotel, which had live entertainment he described as 'you clap, she dances'. He went to the mosque every Friday, liked foreign films, attended worthy lectures at the Goethe Institute, and every summer made a trip to the beach with his sister's family. An honest man, completely without pretension.

An hour later I was dozing off in the long, carpeted naves of the Umayyad Mosque. Ayman had brought me here through the cardamom-scented labyrinth of the souq before disappearing off to meet a client somewhere out of town. He'd told me he spent many hours in the mosque every Friday, and he wanted me to experience something of the power and mystery of the place, so here I was, doing my best.

The Umayyad is rated as the fourth most important Islamic building in the world, and there is no denying its magnificence. The inner courtyard is the size of a giant football stadium, with a light marble floor surrounded on three sides by a two-storeyed arcade, and on the fourth by the giant prayer hall covered with gold and green mosaics. It is so big that it seems to create its own microclimate. On that afternoon the main visitors were Iranians, the men carrying video cameras and the women in chadors fluttering across the courtyard after their children like big black bin bags bowled along by the breeze.

The story of the Umayyad is the region's history in microcosm. There has been a spiritual building here since the ninth century BC, when the Arameans built a temple to their god, Hadad. The Romans enlarged upon it, re-dedicating it to Jupiter, and then, when the Emperor Constantine converted to Christianity, it was rededicated again. Herod was supposed to have dispatched the head of John the Baptist here to prove to the Romans that he was dead. Thereafter, so the story runs, the head was buried and forgotten, until Damascus fell to the Muslim armies and blood started to bubble up through the floor of the church. The floor was torn up, the head discovered, and a shrine created as a fitting resting place.

For a while, during the spread of Islam around AD 700, the buildings became dual use, part basilica and part mosque, with Islam and Christianity existing side by side. But eventually caliph Khaled ibn al-Walid decided it was time to show the world the glory of the new religion through a building the like of which had never been seen before. The site was redeveloped, and the basilica scrapped. In its most magnificent state the new mosque was covered in gold leaf, inlaid with precious stones, and hung with 600 lamps, but earthquakes and invading Mongols have since taken their toll.

It took me some time to get over the feeling of being an unwanted intruder within those walls, steeling myself initially for ejection at any minute by a truck-load of screaming mullahs. But then, after sitting on the rim of the central fountain for a while and being smiled at, I felt emboldened enough to pad barefoot across the courtyard and wander inside the huge, 200-metre-long prayer hall.

It was divided loosely into three naves by rows of tall pillars and carpeted from end to end in a deep, rich red. At one end stood the shrine of John the Baptist, a little conservatory which glowed with green light. There was no overwhelming sense of awe or sanctity, and several people were plainly asleep on the carpets. A group of young mothers were taking advantage of the wide open spaces and the soft landing to encourage their children to take their first footsteps. A handful of robed men in dark glasses sat like a group of race officials on the finishing line next to the shrine; presumably blind holy men are like blind piano tuners, more attuned to the inner harmonies of things.

Sitting against a pillar in these calm, sympathetic surroundings and feeling pretty relaxed from the hamman, I had to stop myself from taking a siesta, reminding myself that back home I wouldn't go for a snooze in a cathedral. Indeed, most congregations in the Christian world would be outraged if their holy places were used as a midday dormitory by passing Muslims. It said something about

Islam that anyone, of any faith, who wished to enter was welcome to settle themselves down to think, sleep, gossip and admire passing children. Here, an infidel in the prayer hall of one of the world's great mosques, I was left to fall calmly, gently . . . a loud burp brought me back from the brink of sleep, and for one ghastly moment I thought it had been me. Then one of the blind men grimaced and reached for his waterbottle. Even holy men have indigestion.

THE ROAD TO BAGHDAD

In *Nemesis*, the final Miss Marple mystery of Agatha's writing career and one of the last and darkest of her books, the spinster detective receives a posthumous letter from a millionaire asking her to undertake a mysterious project on his behalf. Two days later she receives notification that he had booked her a seat, before he died, on a coach tour of England's country homes and gardens. Miss Marple duly boards the bus knowing no one and nothing of what lies ahead of her, but suspecting that the clues to the mystery will be revealed either from the destinations along the way or from among her odd collection of fellow passengers. It turns out to be both.

The coach party which set out for Baghdad at dawn the day after my snooze in the Umayyad mosque reminded me of *Nemesis*. Our itinerary was also ostensibly one of gardens and homes, although in this case you wouldn't find the Garden of Eden, the Hanging Gardens of Babylon and the palaces of Sennacherib and Nebuchadnezzar in the National Trust handbook. These names, along with cities like Nimrud, Ur and Nineveh, feature in the very first chapters of Genesis and are deeply significant in the cultural development of the human race, but it was a strange time to be going delving into prehistory, arriving as we did at much the same moment as the United Nations weapons inspectors. The trip was supposedly a holiday, but who would take a holiday in Iraq at a time when the Cradle of Civilization was about to become a mother of all defenestrations? Accordingly, as had transpired in *Nemesis*, the bus contained an unlikely cast list of characters, and not all of them had tourism in mind.

I hadn't heard such a clutch of pukka British voices since I'd left the Venice-Simplon Orient Express, all those weeks ago. As there had been on Miss Marple's bus, the group contained the inevitable sprinkling of retired gentle-folk, but these were of a particularly doughty, lively variety who had concluded that Saddam was unlikely to be interested in them and were prepared to risk it, now that their children were grown up and that (in some cases) their husbands had died. Of four elderly ladies, two were Europeans – one French, one German – and two were English, straight from the pages of one of Agatha's books.

The first of these was a stalwart good sort and veteran of vicarage tea parties for whom the word 'jolly' might have been invented. Kay was the sort of indefatigably optimistic, effervescent personality everyone would want to have on their lifeboat, forever making the best of things. The fount of her indomitable spirit was a deep religious conviction, and she carried a Bible with her at all times, consulting it at regular intervals as if it was her human shield. She was also the only one of the four women with an accompanying husband, a retired (and retiring) physicist with nuclear eyebrows and a giant, ungainly stride that was all angles and ankles.

The second was a tall, slightly bent lady with a very gentle voice that tended to witter on and then tail away when she realized nobody in particular was listening, a mannerism that concealed the fact that she was actually a very shrewd academic from Oxford. She had floppy grey-blonde hair and gold-rimmed glasses, behind which lurked a pair of pale, quiet eyes. Her name was Eugenie, and I had her down as Miss Marple straight away. It turned out she was married to a don who was so locked in to the circuit of college life that he couldn't conceive of giving up his dinners in hall and port wine in the senior common room to head off for somewhere insane like Iraq with his wife. So rather ungallantly he'd let her go off to Saddam's place on her own.

As for the French and German ladies, they were travelling alone but definitely not together; Brigitte was the oldest of all of us at eighty-one, but she wore jeans, monkey boots, had a penchant for vodka and cigarettes and was invariably vigorous and cheerful. Years of smoking had given her a voice like Marlene Dietrich, but hadn't impeded her health a jot and she could skip across ravaged temple sites, all sand and rubble, like a gazelle. Yvette, who had undoubtedly been a beauty in her day, was far less composed. She had a tendency to prattle on about anything and everything. The loss of her husband some years before was still a painful memory, and she had taken to travelling in order to fill the void. She declared, in an early conversation with anyone who'd listen, that she hated the 'ugliness and loneliness' of old age. She and her husband had adored each other right up to the end, she said; 'I used to see him across a crowded room and think, "What a handsome man."' She was also a worrier who showed little real interest in archaeology, and instead spent most of the time pestering drivers, guides and anyone who'd listen about the detail of arrangements. At what time would we be leaving? How far was it? When would we arrive? What would we eat? Would there be an opportunity to buy some postcards?

Of the four younger couples the most instantly notice-able were the Lovebodys, remarkable first for their flamboyant clothes – as if they'd packed for a luxury week in the Caribbean but had decided at the airport to plump for a fortnight in Baghdad instead – and second for the way in which they couldn't keep their hands off each other, which seemed a bit inappropriate given their age (mid-fifties) and the deeply Islamic nations they were passing through. Ms Lovebody was a blowsy blonde, a maturer, heavier, riper version of Goldie Hawn. Mr Lovebody was handsome in a clean, cruel way, and his khaki shorts were as sharply ironed as an Australian high-way patrolman's. On paper they were both fund-raisers for charity, but he was quick to tell us that he had also recently been on holiday in North Korea.

Then there was Charles, a dry-as-a-bone antiques dealer in his late twenties but with attitudes that were already gathering dust. His pallid, Tweedledee physique and cavalry twill wardrobe made him seem much older. He was the sort of person who would join a gentlemen's club at an early age for the pleasure of telling the old buffers what was really wrong with the modern world. With him was his aunt, the bird-spotter of the group, a bustling, brisk, cheery sort with a rucksack bulging with binoculars, waterbottles and first aid equipment. She was prepared for every eventuality, from cranking up the Aga to cope with a few extra guests for Sunday lunch at the Manor to producing all the necessaries to deal with a minor concussion in the Syrian desert. They seemed authentic enough, Charles and his aunt, but they could equally well have been the modern equivalent of Agatha's Tommy and Tuppence Beresford, the ageing couple who seemed to lead a completely average life but repeatedly proved themselves very useful in matters of national security.

Charles and his aunt were a judgemental pair, happy to share their verdicts with anyone who listened, unlike Rita, a small, neat, severe-looking civil servant of oriental parentage. She was travelling with her husband, Simon, a pale, mild man with a scarred face which looked like a badly drawn photofit, partly concealed by a floppy curtain of long blond hair. These two kept their own counsel. Both carried walking sticks and, once we were under way, they appeared in local, flowing clothes, suggesting that they were already completely *au fait* with life in these parts.

The youngest pair were the best-looking of the party, but they were also the most close-mouthed and non-committal. Anne, in her mid-thirties and with a mid-Atlantic twang to her accent, described herself as a graphic artist who worked for television. She cultivated an air of quiet, calm serenity which may have been a true indication of how she was really feeling, but also conveniently served to reduce contact with others. With her was vigorous and handsome Hugh, in his late twenties, who said he was a promoter of boxing matches and who plainly found sitting still a challenge. As a couple, they seemed an unlikely combination, and so they proved; a few days into the itinerary they requested separate rooms on the basis that they were just good friends. They didn't mix much with the rest of us.

Then there were four single men travelling alone: myself, Torsten, Mark and Sean. Torsten was a self-professed playwright in his early twenties, puppy-like, overweight and witty, but always looking for approval. For him, people were a necessary audience who provided an opportunity to fly his intellectual kites. His origins were suspiciously mixed; he sounded English enough and had only recently graduated from Cambridge, but he was half Swiss, he said, and he'd spent much of his youth living on a Glaswegian housing estate. He was eloquent on everything from politics through hairdressing to human rights.

Then there was Mark, a Chinese banker from Hong Kong who divided his time on the bus between sleeping and muttering his way round his necklace of Buddhist beads. His spoken English was so staccato it sounded as if it was fired from a machine-gun and several members of the party had difficulty understanding him. Much of the time he sat by himself.

Last but definitely not least was Sean, the most unlikely of all of us to be making such a trip at such a time. Many of the others could have been spies, but this toothpick-chewing shaven-headed American in baggy shorts was straight out of the movies. He said he ran a restaurant in New York, but everyone assumed he was a Marine, and that the ghetto-blaster he was carrying could be stripped down into something else that would truly blast a ghetto or two. He was deeply distrusted by many, and some of the more conservative members of the group never found anything to talk to him about in the whole two weeks we were together. From early on he staked his claim to the front seats of the bus and I daresay nobody would have been surprised if he had disappeared in a swirl of dust as soon as we'd crossed the border, never to be seen again.

The leader and organizer of this unlikely group was Geoff, a wiry Englishman with grizzled badger's eyebrows who'd been travelling to the country since the 1980s, and who presumably knew more about each individual traveller than he cared to let on. He had developed sufficiently close links with the regime to be able to secure a group tourist visa which would allow this odd collection of cover stories to enter the country at a time when President Bush was announcing that war was 'neither imminent nor unavoidable', but was nevertheless airlifting his command centres into position in nearby Qatar. It was hardly surprising, given the circumstances, that everyone took everyone else's ostensible reason for being on the bus with a very large pinch of salt, especially in a region which had a long and worthy tradition of archaeologists-as-spies.

We may not have been soulmates, but I was happy to be back in the company of fellow countrymen after many weeks on the road. The group ethic gives you the luxury of choosing whether to be the joker, the worrier, the know-it-all or the philosopher of the party, or whether just to sit back and blend in. Moreover we all felt that there was safety and security in numbers, so we were pleased to be on the bus. Initially, at least.

Looking back on it now I can see that it was a classic Christie setting, common to so many of her books and plays, where an odd assortment of people with as yet unknown motives and connections are pitched headlong into a situation from which there is no easy exit. For us the bus was to become both an emotional sanctuary and a virtual prison, like the train in *Murder on the Orient Express* or the river cruiser *Karnak* in *Death on the Nile*. By embarking on the trip we were entering into a sort of voluntary isolation of a degree which would have been practically impossible to achieve anywhere else in the modern world; our mobile phones wouldn't work (and anyway couldn't summon help), we'd have no embassy to turn to in times of trouble and we'd have no freedom to move around as individuals. All we needed to bind us together into a novel was a crime, and I found myself speculating, as we left Damascus, just who on the bus might have the motivation to commit murder, who would be their victim, and what would the title be: Ordeal at the Baghdad Café? The Mystery of the Basra Train? Or just The Ziggurat of Ur? Clearly, if you wanted someone to meet with an 'accidental' death, then Iraq, which is beyond the jurisdiction of Interpol, the CIA or Scotland Yard, would be an excellent place to do it.

Agatha's Damascus to Baghdad journey had its own anxieties, too, but of a rather different sort. In those days the people of Mesopotamia were preoccupied with their own survival and were barely aware of the outside world. For her it was the getting there, not the destination, which was the arduous bit, because Baghdad lies an immense 844 kilometres east of Damascus across the featureless, flat crust of the Syrian desert, so large and empty that even the snakes feel lonely. Moreover, in those days there were no roads across this vast nothingness and the two-day crossing was like a voyage across choppy seas with a navigator riding shotgun by the driver.

Nairn Line was the creation of brothers Gerry and Norman Nairn, New Zealanders by birth, who'd done their time in the transport division of the same British Army which had marched triumphantly into Baghdad in 1917, ousting the Turks and their allies the Germans. It was a victory which 'has shattered the dream which the Germans have been dreaming for more than twenty years', crowed *The Times*. 'The German route to the East is blocked, and the existing terminus of the Baghdad Railway has passed into our hands.'

In the months and years that followed, replacement personnel and civilian post for the British forces in

Baghdad used to travel around by mailship through the Suez Canal to be landed at Basra, a circuitous route that, with stops, could take as long as twenty-four days from the Eastern Mediterranean.

The Nairns saw the opportunity to open up a cross-country link across the featureless desert, straight from the Mediterranean coast at Beirut via Damascus to Baghdad, and in 1923 they set out to prove its feasibility with a couple of specially provisioned Dodge cars. Within weeks their journey time of just four days had won them the postal contract and passenger carriage quickly followed, with a costly one-way fare of £30 for the two-day crossing. In 1926 they carried 1,600 passengers, and by 1928 that number had increased to 2,500, many of them important civil servants looking for a shorter route to British territories who would go on to complete the journey to India by sea from Basra. It was these people, carrying their important messages and their government secrets, who were eventually to provide the backbone of the passenger list on the Orient and Taurus Expresses when the Baghdad rail-link was finally completed in the 1930s, shaving many, many days off what had always been an arduous journey. And putting an end to Nairn Line.

The Nairns packed quantities of food and iced drinks and a couple of guns in case of bandits, and one of their key selling points was that they always used British 'chauffeurs'. Most of the journey was on a natural surface of hard earth on which the vehicles could reach speeds of up to 50 mph, and although much was made of the on-board facilities (small tables were provided so that passengers could play bridge) and the reliability of the service, it must have been an extremely uncomfortable and deeply tedious experience. Navigation partly depended on finding a furrow the army had cut in the desert to aid aircraft flying between Baghdad and Amman, and the Euphrates, when it was reached, had to be crossed on a bridge of boats lashed together. In the early days the expedition bivouacked for a few hours in the night with the male passengers taking turns to keep watch 'to reassure the ladies'.

I daresay that not many thirty-eight-year-old lone women travellers would undertake such an adventure today, especially if they'd just spent the last ten years sitting around in Sunningdale, but Agatha seems to have not minded the inconvenience or the uncertainty. Crossing the desert was, she wrote, like being in a fascinating and rather sinister void. She describes how the Nairns allowed for just one stop in the forty-eight-hour journey, a three-hour rest at a desert fort in the middle of the night, and then brewed up a breakfast of tinned sausages and strong black tea on a primus stove in the desert. There she breathed in the sharp-toned air and watched the dawn creep across the void with colours of pale pink, apricot and blue. 'It was a wonderful ensemble – I was entranced. This was what I longed for.'

In this she is unconsciously echoing the words of Gertrude Bell, diplomat, accomplished mountaineer, and lover of all things oriental. A few years earlier the female equivalent of Lawrence of Arabia had declared, 'I think every day in the Syrian desert must prolong your life by two years.' Like her, Agatha derived pleasure from a situation where others would have only seen pain. And like Gertrude, who would always insist on linen tablecloths and Wedgwood china even in the desert, she never let hardship deter her from observing the niceties of life.

As for us, in our air-conditioned bus, our stamina wasn't tested in anything like the same way as hers, but there was one deprivation that had to be faced: the absence of alcohol. It wouldn't have bothered Agatha, who was teetotal, but few Western travellers these days warm to the idea of a fortnight without a drink, especially in a stressful destination, and the extent to which we use alcohol as a lubricant to oil the wheels of society only becomes evident when you remove it. One of my key anxieties before setting off for Iraq was not what would happen if we got bombed, or what if we got turned into human shields, but what it would be like not to have a drink for two weeks. I'd steeled myself to accept that particular austerity as a necessary (and trivial) test of my own resilience in a place which was, after all, under threat of annihilation, and naïvely I'd assumed that the rest of the party had come to terms with it too. But this was not the case. It soon became obvious that many had brought with them half a cocktail cabinet in their hand luggage.

On the first day we travelled only as far as the Syrian outpost of Palmyra, which 2,000 years ago was a great trading oasis in the final fold of the mountains before the desert proper, the last kicking-off point before the long dry haul to Baghdad. Following its declaration as a 'free city' by the Emperor Hadrian in 130 AD, Palmyra was able to set its own taxes on passing traffic and as a result grew hugely rich, particularly from the sale of water from what was the last spring for hundreds of miles. I could imagine the caravan leaders cresting the hills to the west, looking down on the city and whistling 'Uh-oh, this is going to be expensive' when they saw the lavish urbanization below them.

In fact the city became so prosperous that at one point its ambitious Queen Zenobia – who claimed to be a descendant of Cleopatra – took it upon herself to invade Egypt, Syria and Palestine and had coins minted in Alexandria bearing her image. This was too much for the

Roman Empire, and Emperor Aurelian came to deal with her personally, removing her to Rome and torching Palmyra behind him. Today the city's remains look like cream stitches patterning a beige tunic of sand and rock, some still standing proud, half-unpicked, and some long since ironed flat to the ground. As you get closer you can identify bits of pillared walkway, fragments of arched colonnades, most of a monstrous temple, a reconstructed theatre, the royal baths minus the water, and even traces of where shops once stood. This was a true precursor of the Warner Village, a 2,000-year-old retail park on the bypass.

It was also, and still is, a thriving oasis of date palms and olive trees which spreads in a timeless wig of dusky green across the brow of the old city. While the descendants of Queen Zenobia have long since returned to dust, the olives and dates have kept on coming, providing a perennial income year after year.

Under the shade of these trees the air was sweet with ripe fruit, musty with the smell of donkey shit and thudding gently with the putputtering of a distant diesel pump. The pump distributed water through a series of gurgling culverts which took their turn in transforming parched groves into shallow ponds, bathing the roots of pepper bushes and passionfruit trees. In the heat of the day it made sense to wander through these mud-walled secret gardens, following the spread of the water as it blithely ran hither and thither. A well-watered orchard like this, where the light was filtered and softened and the sandy tracks stained with squashed fruit, is the Koran's vision of earthly paradise, and I could understand why.

I didn't emerge into the ruins of Palmyra proper until the sun had lost much of its bite and most of the rest of the group had returned to the hotel. I was working my way upwards through the pillared colonnade, noting how seasonal sandstorms had weathered the lower stone into the texture of dried leather, with the faces of their creators gradually emerging from the patterns of fissures and veins, when I spotted Sean; he was sitting in the shade deep in conversation with a couple of local boys and I don't think he noticed me pass. Nor did the close-mouthed couple Anne and Hugh, who had their video camera on a tripod on a temple platform, waiting for the sun to go down; it was a clichéd romantic setting, but they were sitting determinedly apart. The Poirot in me thought there was something unexpected in both situations.

A couple of children intercepted me as I climbed higher, asking whether I'd like them to pose for a photograph or 'come to tea with their sister', which sounded alluring until they indicated a squat hut which sat by a spring in a small pubic tangle of green just north of the colonnade. For them, the ruined city was like a field which produced a harvest of wealthy foreigners, threading their way through the columns like weevils through golden corn. They were just the grasshoppers who picked us off.

Several tall towers girdle the rising ground behind Palmyra, looking down towards the city, and many more of them line a silent trough in the hills behind. These solid Tuscan-looking structures are the Towers of the Dead, the last resting places of the wealthy Palmyrans who presumably were interred above ground because the land was simply too intractable to allow the digging of graves. From the side of this westward-leading valley of tombs I reckoned I could see the remains of around 350 such towers, each of which would have had five floors and accommodated 300 sarcophagi standing in rows in niches in the walls. Presumably the remains of the bodies incarcerated inside were air-dried slowly, but the process must have produced an odour in the valley which would in turn have generated clouds of interested insects and had all the local wildlife salivating furiously. There were no flies today, nor even any birds, which was reassuring; I didn't particularly want to be the one who found the padlock broken on the locked gate, who glimpsed a thread lying on one of the stones which led me to the body of one of my fellow travellers wedged into a niche. Battered to death by a ghetto-blaster.

Most of the towers were in ruins and I picked my way around two or three, looking for any shreds of evidence of human pre-existence. Did the stones themselves still hold traces of human DNA after such a long time? How long does it take for sun and wind to blow such traces away? And would we soon be able to take a bit of that DNA and reconstitute it, as dried powder can be turned into milk, to create an individual who could tell us what life was actually like in Palmyra all those centuries ago and whether Queen Zenobia had truly been as beautiful as legend has her, or whether she'd just instructed her scribes to describe her so?

The Queen is remembered these days in the Hotel Zenobia, a low-slung building which sits between the ruins and the small modern town of Padmor. Once upon a time this was the place to stay in Palmyra, and Agatha had returned here a couple of times with Max, relating in *Come Tell Me How You Live* how the hotel was quite charming if you could ignore the overwhelming smell of drains, and how the proprietor had declared, in an attempt to reassure them, 'Mauvaise odeur, oui! malsain non!' While at Palmyra the couple had spent a happy day picking their way across the ruins until they'd eventually come across a group of French ladies on the other side, among the funerary towers, where they'd found one of the party in a state of some distress. Evidently she'd broken the heel off one of her (highly inappropriate) shoes and was declaring herself quite incapable of walking a step further. Normally this wouldn't have been a problem, but the taxi the party had hired had also broken down and couldn't take them back. So Max volunteered to walk back to the hotel to get his car and driver and left Agatha making conversation with the French ladies. Eventually he returned, still on foot, and this time rather cross. It turned out that the self-same broken-down 'taxi' which the French ladies had hired was actually Max and Agatha's vehicle, their driver having decided that there was nothing in his agreement with the English which prohibited him from moonlighting for the French whenever the opportunity arose.

I returned to the fringes of the town as the sun was setting and poked my nose inside the Zenobia. It bore little sign of ever having been charming, but then neither did it smell. I had a beer on the terrace where Agatha and Max would have sat, while the last rays departed from the tumbledown colonnades and the silhouettes of camels disentangled themselves from the fragments of history.

By midday the next day we were approaching the Iraqi border. The road stretched out across a brown sea of dust so immolated by the sun that it couldn't even raise the energy for a wave. It was a distressingly empty, dehumanizing place and the first landscape on my journey which didn't have the inevitable discarded plastic bag blowing across some distant corner of the picture. But nor was there any sign of the profusion of gazelles, hyenas, wolves and foxes described by early travellers on the Nairn buses. According to a contemporary account, sand-grouse were so numerous here, particularly during the couple of spring months when the wild barley grass grew, that 'a shot fired without aiming would literally have brought down a big bag'.

The desert wasn't completely untouched by human hand, though, because there were regular sets of tyre tracks setting out from the tarmac into the void, where onward navigation would have to be by compass alone. If you gazed long and hard enough in any direction you would occasionally be rewarded with the glimpse of a streak of dust heading east to west, as if a ship was just beyond the horizon and all you could see of its progress was the smoke. These were lorries emulating the Nairns, and literally going overland.

In a time of sanctions the official frontier crossings were carefully watched. Therefore the large amount of un-official trade that still took place was forced to take to the routes of the ancient camel caravans of Palmyran days, and steer their own course across the surface of the desert, which was generally brittle enough to support the weight of lorries. Most of this traffic embarked at night, when the US spyplanes weren't watching, and it must have been a gruelling ride, pitching across the friable plateau with all lights off. Not long after turning on to the Baghdad road we'd passed a parked file of these lorries either resting up from a long, wearying night crossing or waiting for dusk to fall before setting out. They had to abandon the tarmac dozens of miles before the border and return to it dozens of miles afterwards to avoid the series of shallow graves dug by the roadside by the military in a bid to prevent such traffic from leaving the road.

Our last stop before the border was a fuel station in the middle of nowhere, with some of the most malodorous hole-in-the-ground toilets I've ever seen, awash with faeces and discarded hypodermics. A couple of battered orange and white Iraqi taxis stood in the shade, loaded to the ceiling with boxes of dates, Iraq's principal cash crop. Occasionally an old, tattered plastic bag would rise spontaneously into the air on a riff of heat, making a last break for freedom until the hot air dispersed and it crumpled and fell, all hope gone.

The whole settlement had a surreal, post-holocaust atmosphere, ringed by the wrecks of former buildings and vehicles, its tarmac covered in a sludge of oil which radiated out from the pumps for many yards, indicating that a lot more happened here under cover of darkness than daytime visitors ever witnessed. It was a depressing, forbidding place but it also had one totally unexpected cheerful surprise: hundreds of small birds, many in full song. They were migrants and, like the lorries avoiding the spyplanes, they travelled by night for security's sake to avoid malevolent birds of prey, which needed the daytime thermals to do their prowling. In the shade of the fuel station they were conserving their energy from a strength-sapping sun, and had a chance of finding waste water or even discarded food. The only danger was from a young boy with a patch over one eye, wandering around with an air-gun.

The state of the fuel stop served to increase everyone's anxiety about the border itself, and gallows humour descended on the bus as we drew near. 'Welcome to Camp Saddam,' muttered someone as the first official buildings came abreast. 'Ah, the interrogation chambers,' said someone else as we passed a row of burned-out cells. 'No,' said a third, 'surely that was the Cham Palace Border Hotel.' 'Shhh,' whispered Yvette urgently; she was already deeply agitated by Sean's 'Property of New York' T-shirt, which she was convinced was going to get us all into trouble. I didn't think there was much point in being quiet – if the Iraqis were truly interested in us then surely the bus (which had been sent from Baghdad to collect us at Palmyra) was wired already. 'Look,' whispered a scandalized voice behind me, 'he's speaking to someone on an invisible mobile phone.' I looked; it was Mark the Chinese banker, and he was muttering hard over his Buddhist necklace, reciting his way around the beads in Cantonese. He'd already admitted to chickening out of a possible previous trip to Iraq some months before and now he was plainly finding the whole thing difficult. You had to wonder why he was there at all.

As we bumped across the last sleeping policeman in Syria we passed a sign saying, simply, 'Goodbye', which sounded rather final. Geoff briefed us to show no particular interest in anything that looked military, never reach for a camera, make no jokes or remarks about Saddam and not to show anything to anyone unless he or the Iraqi travel agent who was meeting us sanctioned it.

'Distrust everyone, whether or not they're wearing a uniform,' he said.

Then we handed over our passports, disembarked and stood around in an empty concrete building designated 'customs hall'.

Before long a small crowd of Iraqis had gathered to watch us. And it was true, we were the only show in town. Outside, the road refused to deliver any alternative entertainment. Nothing came, nothing went and for a long time only the flies seemed busy, although we understood that our passports were being dealt with in a back room. Then we were asked to make a pile of cameras, all of which were taken away to be examined, and to place all our money in individual envelopes for counting, which also disappeared. In a way it was this last act, the removal of the money, which drove home our complete sense of powerlessness; we were now at the mercy of Iraqi hospitality, whatever that would be.

The Iraqi travel agent reappeared. The paperwork was proceeding well, he announced, and the time had come for AIDS tests for men under sixty and women under fifty years old. 'For once I am happy to be old,' murmured Yvette, but Ms Lovebody was miffed. 'What are they saying – we're not attractive any more?' Her accent started off posh and then seemed to veer downmarket, like a ship going off course. 'Do they think that once you reach fifty you're no longer interested in sex?' She tossed back her mane of blonde hair in disgust; her age was not something she cared to advertise.

We filed across the compound to a low building with a couple of rooms containing tables, chairs and a filing cabinet. This was, said the sign above the door, the AIDS lab, and on the wall was a list detailing all those nations for whom a test was mandatory. It also suggested that you could be exempt if you had a certificate less than two weeks old demonstrating you were AIDS-free; 'Uh-uh,' contradicted Geoff, overhearing someone read it out. 'That won't wash. It's not the test which matters here, it's the $50 fee.'

We were called from the waiting-room one by one. The man administering the test looked disturbingly like the dentist who tortures Dustin Hoffmann in *Marathon Man*, complete with round, glacier-mint glasses. Grateful that there wasn't a 'no unfilled cavities' entry criteria for Iraq too, I handed over my own needle and sat down.

'You afraid,' he said; it was a statement of fact, not a question.

'Yes,' I agreed.

'I can make it soft.' He looked at me expectantly. I suppose he was asking for a small contribution, but I had no money left on me. He shrugged, unwrapped the needle and plunged it into my arm with well-practised dexterity.

'You have good blood,' he continued, showing me the phial he'd collected.

'Does that mean I've passed?' I asked. Was that the science part, holding the phial up to the light to check that there are no little green HIV viruses jumping about in it? But he was already beckoning the next person and I was so grateful to get out of there that it wasn't until some minutes later that I realized he hadn't even bothered to mark the sample with my name. So much for the probity of that test.

Back in the customs hall our money and cameras were back and two new men stood among the passengers, chatting amiably. The tall, rather laconic one turned out to be Ahmed, who was to be our guide, and the shorter, plumper and smilier one was the minder from the ministry, Mohammed. Everything was in order, they said, and we were clear to proceed, so we all clambered back on to the bus, much relieved.

That relief didn't last long. As we were progressing towards the open road past the last border checkpoint a soldier who'd been sitting on his chair in the sun suddenly jumped up and waved his gun at the driver. The bus stopped, the door opened and the soldier shouted something up to Mohammed, pointing towards the rear windows. He in turn summoned Geoff, who returned back down the aisle of the bus towards Anne, his face contused with anger; the border guard had seen a video camera in her hands.

For a moment everyone held their breath. Anne protested that she'd thought we'd left the border proper and was only taking a picture of a sign saying 'Welcome to Iraq', and after a long whispered conference the Iraqis finally gave her the benefit of the doubt. Mohammed, who was visibly sweating with anxiety, waved the border guard away and urged the driver to continue, and an audible series of sighs ran right around the bus followed by a tut-tutting in which the word 'stupid' was frequently heard. Charles, across the aisle from me, said loudly, 'That idiot woman could have got us all killed.'

At a petrol station a mile or so further on, the bus driver filled his tanks up for the Iraqi dinar equivalent of £1. Then we were off on the open road – which unlike the single potholed ribbon of tarmac on the Syrian side was a brand new dual carriageway empty of traffic but replete with lunch stops with concrete umbrellas. It was hard to think of anywhere less alluring for a picnic.

There are 400 miles of open desert between the border and Baghdad, and although the dual carriageway maintained a gentle slalom, supposedly to prevent any enemy aircraft using it as a convenient landing strip, it could equally well have drawn a bead upon the very distant city centre and headed straight for it. The crash barriers were dented at regular intervals where drivers had fallen asleep from the tedium of it all. It was hard to see what Agatha had found so pleasing in such an unrelentingly drear meeting of land and sky. It was the sort of place where you begin to appreciate the usefulness of eyelids.

An hour or so after the border any lingering conversation on the bus had trailed away into silence, and most of the party were either reading or asleep as the vehicle churned interminably on through that raw, beige sea. On my knee I had *Absent in the Spring*, a book Agatha wrote under the pseudonym Mary Westmacott, the name she used for her non-crime fiction. The Westmacott novels never matched the success of the rest of her output but this one had a particular resonance. It was the story of a rather self-centred prig of a woman who was catching a train home from visiting her daughter in Baghdad when unseasonably heavy rain washed away the tracks and isolated her in a station rest-house in the middle of a Mesopotamian no man's land, where she had been the only guest. The absence of anything to do, anything to look at and anyone to talk to prompted a mood of intro-spection which would normally have been totally alien to her, and allowed the unpleasant self-realizations which she'd always suppressed to float to the surface. The result was a real crisis of identity brought on by silence, loneli-ness, the desert sun and middle age, during which the superficial character which she'd spent years building up crumbled steadily away to reveal all the insecurities hidden below.

I'm not saying that anything similar happened to me on that bus journey towards Baghdad, but staring out at that unrolling sheet of nothing you could begin to appreciate what Agatha was suggesting in the book – that prolonged exposure to nothingness can have a disturbing effect on the psyche, and that in general our sense of our own personalities is founded on our relationships with others. A happy, cheerful, witty person can be none of the above without someone else to be happy, cheerful and witty towards.

The one exception to the silence that reigned over most of the bus was up at the front, where Sean was riding shotgun flanked on either side by Ahmed and Mohammed. In theory this looked like a potentially alarming combination of US infiltrator and Iraqi security men, but after a slow start the three men were now getting on like a house on fire, grinning and slapping each other on the back. When we finally stopped at a roadside café, where rows of cooling orange and white taxis had their bonnets open like crocodiles waiting to be fed, I tackled the American; what had they been talking about with such evident pleasure?

'Boning.' Sean spoke out of one side of his mouth because the other was invariably occupied with a toothpick. 'They wanted to talk about girls. They wanted to know whether we were gonna want to go to any girly bars.'

I looked at him, and then we both looked around at our collection of fellow passengers. 'Unlikely,' I said.

'Uh-huh, that's kinda what I said too,' mused Sean, rolling the toothpick between his molars. 'Shame. I got the feeling that being with foreigners is their only chance of having a good time. Hey, isn't that a supergun?' He nodded in the direction of a pair of lorries bearing giant metal pipes.

'I hope not,' I said, trying not to look too closely, and then we were inside the cafeteria being greeted by the smiling staff, the smell of freshly baked flat breads and walls covered in posters showing a fantasy land that was steep, cool and green. And standing in front of them was Charles, reiterating his opinions on the idiocy of 'that woman with the video camera'.

'In fact, anyone even making notes in a notebook is jeopardizing the safety of everyone,' he declared, looking pointedly in my direction. I felt as guilty as hell.

It had long been dark by the time we arrived in Baghdad. The city rose in silent and dark squares out of the desert, only to be lassooed by ambitious motorway flyovers so numerous that I wondered whether the government had done a deal along the lines of buy-one-get-one-thousand-free. It looked like a giant, low-rise suburb, well-lit and orderly but with little in the way of neon or advertising, and all relatively recently built. The larger houses stood in walled compounds and showed signs of architectural flourish – modernist glass and steel and echoes of Palmyran colonnades – and there were plenty of new-looking cars on the roads. It didn't look like a city ground down by sanctions and cowed by the threat of war. At every intersection stood a public monument, varying from images taken from the Sinbad stories to the statue of an Iraqi soldier standing on a crashed American warplane, and outside every major building stood a giant portrait of Saddam Hussein, dressed in lawyer's robes, a medical gown or military uniform depending on the nature of the institution. Through the middle of it all ran the Tigris, a dark ribbon of shiny tarmac pursuing its relentless course.

The anxiety we felt about the reception handed out to foreigners had already been diminished by the behaviour of our minders and the Iraqis in the tea stops we'd made *en route*, and now that we were in the city any remaining fears evaporated fast. As we moved through the streets in our smart bus, like a cruise ship entering harbour, we found ourselves mobbed by little tugboats – minibuses full of locals. And instead of giving us the cold shoulder, almost all of their passengers were smiling and waving in our direction. We smiled and waved back. It was a bit like being a teenager at a disco looking across to the opposite sex on the other side of the dance floor, aware that both sides wanted to disappear into the bushes and snog. But neither side would dare to make the first move. And besides, what sort of chat-up lines do you use on a nation with whom you are about to go to war?

SADDAM CITY

My expectations of the Iraqi capital were high, too high. I wanted to scratch it and sniff the history, and perhaps even the fear. This was, after all, the city which had made a name for itself through centuries of trade in Chinese porcelain and Egyptian grain, in Indian sandalwood, ebony and rubies, and in gold, ivory, salt and slaves from Africa. It was also the city which was about to be pounded by the mighty fist of America.

A thousand-odd years ago Baghdad was supposedly the most prosperous settlement in the world, at the heart of an empire which extended from the Mediterranean to India. Its mystical, romantic character was first lodged in western psyches thanks to Harun al Rashid, the ninth-century emperor who used to wander through the streets in disguise to meet his people. He was a great patron of the arts, and would apparently pay a poet who wrote him a good sonnet with gold pieces, Greek slave girls and horses from the royal stables – a payment rate which today's poetry press fails dismally to match. Harun employed a court full of storytellers to feed his imagination and one of the products of his creative empire was *Tales from the Arabian Nights*, so called because the king's bride has to tell a story every night to prevent her head from being chopped off in the morning. This set of stories effectively mythologized the city into a fabled oasis populated by Sinbads, Aladdins and Ali Babas, while the dangerous desert crossing which shielded it from the out-side world sealed it off from more realistic contemporary accounts, thus preserving the image of souqs, magicians, and flying carpets.

Baghdad's mystique continued well into the beginning of the twentieth century. 'One cannot catalogue what there is to see in Baghdad, any more than one can catalogue the colours of a sunset, the shape of rising clouds or the voices in Babel,' burbles the author of Thomas Cook's 1928 brochure (probably the very same never-east-of-Ramsgate author encountered earlier, but now with the benefit of a couple of gins). The brochure promoted Orient-Express-based trips to Syria, Palestine and Mesopotamia priced at around £120 for forty days.

A certain Mrs Stevens, writing about Baghdad in 1923, described markets where 'green-turbanned seyyids sell silk and spices and a dwarf, who surely stepped straight from a tale by the caliph's consort, has a shop as tiny as him-self, a mere slit in the wall about a few feet high from which he gravely dispenses nuts'. That same dwarf is later 'carried off by a eunuch for a frolic in a vizier's harem'. This piece of over-purpled prose must have been written at around the same time as Gertrude Bell, champion of independent Iraq, was taking an overdose of sleeping tablets in the city, and despite the profusion of viziers, seyyids and sunsets, dying all alone. Nobody has ever been sure whether it was suicide, or an accident.

Agatha the storyteller's experience of Baghdad was a

bit more prosaic and considerably more genteel. Describing her arrival here in 1928, a total of eight days after leaving London, she talks in vague terms of a suitably exotic scene of crowded streets with rickety wooden houses, a spice souq, a copper souq, a large buffalo market and turquoise domes of mosques floating above. This vagueness may be attributable to the fact that at the time she was whisked off by a loud-voiced British memsahib whom she'd been forced to travel with on the journey across the desert, and whom she christened the Duchess of Alwiyah after the upmarket residential district of Baghdad in which she lived. Although by this time Iraq had been nominally set on the path to independence, partly thanks to Gertrude Bell, it was still bound by treaty to take account of the financial obligations and interests of Britain. That meant that every individual ministry had its British advisers, and there was a large expat community, mostly rooted in Alwiyah.

I suspect that in the end Agatha saw little of downtown Baghdad, which was thought unsuitable for European women walking alone. Her descriptive vagueness may also indicate that she had been disappointed with what she found, because the city was nothing like the fabled orient of the Cook's brochure, being sadly decayed after several bad floods, plague epidemics and decades of Turkish rule. On later trips, however, she spent more time here, and in the 1950s she and Max eventually bought a house on the banks of the Tigris. It was built in traditional style around an inner courtyard with rooms cooled by air shafts which led up to the roof, and there are photographs of her sitting on the balcony beside the river, drinking tea and pomegranate juice. By that time she was so well known and successful that her publishers would fly out special delicacies for her, along with her regular copies of *The Times*.

For many years Max and Agatha used to spend a month in their Baghdad house before each dig season properly began, visiting art galleries and curio dealers, browsing the markets for local kelims and furniture inlaid with mother-of-pearl. Little remained of the Abbasid city but Baghdad was still quite a centre of learning and there were resources for researching, writing and preparing for the months in the wilds. One of the priorities in this preparation was finding a cook, usually an Indian who'd arrived here in the support services for the British Army, and usually recruited through a coffee house in a riverside district called Abu Nawas, which is still a popular restaurant area today.

In those days much of the city's intellectual life centred on the prosperous Jewish community, which had been granted religious freedom and autonomy by the puppet King Faisal, enthroned by the British in 1917, and coached by Gertrude Bell on the niceties of diplomatic kingship. Back in the mists of time the Jews had been imported to Babylon as slaves when Nebuchadnezzar's son defeated the King of Judah, but over the succeeding thousands of years the Iraq-based community had prospered and grown to become the religious, cultural and scholarly centre of the Jewish world (the state of Israel had yet to be created). Even as recently as the 1940s there were 150,000 Jews in Baghdad, many of them working in the railways and the textile business. Names like Saatchi (as in the advertising agency and art collecting brothers) and Sassoon (as in the author and poet) were among the elite, sending their children to Jewish academies, their sick to Jewish hospitals and spending their leisure time in Jewish social clubs. But the tide began to turn against them in the 1930s, when the German embassy in Baghdad started to disseminate anti-Jewish propaganda which the British did nothing to stop. The formation of Israel after the war further incensed the Arabs, and in 1948 Zionism became a crime punishable by death in Iraq. The Baghdad community saw the writing on the wall and a massive airlift operation was mounted, removing 110,000 Jews in 1951 alone, some of whom came to Britain, where they settled around the Lauderdale Road Synagogue in London and where they still tend to marry only other Iraqi Jews. By the 1960s the number left in Iraq had declined to 6,000 and by the end of the decade there were just forty remaining; there are none today.

Throughout that period the city must have been an unsettled place, and Agatha captures some of this sense of distrust and foreboding in *They Came to Baghdad*, a strange and prescient thriller which was first published in the same year as the Jewish airlift. It features the attempt of a shadowy organization to subvert world peace economically and politically, as well as having 'vast installations and underground laboratories functioning in a remote valley beyond the bounds of civilization'. She could have been talking about Al Qaeda.

The book describes the city as full of noise and swirling dust, with the persistent honking of horns and shouting of vendors, and where sweetmeats, oranges, combs, razor blades and other assorted merchandise were carried rapidly through the streets on trays. There's little of that whimsical frolicking-with-eunuchs ambience ascribed to a place where throat-clearing and spitting was habitual, as were 'hot disputes between small groups of people who seemed ready to murder each other but were really fast friends'. The main action takes place in hotels, bookshops and embassy buildings and rarely involves any of the locals, but the images of the city are robust and pungent. Settings range from the copper souq with its clanging hammers and roaring blowlamps to the fictional Hotel Tio, where a typical room contains a brass bedstead, Victorian wardrobe, plush chairs and a French dressing-table, and the porter is a very old man with yellow face and white whiskers.

In *They Came to Baghdad* the view from the Hotel Tio's window is described as a 'delicate tracery of palm trees and irregularly placed houses along the bank of the Tigris', which at that time was busy with boats, particularly the ferryman's favourite, the *guffa*, a local flat-bottomed coracle made of reeds. When we came to Baghdad we had a similar view from the fifteenth floor of the Al-Mansour, but there was no sign of any brass bedstead or Victorian wardrobe in the rooms, no palm trees on the riverbank, and the Tigris itself was a sullen blade of *guffa*-free water which slid through between concrete embankments, unacknowledged from either side.

During Agatha's time the main hotels were the very British-sounding Waverley, Carlton and Maude, the latter proudly advertising its 'American Bar'. None of them have survived, and in their place stand the likes of the Al-Mansour, a giant block which was built in the 1980s. In those days Saddam Hussein was still on friendly terms with the West and had a vision of tourists as a 'river of gold' which just required diverting into the country's coffers. The hotel was created as part of that ambition, but in recent years it had been sadly left to drift. The friendly-nation flagpoles which lined the fountains outside were bare of any cloth, suggesting no friends. Inside, it seemed empty apart from a young Indian entrepreneur who didn't attempt to conceal his delight at how much business he was doing in Iraq, busting every sanction under the sun. The gift shop was full of Saddam memorabilia and the lift wore a raft of signs with the pride of a war hero wearing his medals. There was, I read, a casino, beauty salon and cocktail bar, as well as restaurants serving Italian and Chinese food, but the baggage boy shook his head; none existed any more, although he was keen to let us know that there was water in the swimming-pool. The lift itself was moody and erratic, as were all lifts we encountered across the country. They may not have been weapons of mass destruction, but they were capable of extreme behaviour which terrorized members of the group on several occasions.

My room in the Al-Mansour had a television with only two channels, both Iraqi, and both of which showed footage of Saddam greeting his people on what seemed to be a continuous loop of music videos, many of which were evidently several years old. After an hour of watching I couldn't help but feel sorry for those thrusting young media graduates who must have gone into the television industry bursting with creative ideas, only to become mired in a propaganda machine where you had to accept the pre-eminence of the creativity of the dictatorship. Their only editorial decisions would be to reverse the running order occasionally.

Even from the hotel room window it was clear that the city was much changed since the days of Cook's tourists. My first impression was of a place that was monochrome, traffic-clogged, orderly and prosaic. The house that Agatha and Max had lived in had apparently long since gone – bombed in the Gulf War was the official line – but so had virtually everything else of architectural interest, although there were still, as a hangover from British days, red double-decker buses, albeit made in India. When Thomas Cook started to send significant numbers of visitors here, in the early 1930s, a correspondent reported countless camel caravans and 'little sign of the modern progress which tends to make some oriental cities disappointing'. Alas, no longer. The city had plainly had an ambitious makeover in the last couple of decades which had bulldozed away all the old housing and narrow streets and replaced them with arterial routes, roundabouts, monuments and bunker-like architecture in stone, concrete and glass, most of it beige and covered in dust. A lot of history had been lost, but no doubt the plumbing was much improved.

Over the next couple of days we were taken to the few officially approved tourist sights, but there was to be no visit to the modernist Saddam City, which looks in pictures like a film set from *Star Wars* or *Blade Runner*, and the ceremonial Imperial Way, the equivalent of Beijing's Red Square, from where came all the television footage of rank upon rank of military hardware filing past the dictator on his podium. The nation's re-election of Saddam was only days away and the television was showing scenes of jubilant support from Saddam City, so perhaps allowing us in among those crowds would have been a bit like throwing slaves to the lions – or perhaps our minders wanted to hide the fact that the TV footage, like the videos, was old, and that nothing was actually happening on the ground. Certainly, when I drove illegally through the district one evening in a taxi there was little sign of any jubilant crowds. Or anyone at all.

Our first sortie was to the Iraqi Museum founded by Gertrude Bell, the museum which was reported to have been so thoroughly looted, with much international indignation, four months later. I was hoping that here, at least, would be some evidence of Max's findings, but very few of the thousands of exhibits in these vast and echoing galleries were actually labelled, and when they were they had such titles as 'a collection of clay tablets in different shapes containing different subjects'. The 45,000-year-old skeleton was interesting, though, as was the pebble with twelve incisions thought to be the first ever calendar, and the stumpy fertility figures with large derrières and startled wide eyes, looking as if someone had just informed them what being fertile actually involved. But even in the museum the threat of war was having its effect, and every room was equipped with a metal trunk into which the more valuable items would be packed post-haste when the bombs started to fall. The endless rows of unidentified limbs and torsos seemed to prefigure what was about to happen in the streets outside, and after an hour or so I couldn't stomach any more. The sad truth is that the British Museum has a far better collection in far better condition, thanks to all those British archaeologists who'd sent the best bits home. That collection should by rights be here, but it is actually far better off and far more widely seen in London. Not a good defence for antiquities theft, but a pragmatic one.

Emerging from the entrance to sit in the sun and await the more hardcore archaeology-fanciers of the group, I found myself being summoned across the tarmac by Kalashnikov-waving soldiers on the gate. I expected a reprimand, but instead was offered a seat in the shade. The 'shims', said the older of the two, was too hot. He had the obligatory Saddam moustache, as did virtually every other soldier. We agreed that his English was *schuay-schuay* (very little) but that his Arabic was very good, and that I, on the other hand, spoke *schuay-schuay* Arabic but my English was very good, which neat symmetry was the cause of much laughter. We even managed to have a semi-conversation about football, thanks to the team-sheet of Manchester United. I learned from him that the only inter-national football match the Iraqis play these days is against the Russians – nobody else would have them – and more importantly I concluded that even men in uniform and Saddam moustaches were only too pleased to see foreigners in their country.

Those early days in Baghdad illustrated how powerful a simple smile could be. Iraqis in general were delighted to see a group of foreigners and although they kept their distance – apparently they could smell a security man from 500 yards – you'd only to make eye contact to trigger a hand-to-heart gesture and a murmured *salaam wa'aleikhoom*. Perhaps some viewed us as involuntary human shields, the simple fact of our presence guaranteeing an invasion-free fortnight, but from later contact with individuals it became evident that they were instinctively hospitable, friendly and prejudice-free, perhaps even naïvely so. They seemed resigned to what was about to happen to them. Birth had put them in that country, economics had forced large numbers into uniform, politics had propelled the nation into conflict, and now History and Allah's will was about to be done.

Our government-agreed itinerary allowed for little human contact other than through the bus window, but the excursion to the Abbasid Palace did at least permit a glimpse of Baghdad as it once might have looked in Agatha's day. The Palace itself was impressive for the carved niches in its galleried courtyard, which inverted themselves over and over again in sandstone somersaults like something by M. C. Escher, but more significantly it gave us the chance to wander out on to Rashid Street into the Baghdad of crowds, the clanging of hammers on copper, the trays of sweetmeats, the shouting fish-merchants with handcarts and the arguing taxi drivers. The human tide parted a little and fell quiet as we moved through in the wake of our minders.

Rashid Street is the old city centre, a sort of Tuileries of the Middle East, and it was still lined with pillar-fronted old-fashioned shops like something out of old Rangoon. Gentlemen's tailors had their premises here, measuring old-fashioned gentlemen for old-fashioned suits, and clambering up wooden ladders to retrieve rolls of pin-stripe and flannel which would be thrown with a flourish across tabletops. The pavements outside were worked by itinerant jacket sellers selling best quality, secondhand. I stopped one to inspect the labels and found Dior and Moss Bros among them. 'London, Paris,' repeated the salesman, very keen that I should buy, but not comfort-able with any attempt at conversation.

Wherever we stopped to eat the menu was the same, dictated by the invisible hand of the United Nation's Food for Oil programme. The only real difference between restaurants was the ambience and the colour of the table-cloth. A selection of mezze was always brought straight to the table as we sat down – hummus, tabouleh, olives, cucumber salad, chickpeas – served with excellent freshly made warm flat breads sometimes sprinkled with sesame seeds. The main course was invariably grilled lamb or chicken with rice, delivered suspiciously soon after ordering. There was, of course, no alcohol but plenty of Coca-Cola or Seven-Up, despite the sanctions blockade. Presumably both were made locally under licence, but was the Coca-Cola company getting its royalties? It didn't seem likely.

Given our considerable buying power and a govern-ment brief to give us a good impression, we ate only at the best addresses. One of these was the Al-Goata Gardens, which turned out to be the place of choice for those elite Baghdadis who'd not yet managed to secure themselves a berth overseas, particularly well-padded and well-heeled ladies wearing lots of gold, with their chauffeur-driven Mercedes parked outside. Near us sat a police chief, casting benevolent glances in our direction, and further away I spotted a family with a twenty-something daughter who was dressed in jeans and T-shirt – quite a rarity in the city – and whose open face and frank, aware look suggested that she had seen plenty of Westerners in her time. Many of the women were doing the typical elite thing of ignoring their lunch partners and chattering away instead into rather chunky-looking walkie-talkies, which were Baghdad's substitute for mobile phones. Iraq may have motorway flyovers galore but it has no mobile network (wire-free calls would have been too difficult for the regime to monitor), so the privileged turned to shortwave radio instead.

Baghdad does have one local speciality, mazgouf, a fish which is supposedly taken from the waters of the Tigris itself. It was to taste mazgouf that our minders suggested we had dinner at one of the riverside restaurants at Abu Nawas, the place where Max and Agatha had recruited their cooks. The original couple of coffee shops have multiplied over the years into quite a little resort of restaurants, nicely landscaped on terraces descending the riverbank and well lit with strings of coloured bulbs. Here, at last, were river boats offering romantic rides, a sort of disco barge which looked, as it loitered rhythmically by, as if it was entirely monopolized by men, and a car park attendant in a very heavily-stained comedy bear suit. It was the only place to relax in a very tense city.

The Tigris, velvet and rippling with the reflected lights from the shore, smelled pungent – Saddam's chemical factories are upriver, whispered someone – which didn't make the idea of eating its fish particularly appealing. The restaurant manager assured us it was good, and to prove it he showed us where the fish – they looked like carp – were still swimming around in freshwater tanks prior to their *coup de grâce*. They were put into tanks, he explained, at least twenty-four hours before they were eaten in order to clean out the system, in a sort of pre-sacrificial detox. And then they were netted, split in two and staked out in a wide circle around the embers of a log fire. As a cooking method it looked dramatic and smelled sufficiently enticing to convince most of the party to give it a try, but when the fish arrived it turned out to be muddy-flavoured and full of tiny bones. At least two of the group disappeared hastily towards the toilets before the evening was out.

By now our version of *Nemesis* had been going for four days and the idiosyncracies of individuals were beginning to show. Mark, the Chinese banker, carried bottles of soy sauce and chilli with him into every restaurant, and for this occasion had produced a sachet of Aji-no-Moto, monosodium glutamate, 'because fish taste like cardboard'. Down the table a couple of the hard-travelling older ladies were comparing notes about how to dry your blouse overnight by rolling it in a towel, and there was some friction between them and Ms Lovebody, who certainly didn't subscribe to overnight wash-and-dry techniques and instead appeared in a new outfit for every day. Sure it meant lots of luggage, she said gaily, but what were men for? All you had to do was tip a bit more, and it was worth it to look your best.

There was some mouth-tightening around her as the implications of these words sank home, but I don't think Ms Lovebody intended to be insulting. She didn't really know how to be friendly with other women, and she had a raucous, dirty laugh that rang out at regular intervals in response to some passing remark, usually one made by her man. By the amount of hand-holding and close physical contact, she and Mr Lovebody were evidently not long a couple, and it looked a dangerous combination. There was something about him I didn't warm to, something vain, hard-nosed and institutional, and his clothes were far too neat. He had a way of walking and of standing with his feet well planted astride as if he had the crown jewels between his thighs, and a quick and cocky repartee that could only have been honed through years spent in the company of like-minded others – the army? the police force? Smithfield meat market? Whichever it was, it bred the sort of humour which managed to be amusing at someone else's expense. He didn't sound like a charity fund-raiser.

Next to the Lovebodys sat Yvette and Charles, two individuals as unlike in their interests as it was possible to be. She the former society beauty depressed by the loss of her looks, and he the rather pompous young fogey. Yvette was wondering out loud to no one in particular about which ageing starlets still had a certain something – she did sometimes disappear off on conversational tangents – whereupon Charles fixed her with a steely eye and said witheringly that he wasn't remotely interested in whether or not Joan Collins had any sex appeal. After that they both carefully avoided sitting anywhere near each other.

Then there were those of us who were not quite what we seemed, and who would never have got on the group visa if we'd confessed to how we really made a living. By now most people suspected that Anne and Hugh were trying to make a television programme on the quiet, but nobody had confronted them, because that wasn't the British way. When pushed, Hugh had shown some knowledge of the boxing world, but it was knowledge that could easily have been acquired in the making of a documentary, and in any case he was on safe ground among a busload of amateur archaeologists. Anne's claim to specialize in the title sequences of television programmes was a clever choice, being nicely lodged in the television business without actually tipping into the danger area of programme-making. I too had my cover story, pretending to be a translator of technical texts from German and French to English, although I was very happy to reveal my Agatha interest to my fellow travellers; it was, after all, my reason for being there.

As for Sean the muscular Marine, he who we all assumed was the biggest cover story of all – he was indeed turning out to be a loose cannon, but he wasn't firing in the direction that anyone expected. The ghetto-blaster had turned out to be genuine, and every evening we could hear loud rhythm and blues emerging from his hotel room.

That evening on the banks of the Tigris he told me that he was the great-grandson of an Irish-American who'd been a successful bootlegger during the Prohibition years. He had started his adult life as an amateur boxer, street punk and self-styled 'little bad kid' running wild in New York, getting into scrapes and frequently ending up with cuts and broken bones. 'I thought I was real smart, doing a bit of this, bit of that, bar-tending, digging up the roads – I was happiest with a jackhammer in my hands – and then I got some production work on *Saturday Night Live*.'

He soon had a reputation as a street-savvy location fixer with enough nerve to float the *Ark Royal* who could get TV and film-making crews into rough neighbour-hoods, for which he could charge a fortune. A tough nut with connections. 'They wanted a Brooklyn water-front with graffiti all over? They had to come to me. I was the only one who could deal with the guys on the ground.'

By the time he was thirty he'd made enough money to buy a restaurant serving Cuban food which he'd originally conceived as 'a socialist thing, a neighbourhood place for everybody', although the years had watered that ideology down a bit. He'd also taken over the local gym to keep those 'little bad kids' like him out of serious trouble and even given some of them jobs in his restaurant. The business had done particularly well since 9/11, he said, while all the more ostentatious places in downtown had been doing badly. He also had an on-off movie career which I suspected was more significant than his dismissive attitude towards it suggested.

As for his reasons for being on this trip, he'd come, he said, on impulse, partly out of surprise that it was even possible.

'I wanted to go see it, mainly because I knew you really weren't supposed to. Big kid, huh?' He grinned. He pretended no interest in anything remotely archaeological but wanted to see for himself whether all the things that the American people were being told about Iraq were true – and to tell the Eye-raqis that not every US citizen wanted to carpet-bomb them to oblivion. And when he'd done that, he said, he was going to go back to America to tell as many people as would listen what Iraq was really like. He paused. 'I guess I really am one of those people who wants to change the world.'

I murmured something about our group being a very unlikely collection of individuals. This brought him back to life.

'Yuh, what is it about you Brits? I may be naïve but I know when people are talking about me.' I agreed there had been a certain amount of gossip in the darker reaches of the bus about what he was doing here, why he always sat in the front seat and talked only to the minders.

'That's what I don't get,' he growled, annoyed. 'Everyone is very polite to my face, but behind my back ... yak, yak, yak. Where I come from, if you have a problem with someone, you tell him.'

By now the fish had been removed from the tables and Mohammed and Ahmed had come to join us for the glass of sweet mint tea that always came at the end of every meal. In theory, Mohammed was meant to be in charge, but he was too pudgy and eager to please to be threatening, and he had already confessed rather touchingly that the responsibility of keeping our passports safe made him wake up at night in a cold sweat. Ahmed, on the other hand, was a watcher, far more intelligent, and if any decision had to be made then Mohammed usually deferred to him. This may have been sheer force of personality at work, but if either of them was the senior man from the ministry, then it was Ahmed. Both, though, were unfailingly polite and never said no to anything, even when the request was plainly impossible. They would just nod, smile, and hope it wasn't mentioned again.

On this occasion Mohammed turned the conversation back to the main topic all single males have in common besides football – girls – and started to wax lyrical on the subject of Iraqi women, especially big ones. 'Ah,' he said, 'big mamma need big' – here he made a phallic gesture. 'Iraqi women very strong, very white. And very special inside.'

Sean went along with the detailed discussion that followed, but it was a bit too graphic for me.

The next evening I claimed sickness – delayed reaction to the fish – and said I'd skip dinner, partly taking my cue from Sean, who by now was regularly doing his own thing without seeming to create too much friction with the minders. In any case the two of them had little chance of keeping tabs on us all, and there were no security people posted on the hotel door with orders to keep us either in sight or inside.

It was a hot night, with a bullying wind that threatened worse to come. Back on Rashid Street the busy daytime scene had evaporated and the second-hand suit sellers on the pavements had retreated to become dark shapes squatting against shop pillars in the shadows, picking at their teeth and absent-mindedly working their way around their bracelets of Koranic beads. If I was looking for activity, it certainly wasn't here.

There was, though, one shop, a chemist's, still spilling out a pool of light. From the outside it didn't look like much, and inside it receded a long way, down a wide corridor of dusty wooden display cabinets which ran from floor to ceiling, all of them empty. On a pillar half-way down was a colour print entitled 'The Doctor's Waiting Room' and beyond it the unpolished parquet floor was brought to an abrupt stop by a counter on which stood a large, equally empty case which bore the names Wellcome & Burroughs, itself plainly an antique. In the space behind the counter was a marble-topped desk at which sat a little old man with a generous tub of pills on one side and a stack of tiny paper bags on the other. He was dressed like my late grandfather, his body shrinking away slowly inside a charcoal-grey suit patched at the elbows, in a yellowing white shirt and a knotted tie shiny with grease. Wrists as thin as sash cords rattled in and out of his disintegrating cuffs as he counted the pills out of the container into groups of ten, slipping each group into its own bag and then marking them 'Aspirin x 10' first in English and then in Arabic. It was a process he had obviously done thousands of times before, and by the thickness of his horn-rimmed glasses and the parchment that passed for his skin he was plainly both very short-sighted and very old. There was something Dickensian about the whole scene.

I coughed discreetly to announce my presence, but the reaction came from an unexpected quarter. A door which I hadn't noticed before swung open and the sound of Saddam TV flooded the shop, bringing with it a much younger shop assistant. He stood before me expectantly, so I explained, nodding towards the desk, that I would like some aspirin. At the sound of English being spoken the old man, who until then had seemed oblivious to the world, stopped and raised his head to peer owlishly up at me, revealing an unshaven collar of hair under his chin, like an Elizabethan ruff. Then he stood slowly, shuffled around the desk and held out his hand. 'Good evening,' he said in hesitant but barely accented English, 'my name is Sarkies,' and from a pile under the counter he produced a carefully printed visiting card in its own special envelope. I had to apologize for not having one to give him in return.

'I hope you don't think I am nosy, but I noticed you were writing in English,' I said.

Mr Sarkies looked at me intently, digesting what I'd just said. 'English is the language of business.'

'Even in modern Baghdad?' I was surprised.

He looked around him, as if searching for a reply from his walls. There was little sign of modern Baghdad in his immediate surroundings, so I started again. 'Do you have a problem getting medicines?' I indicated the empty glass cases.

Mr Sarkies examined me carefully before answering. 'It's not too bad, not too bad.'

It was not what I had expected to hear, so I pressed him. 'No problem with sanctions?'

Mr Sarkies shook his head. 'No, no, my problem is loneliness,' he said. 'Life has been miserable since my wife died. That's why I keep working, keep the shop open, you see. Don't like being by myself.' He shivered at the idea.

I steered the conversation on to more comfortable subjects. It transpired that Mr Sarkies was eighty-five years old and the youngest of five brothers born into an Armenian family. He'd gone to school during the British Mandate, which partly explained his good English, and had married an Iraqi Arab against the desires of his parents. Accordingly, when the rest of his family had left the country, he had stayed behind to support her mother and father. Since then his brothers had all died and his nephews and nieces were so widely spread around the world that English was the only language in which they could properly communicate. He was all that was left of the Sarkies dynasty in Iraq, and he'd resisted all offers to sell the shop that had been his life for the last fifty years. Only work, he said, kept him alive.

I asked about Agatha, hoping that I might stumble across a fortunate connection, but it was not to be. She had been 'very famous' in Baghdad, agreed Mr Sarkies, and she had done her shopping in Rashid Street, but he wasn't aware of her having come into his shop. Since then Rashid Street had faded; the new commercial heart of the city was Sadoun Street, a couple of blocks away. If I wanted to see street life, then that was where I should go. So I bade him farewell, and he was back labelling aspirins, his wrists rattling in his cuffs, before I'd reached the shop door.

Sadoun Street was certainly busy, but it was a characterless wide boulevard lined with watch and camera shops, jewellery stores and fashion boutiques, with products plonked in the window with little or no attempt at creative display. The brands for sale were largely unfamiliar; instead of Rolex they had Jack Swiss, instead of Kodak it was Chinese-made Lucky Film, and the Bata-substitute was Palestinian-made Golden Shoes. Designer menswear labels like Freeman and Closed meant nothing to me either, but it was actually rather stimulating to be in a retail environment which wasn't full of the same old household names. Would it have been any different without sanctions, I wondered? Or were many of these products actually still made by the major manufacturers but sold under unfamiliar names so as not to be seen to be breaking the embargo?

In the moneychanger's I asked the proprietor whether sanctions had made much difference to the shops around him, but it wasn't sanctions he was worried about. 'We wish you could do something,' he said, handing over a small bale of dinars for my single $20 bill – despite it being the currency of the enemy, the imperialist dollar was what Iraqis wanted most of all. 'Before we were worried about sanctions, but now we are worried about war.'

Outside, something was happening, but it wasn't missiles. The wind was rising, throwing litter into the air, tugging at street banners and threatening to overturn the vendors' trestle tables. Whereas previously people had largely been ignoring it, now they were moving hastily, and the pavements were emptying fast. I stopped beside a man who was stuffing his collection of plastic hair-grips quickly back into his bag. 'Horses,' he said, grinning up at me and nodding towards the sky. 'Horses.'

A moment later an overhead banner celebrating the President shredded with a crack and the thin rope which had been holding it started whipping at random, lethal to anyone standing near. I skipped quickly away just as the street lights bounced, juddered and then dimmed several volts. The first billow of sand had arrived, heralding a searing, scouring fog which got up your nose, in your eyes and dried out the back of your throat in an instant. Any vehicle that didn't have windscreen wipers crabbed sideways to the gutter, crawling along like a blind man with his stick on the kerb. This was what everyone had been trying to escape, an atmospheric sandpapering, a demoisturizing, abrasive blizzard that shrieked, whistled and howled as it went about its business, removing the surface from everything it touched.

I started to walk with the wind at my back, because it was actually less physically tiring than trying to stand still. Even to raise one's head to look around was uncomfortable and it would have been impossible to read a street sign or haul out a map to find out in which direction I was headed. I knew I should really find a shop or a restaurant in which to take refuge like everyone else, but I'd never been in a sandstorm before and I was impressed by the way it turned a shopping street into a scene from Armageddon, peopled by cowed shadows who leaned rather than stood, and whose heads had largely disappeared. I was half expecting the Horsemen of the Apocalypse to come riding through, and it was only when the top of a tree came skidding down the pavement towards me that I knew the time had come to seek cover. There were no trees in that part of Sadoun Street.

A few cars were still crawling along, being viciously assaulted every few yards by rabid plastic bags. I stood at the edge of the pavement looking hopefully down the road for a taxi, whereupon every approaching car tacked towards me, flickering its headlights, and then tacked away again when I didn't react. After standing there for several minutes, losing the battle to keep sand out of my eyes, it occurred to me that not all taxis necessarily had signs identifying themselves as such, so as the next vehicle lurched drunkenly in my direction I flung out an arm. The car stopped dead where it was, as if fearful of coming too close to the kerb. I hauled the door open. 'Taxi?' I hollered unnecessarily loudly into the dark, calm interior. The driver, a little bespectacled old man who wasn't so much behind the wheel as jammed in the space between it and the seat, nodded; taxi he was.

With the door shut, everything seemed suddenly peaceful again. The taxi driver was staring at me, astonished and a little bit frightened, as if President Bush himself had climbed into his cab and demanded to be taken to see Saddam. I daresay that my silhouette on the kerbside hadn't suggested I was a foreigner; actually, I daresay from the way he peered at me through pebble glasses he was only partially sighted anyway. Not good news in a taxi driver.

For a good thirty seconds we both sat and looked at each other as the wind raced around the car, wondering where I'd gone to. I was savouring the softness of sand-free air, and he no doubt was feeling some degree of panic about what might happen next.

'Station, please,' I said eventually. 'Railway station.' I'd found the right expression in the back of my guidebook, but it took a few stabs at it before the driver echoed the words back at me with obvious comprehension. He edged off down the street, trying to dodge the larger flying objects, wincing whenever something clanged into the car's bodywork and muttering imprecations whenever something lodged momentarily on the windscreen. It was like being caught in a huge domestic argument in a wind tunnel.

I settled back, wondering whether taxi drivers had strict instructions to return all wandering foreigners to the headquarters of the secret police. I knew the railway station was officially off-limits, but did the taxi driver know that too? The word was that the Iraqis moved their military hardware around by rail – there were only a couple of passenger trains on the whole network – so by insisting on visiting the station I was in danger of identifying myself as a spy sent to case the joint before calling in the bombers. The Iraqis didn't strike me as the sort of nation who'd be familiar with the concept of a 'trainspotter' and I doubted whether my Agatha interest – although she'd not arrived this way in 1928, she'd regularly used Baghdad station once the line had been completed four years later – would have rung any bells. It was simpler to remain merely a stupid tourist.

By now the taxi was crossing the river and the sandstorm was quickly abating. From the sudden aggrandizement of the buildings and the appearance of upward lighting and strange-shaped towers, I realized that we were passing through the forbidden Saddam City. There were practically no pedestrians, but every traffic light boasted a couple of policemen. I found myself behaving like the star of a clichéd action movie, sliding surreptitiously downwards in the back seat to get out of sight. Fortunately my driver was so focused on the hazards of the road, squinting short-sightedly through the windscreen, that he showed no sign of having noticed this incriminating behaviour. He drove with the exaggerated care of someone who had an unexploded bomb to deliver, and I was relieved and grateful when we finally did pull up outside the railway station, and not the police station. Even more surprising was his refusal to take any money, with the words, 'I love English, you no pay.'

In the end we agreed a compromise which involved him

taking a small wad of notes so he could buy presents for his children.

Baghdad railway station is a huge, imposing red brick building which was built by the British in the early 1930s, and looks from the outside like a cross between the Bankside power station and the domed reading-room at the British Museum. Its main façade would be all the more grand if it were not interrupted by a giant billboard celebrating Saddam, in this case portrayed as godfather of all the railways in the world. Agatha may not have arrived here in 1928, but she did use the railway that year for her onward journey south to Ur, and indeed at the time Iraq was proudly advertising its new electrically lit coaches as the best method of travelling to the various archaeological sites. Ur station, for example, was within twenty minutes' walk of the Ziggurat, the famous pyramidal tower with the temple on top which everyone wanted to see. In fact, so amenable was the railway company to tourist needs and so poor was the local accommodation that travellers were advised that for a small financial consideration, a coach could be slipped off the main train. It would then be left in a siding as somewhere safe and clean for the tourists to sleep in and to retreat to during the heat of midday.

My own experience of Iraqi railways was not destined to be nearly so accommodating. The main station approach, through an ornamental garden, was barred by railings, so I searched out an open entrance around the side. Here I was immediately hauled over by a soldier, who wanted to look inside my bag. At the sight of my camera he looked so worried that I almost expected him to burst into tears.

'Photo,' he said, pointing.

'Photo,' I nodded. There was no denying it.

He gestured to me to follow him in the direction of the guardroom, and I felt that dreadful plummeting sensation in my stomach when you realize that you've just made a hideous error of judgement. What would my wife say to the children in years to come? 'Your father, he was a good man. That moment when he marched into Baghdad station waving a camera around was completely out of character . . . I know he wouldn't have done such a thing if he'd thought for a moment it would leave you fatherless and me a widow . . .'

Another soldier joined us, and together we marched into an office with a phone and a desk. The first soldier indicated I should sit down. Moments later a man in an off-white shirt strolled in, looking relaxed.

'Where from?' he said, smiling. I explained I was from England, realizing as I did so that Mohammed had my passport so I had no form of identification to back up anything I said. But the man didn't seem bothered.

'Very nice, England,' he declared, with such conviction that I asked him whether he'd ever been there. He shook his head.

'Maybe one day,' I said, declining his offer of a cigarette. My interrogator lit up, thoughtfully, in the time-honoured way of all interrogations.

'Tourist?' was his next question. I nodded vigorously. I was completely and utterly a tourist, completely. Utterly. I hoped my frantic nodding conveyed that.

'You wife?' Again I nodded, conveying with a mixture of gestures and words that I had two children. It turned out that he had eleven, and this virility one-upmanship prompted much amusement for him and the soldiers. At least, he was amused first and the soldiers dutifully followed suit.

Another long pause.

'England raining?'

'Oh yes,' I said hastily. 'Must be. Bound to be.' This too was the cause of much amusement, especially once the boss had explained to his troops that it rained all the time in England. Somehow or other this reflection on the awfulness of my weather, combined with my complete inadequacy in the fathering department, must have earned me the sympathy vote.

'So, tourist, please,' said my man, indicating that I could get up. 'Walking, looking OK.' And he waggled his finger. 'But no photo.'

Bowing, stupidly grateful and stupidly repeating 'No photo' as if I'd come over all Japanese, I retreated backwards through the door and out on to the station concourse. Even if I had wanted to take a photograph my hand would have been trembling far too much for a clean shot. I walked out to the roofless platform area, looked around cursorily to establish that there was no sign of any trains whatsoever, and then retreated into the slender-pillared, chandeliered and domed booking-hall, where no footsteps other than mine echoed across the marble floor. The only sign I could read said 'Trains for Mosul' above one of three ticket windows, none of which was open. Then I walked out of the front entrance, strode through the small garden with snakes of sand chasing my ankles, and hailed a taxi back to the hotel. I'd seen the station, it had turned out to be a great white elephant, and it had nearly given me a heart attack.

NINEVEH, JONAH AND LUCIFER

My return to the Al-Mansour after the close encounter at the railway station went completely unnoticed thanks to drumming, ululating crowds in the car park and a blizzard of camera flashes at the hotel entrance. Fortunately this wasn't a reception committee for the Englishman who thought he was lost and gone for ever, but a once-weekly ritual on which the Al-Mansour depended for its continued survival. It was Friday, the most propitious day of the week for getting married, and on this particular Friday a staggering ninety-four couples had booked into the hotel for one night of privacy and clean sheets, and it was their business which was keeping the hotel afloat in a time of sanctions. Of course the Al-Mansour's one-night-stand package was only for those families who could afford a honeymoon; in the dire state of the economy and the absence of any freedom to travel, a night on the fourteenth floor was the best they could do.

Not that the brides and grooms looked particularly excited by the prospect. Standing in the foyer, watching these couples pose for their official pictures, I couldn't say that any seemed to be savouring the moment sufficiently to want to tell their grandchildren about it. Perhaps it was a tradition that the brides, in stiff, wide, hooped white dresses, and the grooms, in ill-fitting second-hand suits (no doubt bought from the pavement salesman of Rashid Street), were obliged to look deeply uncertain about the prospect of newly wedded bliss, while all around them whooped and grinned.

From the foyer a posse of closest relatives accompanied the unhappy couples to the lift and up to the relevant floor, chattering gaily. There, eventually, they left them to consummate the beginning of their new lives with Saddam TV playing out in the background and their glorious President himself symbolically shooting off his rifle whenever the occasion demanded. In theory, 188 virginities were going to be lost in that hotel that night, and it didn't look as if it was going to be a joyful experience.

We didn't stick around long enough the following morning to see whether the newly-weds had become any more comfortable in each other's company, post-coitally, although we didn't leave quite as early as intended. A new bus had turned up to take us north but several of the party had refused to travel in it, claiming that it was 'full of vomit'. A baggage boy was sent to fetch a bucket and a cloth, and while he set about his task, we gathered in gossiping, tut-tutting groups. Now that the excitement of being in Iraq had started to wear off and it was becoming clear we were welcome, even valued, guests, some members of the group had begun to find fault with facilities and arrangements. Cliques were starting to form as people sought out the company of others who held a similar point of view. And as tends to happen when a group of complete strangers comes together, the dynamics of our interpersonal relationships were becoming just as absorbing as the destination.

Two main camps were forming, the first being of the complainers who liked to grouch at every small change, and the second of the non-complainers who were grateful to be in Iraq and just wanted to get on with it and see the archaeology. On the bus these positions had begun to polarize. The pushier people were percolating forwards towards the front, where they could moan into the ears of authority, while the non-complainers drifted towards the back, where their little-heard views were easily ignored. This is the way that schisms begin, and I could see the two groups becoming the Sunnis and Shias or the hawks and doves of the trip. I sat uncomfortably between the two, trying not to become involved too much on either side, and keeping my guilty note-making as surreptitious as possible lest it antagonize Charles or even (less likely) the minders.

The unexpected substitution of the bus was more grist to the complainers' mill, but fortunately on this particular occasion there were other issues to discuss. The toothsome television twosome, Anne and Hugh, had left the country the previous day in a cloud of question marks, taking a long-distance taxi back to the border accompanied by a minder provided by the ministry. They were to proceed from there all the way back to Damascus, and Mark, the banker from Hong Kong, had gone with them.

Mark's main motivation for being in Iraq had emerged fairly soon after our arrival. He had no interest in the nation or its history; he wanted to buy pearls, Basra pearls, which were supposed to be the best and the most valuable in the world and had been made all the more sought-after by the country's political and economic isolation. To this end he'd disappeared off with one of the minders on a couple of occasions and word was that he'd been prepared to spend tens of thousands of dollars, but although he'd been shown some good examples, he hadn't bought anything – or so he said. Perhaps he'd just been investigating potential sources of supply for a business when sanctions were over, or perhaps it was all a smokescreen. I don't think many of us were sorry to see the back of him; he'd made a scene in the Al-Mansour's restaurant the previous evening, when he'd ordered his meal, waited five minutes and then stood up and barked, 'Food, drink, now!' across the room at the frightened waitress. The Lovebodys, who'd been there at the time, had found this tableau very amusing.

It was only when Mark had gone that I realized that so too had a protagonist of one of my potential Agatha Christie plots: the celebrated international jewel thief who does his business and then departs long before the crime is discovered. The question was – had he been successful, and if so, who or what was his actual target? Nobody on the bus was likely to be carrying any jewels, so perhaps he'd taken something from the Iraqi Museum.

I was still contemplating the ins and outs of Mark's potential criminality as the bus (the vomit had turned out to be a patch of spilt paint) shrugged off the last of the suburbs. The air was still so full of dust after the previous night's sandstorm that the stem of a distant pipeline burn-off beacon was completely invisible, leaving just the flame to hover in the sky above Baghdad like an archangel's torch, foretelling doom.

There was dust, too, on the crops growing on either side of the road, rendering them, and the trees that stood among them, a sort of dusky ashen green, as if they'd somehow become disused. I caught glimpses of a donkey and cart and a man on his knees among his vegetables, praying. The whole scene was so muted and monochrome that you wondered whether something hadn't been injected into the bus glass to extract the life from things. Clearly this was an austere, difficult place where existence was only made possible by the gift of two rivers flowing through the desert, and you can see why in these circumstances man would either blindly obey a strong leader or turn to his god. You could also see why the British soldiers in the 1917 invasion had nicknamed the place 'Messpot', and one had reportedly announced, as he marched up from Basra, 'This 'ere is the land of sweet F-all with a river up it.' Similar sentences were probably being said on the Basra road four months later, this time within the privacy of Challenger tanks.

It wasn't quite F-all, though. As the road developed, so it became bordered by wheatfields of a size small enough to be manageable without the aid of machinery, interspersed with groups of date palms, pomegranate orchards, sunflower fields, cabbage patches and even quite considerable stretches of vineyards, although presumably their fruit was never used for wine. Occasionally there'd be a figure walking through this landscape with a long-handled spade over his shoulder, and at one point we passed a scrubland where military helicopters were squatting down among the bushes, their rotors rearranged to make them look like rabbits with their ears back, ready to run. I wondered if the weapons inspectors knew.

From a couple of seats in front of me on the bus I could hear a conversation about porridge, and how it should always be eaten every morning between November and March, a conversation which then moved on to the different methods which could be employed to clean the porridge pot. At the time it seemed absurdly out of place given the context, but looking back on it now I realize that Agatha could well have been having just such a conversation on just such a road, seventy years before, also heading north. She would almost certainly have included porridge in her provisions for the December through to March seasons at the northern digs of Nimrud and Nineveh, and she would have been talking to her new cook, freshly recruited from the banks of the Tigris at Abu Nawas. Every year she'd try to educate these cooks in the likes of how to correctly arrange the cutlery on the table and how to prepare a proper roast. There wasn't much adoption of the native cuisine, let alone the native lifestyle, on these expeditions. The archaeologists were pipe-smoking scholarly types who gave each other nicknames like Bumps and CT and would have been equally at home (and probably were) in the dining halls of Oxford and Cambridge, discussing cricket and claret. Only under extreme conditions would they forgo a jacket and tie. A couple were ex-monks, and Robin Macartney was the son of the consul-general for Chinese Turkestan. For this lot, Asia Minor was a school trip for grown-ups.

Agatha was no different. Even when living in the desert, sleeping in tents beside the dig house, she still dressed for dinner, had Stilton cheese and chocolate imported from London, and instructed her cooks in producing éclairs made with cream from water-buffalo milk, and walnut soufflés cooked in a square tin can. In fact soufflé was her perennial favourite, and she had one cook who, whenever a soufflé collapsed, would come running to his mistress wringing his hands and exclaiming, 'Squeeze me, madam, squeeze me.'

Our first stop was Samarra, former capital and source of some of the oldest Mesopotamian pottery, dating back to 5000 BC. Since then the city has been rebuilt many, many times, and the visible ruins are a mere 1,500 years old, too youthful for archaeologists to show any real interest. Nevertheless they have suffered the same fate as all their more ancient colleagues, dissolving into a huge, pitted and rutted biscuit-coloured expanse covering many square miles, from where the feeble arm of half an arch occasionally raises itself like a suppliant survivor in a sea of immolation.

Unfortunately there has never been much in the way of quarryable stone in Mesopotamia, so the palaces and the cities were built in the only material that was readily available: mud brick. The brick served its purpose well enough at the time, but over succeeding centuries the combined assault of wind, sun and seasonal heavy rain has largely reduced everything manmade to weeping heaps, dissolving back into the land from whence it came. Half close your eyes, and you could almost be among the desolation of the trenches in World War I, but without any of the mud. It's a real-life dust-to-dust situation, and only the sheer size of the Mesopotamian sites hint at what lay there before – the urbanizations of grand and cultured civilizations which date back earlier than their Egyptian equivalents, but which have left far fewer souvenirs. The Egyptians had stone to build with, so their sites don't require such a leap of the imagination.

In those days, palace- and city-building were an essential part of kingship. When Samarra was at its most glorious its creator, Caliph Al-Mutawakhil, wrote, 'Now I know that I am indeed a king for I have built myself a city and live in it.' He's not the last person to believe that the property maketh the man. We may have all scoffed by now at Saddam's obscenely opulent palaces, but Britain is full of country mansions which were built for similarly egotistical reasons, and even in contemporary British society our houses are increasingly both the realizations of our dreams and the focus of our ambitions. A person's sense of self is to a considerable extent based on the size and value of his or her home, just as Al-Mutawakhil's was, before the passage of time reduced it to rubble.

One notable bit of his architecture still stands pretty much intact: the Minaret of Samarra, a sort of Eiffel Tower for Asia Minor, albeit 1,500 years older. Samarra's spiral, shaped like a generous and gentle helter-skelter, is one of Iraq's key symbols, and if ever the nation has a popular selection of postcards then it will be on many of them. At fifty-two metres it is not particularly high, but its beauty lies in the simplicity of its design. The parchment-coloured Minaret is girdled by an external climbing ramp which is wide enough to ride a horse up, although it gets increasingly narrow as it completes its five revolutions, and you'd have a problem turning your horse around at the top to come down again. The effect is of a pathway to the sky like the yellow brick road in *The Wizard of Oz*, and its rapid diminution in size makes you feel as if you are climbing far higher and far further than you really are. Spiralling upwards, watching the land below fall away and the near distance slowly reveal itself through 360 degrees, I couldn't help but wonder why such a simple design hadn't been copied elsewhere – although the addition of some sort of safety rail would have been welcome. It would have been an easy place to commit a murder and make it look like an accident, but most of my suspects from the bus stayed firmly on the ground, and there were too many people around to be sure of pushing someone off unobserved. At ground level there'd been little breeze, but as I climbed higher and the ramp narrowed so the wind started to tug at my clothes and make my eyes water, until finally, on the very top, I found myself standing on a crowded open platform amid a group of Iraqi teenagers making as much noise as possible and joshing each other to show they were not scared of the steep drop on all sides. In their midst was the Wizard of Oz himself, grinning and saluting them all with high fives: Sean.

He told me later that he couldn't stop thinking, while he handed around his camera for everyone to have a go, how these lads would be shoved into uniform and pushed into the front line when war broke out, where they would be the first to be killed. And yet here they were, excited and pleased to be having their photograph taken with an American.

'If I was an Iraqi who'd had the nerve to go on holiday in the US,' he'd said, 'I'd be crucified. If I'd come out with a machine-gun and mown some of those guys down I'd be a national hero back home. But because I've come out to express my friendship, they'll think I'm a national traitor.'

We broke the long journey to Mosul with an overnight stop in a government rest-house near the archaeological site of Hatra. Although the desert colours still seemed the same admixtures of beige and cream – do the bedouin have as many adjectives for desert as the Inuits have for snow? – the surface was like a choppy sea, pre-figuring the mountains of Iraqi Kurdistan. It may have looked arid and inhospitable, but the dimples in that sea were full of small birds, herders with goats, the sound of distant chickens and geese rootling around small mud houses.

This was the heartland of the Assyrians, an aggressive 4,500-year-old dynasty whose cities at Nimrud and Nineveh grew to rival the earlier southern empires based around Babylon and Ur, and who were to become the focus of Max and Agatha's attention. The Assyrians were the baddies of the Bible and their King Sennacherib's fearsome campaign against Hezekiah, King of Judah, in 700 BC is recorded in some detail in the Second Book of Kings, which reveals that 'the kings of Assyria have exterminated all the nations, they have thrown their gods on the fire'. The siege of Jerusalem inspired Lord Byron to write *The Destruction of Sennacherib*:

> The Assyrian came down like a wolf on the fold
> And his cohorts were gleaming in purple and gold;
> And the sheen of their spears was like stars on the sea
> When the blue wave rolls nightly on deep Galilee.

Although on that occasion Sennacherib didn't manage to take Jerusalem, the Assyrians were habitually victorious. They would wrap the skin of their enemies around the entrance pillars to their cities, alongside the giant stone winged bulls which stood there as a symbol of their power. But the Assyrians didn't manage to hold on to what they conquered, long-term, and today only their winged bulls remain. Thanks to the work of CT and his colleagues, the best of them are no longer to be found anywhere near the place of their creation, but stand instead in the British Museum.

At the Hatra guest-house there was another, unforeseen, Agatha connection: the manager was a Yezidi, one of the oldest and most maligned religions in the world. The Yezidis are the followers of Lucifer. But while Christians believe Lucifer fell from grace to become the Devil, the Yezidis believe that he was pardoned and returned from hell to take his position at the right hand of God, from where he runs the world as a sort of chief executive, with the Almighty as his non-executive director.

Because of their faith in Lucifer the sect is rather easily and misleadingly labelled as devil-worshippers, and persecuted as such. They do, it is true, have a strange code of beliefs, including a peacock god, a pathological fear of lettuce and of the colour green (which unfortunately for them is the Islamic holy colour), but there's nothing remotely devilish about them.

Yezidis had been among the team of men recruited by Max and Agatha to work on their digs. They soon came to the couple's attention because they were plainly being picked on by the Muslims, who would claim to have contaminated the daily drinking water with lettuce so that the Yezidis would have to go thirsty. On one occasion during the dig at Chagar Bazar the persecution had become so severe that Max had to gather the whole workforce together and threaten the persecutors with fines. As for Agatha, her interest was piqued by the Yezidis' stoic, uncomplaining nature, and they were so unlike their devil-worshipping image that she and Max eventually felt they must make the journey to the Yezidi holy shrine in the hills near Mosul, a place she found to be beautiful, peaceful, calm, gentle and pure.

Nobody really knows how many Yezidis there are left in their homeland, where the Turkish, Syrian and Iraqi borders meet. Recent reports suggested there were as few as 750 remaining in Iraq, so to have come across Hazim Arker Chamo at the Hatra rest-house was a lucky chance. He too seemed a gentle, sincere man, and he was certainly diligent and meticulous in his approach to his work. He had a three- or four-person staff lurking in the shadows but he insisted on doing all the table-waiting himself, beads of sweat dribbling down his temples. In truth he didn't look much different from anyone else, which wasn't surprising, given that the Yezidis are fundamentally of

Kurdish origin, as are many of the northern Iraqis. When he'd finished clearing after dinner I cornered him, and questioned him with the help of the rest-house's accountant, who spoke some English. He was nervous and defensive, presumably because being a Yezidi usually got him into trouble. And given that the accountant was a Muslim, I'm not sure whether my questions were translated correctly or whether I was only given a distorted interpretation of the answers.

Hazim said, first of all, that the Yezidis were flourishing. According to him a community of at least 500,000 was divided between Turkey and Iraq. They were all meant to be descended from Adam and Eve's son Abel, although given that the Bible suggests that Cain had murdered Abel before the latter had had a chance to have any children, it was hard to see how that stacked up. The Yezidis considered themselves, he continued, to be Christians, although the Christian community – quite substantial in Northern Iraq – refused to acknowledge them thanks to their Lucifer connection. As for the question of what Yezidis actually believed in, Hazim was a bit vague. Centuries of persecution meant that it had become hard for them to maintain a distinct theology, and the Black Book, which was the Yezidi equivalent of the Bible and the fount of all teaching, had been removed to Germany for safe-keeping by the 30,000-strong community of Yezidi asylum-seekers living over there. Worship had become less a matter of doctrine, and more a question of heredity and habit.

He agreed, nervously, that he did have a problem with lettuce, the colour green and certain sorts of fish. As for devil-worshipping, he said the Yezidis had chosen to revere the peacock symbol because the word for peacock was the very antithesis of Satan. He also said that Yezidis could not inter-marry with non-Yezidis and that their churches were basically just shrines, too small to enter, so worshippers walked around the outside. His own thrice-daily worship was performed by holding up his hands to the sun.

All the above information was dragged out of him with some effort. The poor man looked deeply uncomfortable, as if we were forcing him to reveal details of some dirty habit, and he seemed reluctant to volunteer any extra information over and above the direct answers to my questions. It could have been that he was unused to anyone taking anything but a negative interest in his religion, and he may also have found it an uncomfortable experience speaking out about it in front of his accountant and Ahmed, who had also joined us. I wondered whether I should feel bad about getting him to expose himself like this, but given that the rest-house was government-run and that, despite being a Yezidi, he had risen to management level, I concluded that it hadn't done him any harm up till now.

Afterwards, Ahmed added a bit of extra gloss. The Yezidis were effectively atheists, he said, and not civilized people. Every day they kissed the stone on which the first of that day's sun's rays fell – but he stopped short of calling them the worshippers of Satan. He did, however, refuse my suggestion that the bus should make a diversion via the main Yezidi shrine at Lalish. It wasn't, he said, government-approved.

Agatha Christie wrote the foreword to her autobiography in the mud-brick dig house at Nimrud. In it she describes, with much affection, how she first sat down to record her life story with various 'hindrances to concentration' going on all around: the Arab workmen yelling happily to each other on the roof, the barking of dogs, the gobbling of turkeys and the policeman's horse clanking his chain outside. She details her room, with its rush mats on the floor and its view out towards the snow-topped mountains of Kurdistan, and the sign on the door on which was printed, in cuneiform, Beit Agatha – Agatha's House. She spent some of the happiest years of her life here, presiding over a family of archaeologists and local workers and personally organizing (and paying for) a series of Wednesday jaunts, which were usually picnics and expeditions to local attractions. In her will, she specifically requested that 'Nimrod' from Elgar's *Enigma Variations* be played at her funeral.

Her interest in the local workers was a trait not common among archaeologists of the time, and is reflected in the many photographs she took on the dig. They in turn responded with affection towards her. She tells the story of how, many years later, while driving through Baghdad, she heard someone shout 'Mama' above the traffic noise and recognized Ali, who'd been a pot-boy – carrying pots of excavated earth to the heap – at Nimrud. Now he was a policeman, and he was grinning from ear to ear as he held up the traffic to let her through.

From my reading I knew that the dig house at Nimrud was still standing, so I arrived there full of hope that I might be able to stand inside Beit Agatha and look out of that self-same window towards the mountains of Kurdistan. Sadly I was two years too late. The original mud-brick dig house is still complete with sash windows, but Agatha's extension had fallen down and had been replaced by a store-room made of breeze blocks. That apart, the house was everything I could have imagined. It had its own little fenced compound, vegetable patch and chickens, and it seemed to be occupied by a large family with several tousle-haired children, many of whom were sitting outside on an old iron bedstead giggling at the sudden visitation of foreigners. It still had a sympathetic, engaging atmosphere, and a lovely view.

From 1949 to 1957 Max and Agatha had spent every season here, during which time Max excavated the palace of the Assyrian King Ashurnasirpal II, finding a stela covered in cuneiform writing on which Ashurnasirpal recorded how 69,000 guests had come to his palace house-warming. Ashurnasirpal was prone to recording things, sending his scribes out to create a sort of Domesday Book of the world around, which they then recorded in cuneiform on stone tablets and stored in his library. As a result we know as much about life in Northern Mesopotamia in 700 BC as we do about medieval Britain. He also had them chisel his standard in-scription in a decorative band on almost every temple and palace wall, to read thus: 'I am Ashurnasirpal, the celebrated prince, who reveres the Great Gods, the fierce dragon, conqueror of the cities and mountains to their furthest extent, king of rulers who has tamed the stiff-necked peoples, who is crowned with splendour, who is not afraid of battle, the champion who shakes resistance, the glorious king, the shepherd, the protector of the whole world, the king, the word of whose mouth destroys mountains and seas, who by his lordly attack has forced merciless kings from the rising and the setting sun to acknowledge one rule.' Reading this, I remembered the words of the Syrian hubble-bubble dealer on the train from Istanbul about the need for a ruler to be seen to be strong. In 3,000 years the tradition of leadership has little changed.

Besides various friezes, Max also found a lot of ivories in a couple of the palace wells at Nimrud, where they were likely to have been thrown when the city came under attack by the Babylonians, for recovery later. (As it turned out, much later.) Among these finds a couple of carved heads were widely applauded at the time, getting similar editorial coverage in the *Illustrated London News* to some of Leonard Woolley's finds at Ur. The dig staff christened the first 2,600-year-old Mona Lisa 'the Lady of the Well', and the second the 'Ugly Sister', names which they still carry in museum collections today. Agatha describes the heads' discovery as one of the most exciting days of her life, telling how the workmen came running, shouting, 'We've found a woman in the well!'

She acclimatized the Lady of the Well and her Ugly Sister to their new and arid climate by nursing them under damp towels for several weeks, gradually reducing the humidity until they became accustomed to the drier atmosphere, like ageing starlets after their face-lifts. She then used her valuable stock of face cream to clean them off. It makes an intriguing picture, the elderly (by now she'd turned sixty-six) crime novelist bending over heads which had inexplicably been thrown down a well 2,600 years before, her hands mechanically wiping the features clean while her mind sorted out plots and obscure methods of death.

An archaeologist who came to visit Max at Nimrud wrote that the Agatha he saw on site was quite different from the Agatha he'd met in England. There were no shy psychological hang-ups. Here was a woman in a man's world who knew she was being accepted at face value. 'She worked like a beaver . . . no professional would have done it better.' The truth is, she liked jobs, particularly those where she worked with other people, as she had done in the hospital in wartime. It made a welcome contrast to the solitary world of the writer and gave her a sense of her own value, a sense of self-image which her writing did not. The archaeologist also described her as being largely responsible for the prevailing mood of great good humour that existed on the dig, where she developed a tradition of penning special poems for expedition members to take away as leaving presents. One of these Nimrud odes records her frustration with the laying of a new tarmac road right past the site, which meant that the number of daily visitors increased to intrusive levels. Those visitors were often more interested in her than in the dig.

A guaranteed Epigraphist
In Kurdish trousers gay
For fifty fils will write your name
In cuneiform on clay.
A famous Novelist's on view
For forty fils a peep,
But if you want a photograph
It will not be so cheap!

The discoveries made at Nimrud were sufficient to establish Max among the major league of British archaeologists, but he failed to spot a crucial clue which would have led to him finding something much, much bigger. It is probably just as well that he and his wife had both died by the time that news of this later discovery came out.

The legacy of that later find is that Nimrud today is a rarity in modern Iraq: an archaeological dig still in operation. Its Ziggurat rises out of a floodplain of cotton fields, so misshapen by decay that it could be just another hill – although there are no other hills around. Climb that hump, and you look down on a small plateau with a fenced-off compound where the excavated remains of the palace of Ashurnasirpal II stand, next to an area of recent digging with reconstructed walls and trenches busy with Kurdish men in baggy trousers.

In the middle distance are two conical brick ovens next to pits filled with the ingredients for brick-making – straw, mud and water. Beyond that stands the dig house in its compound, with a newish air-conditioned mobile home where the frustrated hero of Iraqi archaeology, Muzahin Mahmud Husein, has his office, with a sofa, a big desk and several photographs of Saddam Hussein.

Muzahin is a distinguished-looking, lean, dry man dressed in khaki, somewhere between a professor and a military commander. He has been working on this site for thirty-two years, and although he just missed overlapping with Max and Agatha, he said there were still some old people who remembered her. It was he who was responsible for the series of finds, starting back in 1988, which some say are the most valuable in the archaeological world since Tutankhamun. Four hidden royal tombs at Nimrud yielded four gold anklets weighing 1.4 kilos apiece – too heavy to walk with – along with thirty golden rings, seventy-nine gold earrings, six gold necklaces, fourteen armlets, fifteen gold vessels, cups and jars. There were gold bottles, bowls made of crystal and gold safety pins, each with a tiny gold eagle holding the point safely in his beak. And then there was a crown in filigree gold with little bunches of bright blue grapes exquisitely fashioned out of lapis lazuli, as well as the actual remains of three queens and assorted others, plus all their personal possessions, of less material value but great archaeological significance.

As Muzahin ran quickly through the details of his find, seated in his mobile home, he rifled through a series of photographs which he said he would be happy to sell to us. The photographs were as close as we, or anyone, were going to get to his discovery, because his country's political isolation meant that the treasure had remained under lock and key almost since the day it was brought to light. Muzahin had to master his frustration at being the discoverer of something that no one else can see. Only another archaeologist could know what it must be like to make such a major find and not be able to take it with you on a triumphal world tour. Instead he was reduced to effectively selling postcards of it from a mobile home.

After we'd made suitably appreciative noises – hard to do with just a set of photographs – Muzahin took us around the Ashurnasirpal palace, making it clear before we set out that he would not be drawn into general discussions about Iraq.

'My English language is about archaeology only,' he insisted.

He showed us the palace anterooms, with wall friezes like poorly constructed jigsaws with their heads missing thanks to the work of looters. Only one was still largely complete, because the forehead had cracked off while its head and shoulders were in the process of being chiselled apart from the body, so the looters had left it alone.

'How recent?' someone asked.

Muzahin shrugged. 'Not very. Not here. Here we have a fence, an armed guard. But elsewhere. We have so many sites. With sanctions, no archaeologists come from abroad, so we have no budget for guards, so the wire in the fences is stolen. Poverty does the rest.'

Monitoring agencies believe that 4,000 looted Iraqi antiquities have been sold on the international market since 1994, most of them hacked from the remains of those temples and palaces which had been so painstakingly uncovered during happier times.

And then he showed us the scene of his own personal triumph, the palace room from which Max had removed all the sand, but had missed a vital clue staring up at him from under his feet. Thirty-five years later Muzahin had noticed that the exposed floor tiles were not regular, suggesting that at some stage they had been taken up and put back again, and in a royal palace he knew that that could mean an under-floor burial. So he dug up the floor, discovered a vault of bricks and opened a tomb so full of dust it took two weeks to remove before the 'gold shined bright in my eyes'. By the time the Gulf War began in 1991 he had discovered three additional tombs under the floors of neighbouring chambers, each with its own collection of skeletons, jewellery and personal items, together with a curse that threatened tomb-robbers with eternal thirst and restlessness. When he'd finished show-ing us the scene of his triumph, I asked him whether he thought Mallowan had actually been a good archaeologist.

'Of course,' Muzahin replied. 'But in archaeology there is luck as well as judgement.'

Over at the new diggings at the foot of the Ziggurat the workers were brushing down the head and shoulders of a new winged bull, fresh, unscathed and emerging from the earth as if it had been newly born; I wondered if they were going to wrap it, as Agatha had, in wet towels. Muzahin, now beaming like a proud father, asked us not to take photographs. It is an honourable tradition among archaeologists that nothing should be written or published of a new discovery by anyone other than the person who made that discovery – even when that person is politically and intellectually isolated behind a barrier of sanctions. He added that we could, though, 'tell John', by whom he meant John Curtis, the Keeper of the Ancient Near East at the British Museum. He wanted someone in the world outside to know, someone who really understood. For him it must have been like putting a message in a bottle and setting it on the ocean, in the hope that someone who speaks the same language will eventually pick it up.

Afterwards, walking back across the site towards our bus, my boot struck a stone on the edge of a mound. It came away from among a narrow band of stones which probably represented the top of a wall. No doubt a building lay below me, one which Max hadn't had time for and which Muzahin had yet to reach. Somewhere down there it was possible that the statue of a goddess, the figure of a bull or the tomb of a queen shivered with the faint vibration caused by a clumsy foreigner from another era passing by overhead, with his head full of unlikely ideas and his body full of wind.

The two rivers of Iraq, the Tigris and the Euphrates, are as nomadic as the Bedouin, and time-lapse satellite photography over the centuries would show them slithering around the map like a pair of lazy snakes. That movement has come about through the steady accumulation of silt scoured out of the mountains by seasonal rains. The silt fills up the shallow riverbeds, making the water level rise, until a new seasonal flooding easily breaches the banks and the rivers find new, lower routes. In Ashurnasirpal's day the Tigris flowed right past the gates of Nimrud, but now the river's course is barely visible, some miles away, from the top of the Ziggurat. Many of the ancient cities further south are even more remote from the waterside, left high and dry by the wandering rivers. Without a valley to follow or a bed of rock to keep them on course, the waterways are free to roam, and it is up to man either to harness them or to move with them.

North of Nimrud, though, it is a different story. The mountains of Kurdistan and western Turkey have conspired between them to set the Tigris's route in stone, and when it reaches the northern Iraqi city of Mosul it is still sticking religiously to that plan. Thus the old part of Mosul is up on a rocky ledge where it always has been and the Tigris runs obediently past as it has always done, fresh, clean and in a hurry to get to the bits of Iraq where it can trick mankind into building a city on its banks, before slip-sliding away.

On the other side of the river from Mosul is the former site for the great and infamous Assyrian city of Nineveh, from where Agatha went off on her shopping trips to Aleppo. Nineveh is the location of the Palace of Sennacherib, the Assyrian king immortalized by Byron. At the time of Sennacherib the Assyrian empire was huge and its capital was a major urbanization. The Bible described Nineveh as 'an exceeding great city of three days' journey ... wherein are more than six score thousand persons that cannot discern between their right hand and their left hand, and also much cattle'. It was also identified as being full of sin and therefore doomed, which is why God commanded his prophet Jonah to enter Nineveh and tell its people to repent their evil ways. Jonah, who didn't see why he should put himself out to save his enemy from a fate he thought they thoroughly deserved, did a runner, and as a result took a short holiday in the belly of a whale until he saw sense. Today Jonah's shrine and tomb is in the newish mosque of Nebi Yunis, which stands on a mound overlooking Nineveh's ruins, but little remains of the former metropolis to which he eventually returned and preached with good effect. Goats browse among the ocean of rubble and dust by the gates, while fields of barley are prospering on distant acres of dissolved antiquity.

This was the setting for the 'Palace without Rival' built by Sennacherib, which was rediscovered in 1847 by British adventurer Henry Austen Layard, a lawyer who was originally heading for Sri Lanka to start a new practice, but who effectively became the father of British archaeology instead. Layard uncovered seventy-three rooms – the outlines of eleven of them on his very first day – whose walls were covered with stone slabs decorated with reliefs depicting religious, hunting or battle scenes. Many of these Nineveh friezes were carefully crated up and packed off to Britain, and still fill a whole room in the British Museum with their wonderfully clear depictions of lions, birds, horses and hares.

At the time, Nineveh's discovery had an added significance because an account of Sennacherib's failed siege of Jerusalem was written in cuneiform on a palace doorway, providing what was effectively independent, eye-witness corroboration of an event described in the Bible's Second Book of Kings. Christian fundamentalists around the world latched on to this discovery as sure evidence that the Bible was all true.

Nineveh was where Agatha and Max had worked together for the first time, shortly after they were married, on the dig run by Reginald Campbell Thompson. It was a period of great happiness for them, and they'd be horror-struck by what they found if they returned there today. Contemporary Nineveh is the epitome of Muzahin's worst fears: decades of meticulous archaeology reduced to a jumble of ancient rubble by a few short years of sanctions. Until recently the palace had been protected by a roof, a fence and an armed guard and was officially designated a Site Museum, but now it resembles an abandoned quarry. Key parts of all the slabs are missing, and there's barely a carved palm tree or a figure that remains complete, thanks to a combination of rain, vandalism and antiquities theft.

American archaeologist John Malcolm Russell, who went to Nineveh in 1989–90 to document the palace, watched helplessly over the following five years as twelve individual chunks were removed from what he had so recently seen and photographed on site and then appeared in quick succession on the international art market. Russell describes the plundering as a 'world heritage disaster of the first magnitude', and points the finger unwaveringly at the United Nations, whose sanctions 'have finally destroyed Sennacherib's Palace, finishing the work begun by the ancient Medes and Babylonians who sacked Nineveh in 612 BC'.

Mind you, that process was begun long ago by Layard, who calmly strolled away from Nineveh with a group of twenty-eight Assyrian sculptures which he presented to his cousin, Lady Charlotte Guest, mother of ten and wife of the wealthiest industrialist in England. Lady Charlotte displayed them at her home, Canford Manor in Dorset, a building which later became a private school for boys. The bulk of the collection was later sold on to the Metropolitan Museum of Art in New York, but in 1992 John Russell visited Canford School as part of his Nineveh research and realized that an original carving was still in place on the wall of the garden pavilion, which was being used as the school tuck shop. There was never any idea of returning it to the Iraqis, because for the school this discovery represented manna from heaven. The relief eventually sold for £7.7 million, the highest price ever paid for an antiquity at auction.

Agatha had found Mosul a real relief after the heat and the flatness of southern Mesopotamia, and although it doesn't quite have the feeling of a highland city, it is

definitely cooler and clearer than Baghdad. The afternoon
we arrived it actually started to rain, and men were hitch-
ing up their *galibiyyas* to step across gutters which were
purging the streets of accumulated rubbish in a free-
flowing enema. The foyer of the Station Hotel, where
Agatha had stayed and where she recorded with some
amusement that the hotelier's name was Satan, was inches
deep in water. A sleepy Iraqi just looked at me when I
mentioned her name; they had, he said, no rooms. As for
us, we were staying in the more modern university
quarter, next to one of Saddam's palaces. The streets
around were full of young men in white shirts clutching
files and folders, hanging out in the Playstation café, in
grilled chicken restaurants, in juice bars and in a shop
called Virus, which sounded as if it might breed digital
terrorists but actually sold computer software. It could
have been almost anywhere in the Middle East, and just
like students everywhere these young men were wrapped
up in creating their relationships and mapping out
their existences, hoping that world events wouldn't
interfere.

Mosul is a mixed-race, mixed-religion community, with
marked similarities to Aleppo, its next big metropolis to
the west. It's not nearly as relaxed and sophisticated as the
latter, though, which is why Agatha would head for
Aleppo whenever she needed a break from dig life. And
unlike Aleppo's ordered brick arches, the Mosul souq is a
labyrinthine shanty town roofed with a mixture of
tarpaulins and corrugated iron which slides down
towards the river in a tangle of lanes like the mesh of a
net. Arabs, Armenians, Syrians and Kurds are commingled
here, and before the arrival of Islam most of the local
people were Christian. Many still are.

Our itinerary that afternoon focused on local churches,

but I hadn't come all that way to do something I could do equally well at home, so after viewing a couple of ecclesiastical interiors I took the opportunity to slip away, leaving a message with one of the others. 'Tell the minders I'm not feeling well,' I said. 'I've gone to get a taxi back to the hotel.'

Night was falling quickly, and the purpling sky above the narrow, high-walled lanes of old Mosul was suddenly full of skittering bats. Below them, doors in the walls were opening and closing, giving glimpses of inner courtyards, as fathers, freshly washed and clean-shirted, took their young children out on the streets. Figures strolled down alleys, deep in conversation, just as they do in hilltop towns in Andalusia. The place had a relaxed, contemplative rhythm, tolerant of a foreigner walking alone.

I had no real sense of where I was headed, but I kept a wary eye on the 1,000-year-old minaret of the Nurid Mosque, tall, helmeted and famously bent like a giant phallus, looming out of the dark. In a street that seemed to be mainly car repair shops a group of young men pointed at me, started to laugh, chant and follow. It was difficult to tell whether they were being threatening or just curious, but for a moment I was frightened, so I dived back into one of the high-walled lanes, hoping it wasn't a dead end. There, a stone clattered past my feet, thrown by a boy aged around ten or eleven in the alley up ahead. I can't say for sure whether he'd thrown it at me – if he had, it was a poor effort – but a man who'd been walking towards me turned and pursued the boy back up the alley, brought him to the ground and cuffed him hard, repeatedly, until the boy started to cry. In the West it was the sort of scenario which would have put the man, not the boy, up in court, but it was impossible not to feel that a valuable lesson was being learned. I was prepared to thank the man as I walked past, but he didn't look up; perhaps he, not I, had been the intended target.

Twenty minutes later I found myself rounding a corner where a teenager was using a bit of cardboard to fan a makeshift charcoal stove made out of an old petrol can. Two kettles were perched on the stove, and beside him were two benches covered with old scraps of carpet. 'Chai?' said the teenager, seeing me surveying his little enterprise. I nodded and sat down. He pulled out a small glass, swilled it momentarily in a bucket of water, slung the dregs into the gutter, shovelled in the sugar and then filled the glass up to the rim so that the tea drinker's first problem was dealing with the overspill. It was good – minty and fragrant – but it was even better to sit down. Wherever you are in the world, staying on your feet makes you a visible, vulnerable non-belonger, while sitting down helps you become part of the fabric. In this case my teenage host – I guessed he was no more than fourteen – accepted me as his responsibility, and we communicated with a combination of gestures and smiles: was the tea good? It was good. Not too hot? No, not too hot. He shooed away anyone who just wanted to do a 'hello mister', and when anyone sat down on the bench beside me and tried to start a conversation he would sign to me whether they were good people, not so good people, or nutcases to be ignored.

The most striking of these interlocutors was a twenty-four-year-old student, the son of a chicken farmer from the town of Hilla, who seemed nervous.

'You are,' he said haltingly, 'the first foreigner I have met.'

'Ever?'

'Ever.'

It struck me as quite a responsibility. Accordingly, I

would have liked to have a meaningful conversation with him about our mutual situations, but our mutual language was not up to it. He soon got frustrated.

'Why you no translator. You walking, no translator?'

'Most of the time I am with a group. The group has translators, but government translators.'

This prompted an anxious exchange about whether I had lost my group, or whether they'd gone without me. After we'd established I was there voluntarily, he changed tack.

'How much did it cost, to come here?' he wanted to know.

I converted a typical airfare into dinars. He blanched.

'So rich!'

I tried to explain, in words that he understood (and which wouldn't sound too hollow to me) how riches were relative. But it was too difficult. He looked even more confused, made his apologies and left.

By the time I'd been at the tea stall half an hour my teeth were floury with sugar and my insides were getting stained with tannin, but my sense of equilibrium was somewhat restored by these exchanges and I didn't feel my presence quite so resented in the town. I settled up with my teenage host, who had initially refused payment, and wandered out into the main shopping district. There I was instantly latched on to by Ayub, another student, who worked, he said, in a local fish shop.

'You don't smell of fish.' He was dressed in jeans and a leather jacket, and didn't look remotely like a fishmonger.

Ayub smiled apologetically. 'This evening I am not working.'

'Do all fish salesmen speak such good English?'

'You are very kind. My ambition is to be a teacher in England,' he said, a touch too ingratiatingly. I can't say that I liked him as much as I had the chicken farmer's son.

'Is that what your father wants you to do?'

'My father is a businessman in Baghdad.' That could mean anything.

'What kind of business?'

Ayub's otherwise excellent English seemed to fail him on this question. 'Please, we walk, I show you some things. What do you want to buy?'

In Morocco or even Damascus this would have betrayed him as a shop tout looking for commission from tourists, but there were no tourists in Mosul. I thought of trying to dismiss him, but sometimes it is better, when a highly visible foreigner, to accept one street companion if just to deflect the others.

'I don't actually want to buy anything, I just want to look.'

'In that case let me take you to meet my friend who works in a fashion shop.'

I had an instinctive distrust of anywhere where Ayub wanted to take me, so I walked slowly, stopping to look frequently into shop windows. Every time I stopped he'd demand what it was I wanted to buy so that he could go inside and sort it out for me. I lingered particularly over a display of buttons laid out like semi-precious stones in glass cases under lights so bright that you could feel the heat coming off them. Beyond was a series of stalls selling basins full of pickled vegetables, eggs and nuts. The bananas, Ayub announced triumphantly, all came from Ecuador. There were shops selling rotting melons, spices, soap, perfume in unmarked bottles, halva, football shorts, and even a poster of David Beckham.

Whenever anyone else showed an interest in me to the extent of trying to exchange a word or two, Ayub would intercept. They'd have a murmured exchange, and then the other person would pass on, with a nod and a smile.

'I'm telling them that you are from England,' he said, grinning. I wasn't sure I believed him, and began to think that some of these other would-be friends might have been a safer bet.

On two occasions I resisted his attempt to get me into shops 'to meet my friend' on the basis that neither of them sold fashion, and therefore I suspected that neither did they contain his friend, until eventually we reached a small shopping centre which really did have a fashion shop in the basement.

'This,' announced Ayub, on seeing me peering down the steps, 'is where my friend works.' So we went down. It turned out that his friend was absent, and I found myself being requested to sit in the shop and admire the T-shirts until he returned. After five minutes of this I'd had enough both of waiting and of being touted around.

'I think I will walk on,' I said, 'and I'd prefer to go by myself.'

At this Ayub became agitated.

'You must not,' he said, backing away in front of me, practically barring my route back up the steps to the street.

'Why not?'

'Because these streets are evil.'

'They were fine before.'

'No, they are full of very bad men called Yezidis for whom the Devil and God are together.'

I held my tongue.

'Let me arrange a taxi,' said Ayub. 'Take you straight back to the hotel.'

Even now, I still don't know whether I should have been more tolerant of Ayub, and whether his intentions were good. At the time I was aware that I was effectively an ambassador from a world that the regime was telling Iraqis to hate, so I was trying to be at my most benign. But I was also nervous, and maybe therefore I misinterpreted his motives and his over-proprietorial attitude towards me. His motivation may have been simply the kudos of being seen in the company of a foreigner, or he may have been playing a subtle game to get me to go somewhere I didn't want to go. Either way, I couldn't pick which it was, and I certainly didn't like being trapped in that basement waiting for the arrival of someone I didn't particularly want to see.

So I turned my back on him and walked away, having made it clear that I didn't want him to follow. I walked with slow deliberation down the street which he had just described as evil, and then, when I was round the corner and out of his sight, I stopped a taxi and asked the driver to take me back to my hotel.

INCIDENT AT UR

A bad-tempered skirmish took place on the hotel steps on the morning we left Mosul. Ms Lovebody had a tendency to spend a little longer on her morning coiffure than most, and there'd been some behind-the-scenes carping, particularly among the older women, that she was forever holding us up in order to make a grand, last-minute entrance in some completely inappropriate scrap of chiffon. On this particular morning she turned out in an iridescent blue skirt which appeared to go demurely down to the ankle, but turned out to be slit part-way up the thigh on each side. She was also slightly flustered, having no doubt been chivvied along by Mr Lovebody not to be late, and she therefore misinterpreted the not-very-discreet tut-tutting with which her dress was greeted.

'I am not the last,' she insisted angrily, rounding on Yvette, whom she had correctly surmised was at the heart of any disapproval. Yvette couldn't bear any kind of delay to the schedule. 'Count who's here, you will see I am not the last.'

I was glad to be under way again. With the bus eating

up the miles southwards, I was entering on the last leg of the journey towards Agatha's final destination, and the place which had really fired her enthusiasm and catalysed her second life: Ur. It also happened to be one of the focal points in the story of mankind.

Ever since I'd left London I'd been burrowing deeper into history. Through Europe the *amuse-bouche* had been the glorious era of the Orient Express, the turmoil of the Balkans, the antics of Boris of Bulgaria and the transformation of the feared Ottoman Empire into a holiday country called Turkey. In Syria the *hors d'oeuvre* had been the 700-year-old Byzantine ruins, the medieval souq at Aleppo and the desert oasis of Palmyra which dated back to Roman times.

Northern Iraq had hauled me back further to the Assyrian empire of Nimrud and Nineveh of around 700 BC, and now I was being reeled in by the heavyweights of Babylon, the supposed Garden of Eden, and Ur itself – a word which has gone into the German language to signify great age. These remains were to be the main course. They were cities which had started to blossom from around 4000 BC, 1,500 years before the Pyramids and at a time when we Britons were still sitting around in mud huts scratching our arses and wondering whether it was time to start standing some stones up in circles.

Personally, I'd had no idea the Babylonians were so advanced. In the West we tend to think of our civilization as beginning with the Greeks and the Romans and rarely look much further afield. But by the time our Stone Age Britons had started to make rudimentary cups (as in the beaker people), the Babylonians in the 'Cradle of Civilization' had already invented the wheel, started schools, established laws, calculated pi to two decimal points, created the first form of writing, dabbled with astrology and come up with the concept of zero. They were so far ahead it was beautiful.

Looking out at those long hours of empty, harsh land rolling past the bus window, it was hard to conceive why any civilization should have chosen such a difficult place for its early years, but then I suppose it was that very intransigence which forced people to unite. With very limited naturally occurring abundance to hand, people needed to work together to survive. They had to create irrigation schemes and embankments to grow wheat and barley, and introduce concepts such as ownership of property and fair exchange by trade. Hierarchies of management, armies for security and the motivation to annex other people's lands all followed.

Thousands of years later European societies had their foundations in agriculture, too. Whole communities came together around the labour-intensive business of crop planting and harvesting, the establishment of village flour mills and ovens for bread-making. But prior to that we had no imperative to create fields as the Mesopotamians had. There was simply too much available to us through hunter-gathering to bother, for who needed to raise a cow or plant a crop while boar were easily hunted and you only needed to lob a stick into a bush to get a bowl of fruit? For the Sumerians and the Babylonians, God had only provided the Tigris and the Euphrates; the rest of it was up to them.

Appropriately for this southward journey into the earliest beginnings of civilization I was reading the *Epic of Gilgamesh*, the oldest recorded piece of fiction, which had been discovered among all the cuneiform texts at Nineveh and was reckoned to be 4,000 years old. Cuneiform itself had been created to keep account of goods, ownership and trade, and its use for the communication of ideas came later, almost as an afterthought. I wish I could say that *Gilgamesh* is a gripping tale with tremendous narrative and characterization, but that sort of sophistication was still thousands of years ahead. It is, though, entertainingly picaresque in a *Don Quixote* sort of way, being the story of the eponymous hero King Gilgamesh of Uruk, who so threw his weight about at home that his people were desperate to send him away on some conquest or other to keep him out of their hair. Obligingly the Gods created Enkidu the hairy man as a companion with whom the king could absent himself on adventures.

While the bombastic Gilgamesh is just an arrogant bully with too much time on his hands, Enkidu is the prototype noble savage who was born wild, made his friends among the animals he freed from herdsmen's traps, and would have remained running with the wolves if he hadn't spent six days and six nights with Shamhat the harlot, making love. That 'act of humanity' apparently gave him reason – not something usually closely associated with the sex act – and changed his smell to the extent that his former friends the animals no longer trusted him. They forced him out of the wilds and into the company of people, in the king's city of Uruk. There he met Gilgamesh; they fought, could not defeat each other and became friends. At the lively suggestion of Gilgamesh ('Come Enkidu, you spawn of a fish who knows no father,') they set off for various adventures. Eventually Gilgamesh offended the Gods once too often with his brazen ambition, but because he was a king he had ultimate protection, so Enkidu had to be killed in his stead. Gilgamesh realized, too late, that he had lost something truly valuable in the companionship of a friend, and lived out the rest of his life with his consolation prize, the great city he had had built.

There's not much these days to distinguish the remains of Uruk from those of any other of Mesopotamia's early city-states. The Euphrates, of course, had long since slithered away, leaving only a beige wasteland delineated by wind-eroded humps and bumps that were once Uruk's gates and the temples. Here, though, there were also signs of much more recent activity in the shape of bits of a light railway left by a team of German archaeologists. The tracks were laid in short, inconsequent stretches. It looked like the erratic stitching of a sloppy seamstress trying to hold the old city together.

Agatha must have visited this place, because the German-built expedition headquarters at Uruk is widely accepted as the model for the fictional dig house in *Murder in Mesopotamia*. This is her only crime fiction novel which took oriental archaeology as its milieu, and the layout of the dig house was crucial to the crime.

Built out of mud-plastered brick, the house is arranged in a square around a large courtyard, and on the day of our visit it looked to be in very good condition, albeit locked and dusty. The caretaker family living next door said that they hoped the Germans would be back, *inshallah*, next year, and certainly the place looked ready and waiting. Many of the rooms were curtained, but those that weren't contained an iron bedstead and a simple plank table. Three of the sides were plainly just accommodation, while the fourth held a couple of common rooms and the main dig office, with box files, rolled-up charts and several plastic baskets full of unsorted fragments of pottery. I couldn't see up on to the roof, but it was from there that the dig leader and archaeologist Dr Leidner had dropped a millstone, killing his wife Louise outright as she stuck her head out of a window below. Poirot, who happened to have just finished disentangling some military scandal in Syria at the time, had sorted it all out.

We had our own moment of drama at Uruk. Now that we were south of Baghdad again, the heat had climbed up into the low forties and the sunlight was so intense you could feel it penetrate your skin and start to bleach your bones beneath. Some of the group were reluctant to leave the sanctuary of the air-conditioned bus, even though the air-conditioning was struggling to cope, so it was a depleted hardcore who straggled across the rubble of Gilgamesh's creation. There wasn't much specific to look at so we all fanned out, wandering through that scarred landscape, and it was only when the time came to be getting back that we came across Eugenie, the wittering wife of the Oxford don, slumped in a heap in the shadows. She was dizzy, faint and incoherent. She had already been feeling unwell from the previous day's dinner and now the onslaught of heat and light had drained any energy that remained, and her head was rolling. Fortunately, she was only skin and bone; Sean lifted her first, and then I took a turn, and slowly we retraced our steps across the baking plain towards the distant, shimmering lozenge of silver that was the bus.

We made a strange sight, that slow-moving cavalcade bearing a bundle of bones dressed in pastel colours, with Ms Lovebody attempting to shade the sick woman with her frilly parasol. It wouldn't have been particularly surprising if the figure of Poirot had materialized out of nowhere, bringing up the rear, dressed in black, perspiring gently and fresh from disentangling a military scandal or two. The follower of death.

Although Eugenie recovered swiftly once back in the air-conditioned bus, with water to drink and a sweet to suck, concern over her well-being united everyone for a few short hours that afternoon. A member of the group becoming seriously ill would have major repercussions on all of us, and no travel insurance on this earth would have been able to take the drama out of that particular crisis. Underneath that united front, however, relationships were getting increasingly strained. Some of those fault lines gaped open that evening, where we were booked into a basic hotel at Hilla, the home of the chicken farmer's son I'd met in Mosul, on the banks of an irrigation canal near Babylon.

By the time we'd arrived the cocktail-fanciers in the party had long since been busy with their hand-luggage, and two or three of them took one look at their rooms and rebelled. The hotel was disgusting, they said; there were cockroaches in the bathrooms and the sheets were not clean. Knowing that Baghdad was less than an hour away, they demanded that we return to the Al-Mansour, where the standards had been higher. It happened that these dissidents were also those who had little interest in archaeology, and now that the end of the trip was looming they wanted to do some shopping. Mr Lovebody was one of the loudest and the angriest among them, and he wouldn't listen to arguments about how the majority wanted to stick with the itinerary as planned.

'I don't care about anyone else,' he declared, sticking his jaw out aggressively. 'I'm looking after me.'

Eventually judicious room-swapping and the rapid provision of linen and bug spray calmed everyone down sufficiently to keep the itinerary on track, and we retired to bed. But that wasn't the last of that day's melodramas; in the early hours of the morning one of the women lurched along the corridor shrieking hysterically and two or three of us popped our heads out expecting to find a murder at the very least. There was Rita the civil servant, habitually restrained and aloof, but now so dishevelled and delusional as to be almost unrecognizable. She was ranting on about encountering a rat in her bathroom, and demanding a room swap there and then, but strangely she wouldn't let anyone into the room to check on the rat's whereabouts. Even more strangely, there was no sign of Simon.

At breakfast, everyone was muttering about this disturbance, and the views around the table ranged from 'Ridiculous fuss over nothing' to 'Told you we should have gone back to the Al-Mansour.' As for Rita and Simon, they were glued to each other at the hip as normal as if nothing had happened, and they had no comment to make about the whole affair. In fact from that day onward they effectively ceased communicating with the rest of the bus and started talking to each other solely in Esperanto. Their use of an international, mulatto language couldn't have been more appropriate, because that day we were heading for the Tower of Babel.

Babylon is a name which continues to have huge reverberations of paradise and power, despite most people not knowing why, what, or even where. The name itself appears 252 times in the Bible, in the book of Revelation, in Jeremiah, Isaiah, Joshua, Psalms, Daniel and Ezekiel, where it is mostly depicted as an exotic, opulent, powerful city full of strange languages and rich in sin and pride, 'the mother of harlots and abominations of the earth', and fully deserving of being reduced to rubble by the Lord's hand (its eventual fate according to biblical sources). That's the sort of billing which would raise anyone's expectations of a destination; a sort of juiciest bits of Amsterdam mixed with the choicest cuts of Bangkok and tipped into the rump end of Manhattan.

To add to the biblical resonance we stopped *en route* at

a small town called Chifil, where Ezekiel himself was supposed to be buried. The prophet had been tasked by God to go to preach to the Jews in exile, i.e. those who'd been captured by Nebuchadnezzar and taken as slaves to Babylon. It seems that Ezekiel's main responsibility had been to comfort them in their isolation, largely by telling them of the calamities which were to befall their homeland, Judea ('Frankly, my dears, you're better off here'). He also foretold of the restoration of Israel and its happier state in later days ('But your descendants will go home and be more than satisfied').

The place where he was buried is a crossroads town with a small souq in a honeycomb of brick-built vaults, dark, cool, and pierced by occasional shafts of sun, scattering splashes of gold on the floor. The interior of this souq seemed on first entry to be a miniature Hades, with gleaming, sweating bodies slaving in the half-light over roaring, roasting fires. But these were smiling, industrious people going about their daily tasks. On one side Turkish delight was being wrapped in floury pastry, and on the other side bakers were using what looked like a big cushion to stick flat round breads to the domed roof of a brick oven.

The shrine itself, through a stooping doorway and across a scarred stone floor, was a large box-like tomb with a light bulb inside and a hole in one of the corners where male supplicants could go down on their knees to poke banknotes through. Women daubed the walls with streaks of what looked like dried blood or faeces but was actually henna, signifying a marriage wished for, a child born, or a parent dead. Above shoulder level, where the walls were blackened with candle soot, dirt and age, ran several Hebrew inscriptions studded with triangular mirrors. The Jewish community had remained strong here right up until the airlifts of 1950 which had returned them to Israel, thereby finally fulfilling Ezekiel's prophecies. Since then the Chifil shrine had been maintained by the Islamic community, who also revere Ezekiel, just as they revere Jonah up in the north; many of the prophets in the Bible feature in the Koran.

Chifil is the beginning of Shia territory, where the Sunnis of Baghdad and the north start to feel uncomfortable – our Mohammed and Ahmed among them. In Iraq the Shias outnumber the Sunnis, but the power of government and administration was concentrated in Sunni hands. Accordingly the Shias felt at the least under-represented and at the worst persecuted by Saddam. The ill-fated Shia rebellion started here after the Gulf War in 1991, encouraged by the West, but it had no external support and as a result was savagely suppressed, with tens of thousands killed and some key mosques damaged. Brute force doesn't necessarily change people's minds, however, and there was still a sense of nonconformity in the streets.

In Chifil I stumbled across a good example of independent thought in the form of a lean, mahogany-skinned man with a crackly smile and a handsome face, who was sitting in the twilit souq when we walked back through.

'Chai, chai, yes, yes, yes. Please!' he called out as I passed his table. 'Sit!' he commanded. I sat.

'My name is Haider,' he announced, and we shook hands formally.

'All my friends,' grinned Haider, waving a hand at the small gathering ring of onlookers.

'How do you know so many people?'

'My father was the foreman in a local factory. And now I am an electrical engineer in a petrochemical site.' He produced a business card. 'My boss, German man,' he said, as it passed from hand to hand. Judging by the state of the card, it had been passed around many times before.

'Do you speak German, then?'

'No, no, we use English-Arabic mix. You British, don't you have problems with the Germans? Isn't it funny how they can't say the letter v?'

'So why aren't you at work today?'

'It is Friday, my friend,' Haider beamed, slapping the table with his hand. 'Friday, Friday, Friday. The day of rest. Every Friday I pray then I come to the souq for breakfast and to share the news with my friends. Kebabs and bread – you want?'

I shook my head.

'Is there any news?' We had been travelling in a complete bubble with no contact whatsoever with the outside world, and as our journey neared its end we were very keen that the borders should remain open.

'You mean war?'

I nodded.

He was still smiling, but it wasn't for my benefit. 'No war today. I listen to your World Service and the Voice of America, and I don't think we will have war tomorrow. But next week, or maybe next month. It will come.'

It sounded like the weather forecast.

'Are people afraid?'

'Of course we are afraid,' he said, still affable. 'But it is not the people who want war. Not the Iraqis, not the British, not the Americans. It is only the governments. It is a problem between leaderships. Bush, Blair, Saddam, they hate each other. Not us, we don't hate Americans. Or British.'

Before I could respond that I didn't think the British hated the Iraqis, either, Mohammed appeared.

'Mr Andrew. The bus,' he called. He was grinning uncomfortably in the knowledge that something was going on which he shouldn't have allowed.

*

On the slip road which leads to the entrance to Babylon is a giant painting on a concrete canvas. It's a curious mixture of ingredients, with an Assyrian warrior's mask, the head of Nebuchadnezzar, the walls of Babylon, a pair of white stallions with plunging manes, an infantryman with mighty fists, and the supreme profile of Saddam himself, overseeing everything. It is not, therefore, a surprise to learn, when you round the corner, that the President has had Babylon rebuilt, stamping his name on every other stone. Nor is it surprising to see the silhouette of one of his more opulent modern palaces looking down over Babylon from a nearby hill, a hill itself manmade so that he could look down on antiquity from a position closer to God than Nebuchadnezzar ever achieved. In this way Saddam makes his point; he is up there, in the pantheon of Iraq's palace-building despots, the latest and most powerful in a long tradition. It may seem arrogant to us, but such was, and is, the culture of the Middle East, where strength and power are synonymous with good leadership. This leadership style has a direct lineage back to the Assyrians and the Babylonians, where only the palace-building despots ever achieved immortality. Exerting your will over huge quantities of people was and is at the core of government, and it leaves behind it the trappings of glory by which the leader will go down in history as a remarkable man. Power is measured in palaces.

Those ancient rulers were quite right to think along the lines of 'By your works shall ye be judged.' Looking back now, over the centuries, our interest is fixated on the likes of Ashurnasirpal and Nebuchadnezzar, the colourful characters who had their walls adorned with inscriptions reiterating their power, but who were more than likely the Saddams of their day: 'I am Nebuchadnezzar, King of

Babylon, the exalted prince, the favourite of the God Marduk, the beloved of the God Nabu, the arbiter, the possessor of wisdom, whom reverences their Lordship, the untiring governor . . . the wise, the pious, the chief son of Nabopolassar, King of Babylon.' For them, as for Saddam, unity of the people was not achieved through commonality of ideas, but through picking arguments with neighbours.

The other more enlightened leaders, who didn't force their people into unnecessary warfare followed by years of temple-building and who didn't perpetuate their cult on temple walls or television channels, are much less well remembered. Sirus, for example, the king who gave all the Babylonian slaves their freedom, is a hero in the Bible, but regarded locally as a nonentity, having built nothing. However, if there'd been more Siruses and fewer Nebuchadnezzars then maybe the Cradle of Civilization would have had a better chance of getting beyond first base.

Good King Sirus apart, the Bible would have us consider Babylon a place of imprisonment, idolatry, cruelty and misuse of power. 'By the rivers of Babylon, there we sat down, yes, we wept, when we remembered Zion,' runs Psalm 137, relating the sadness of the captive Jews who had been transported there for a lifetime of slavery, building palaces for the king. 'Babylon hath been a golden cup in the Lord's hand, that made all the earth drunken: the nations have drunken of her wine, therefore the nations are mad,' says Revelation, accusing the city of being the fountainhead of all false religion.

And then there's the legend of Babel, where man tried to reach the heavens by a tall tower and was cast down. Genesis tells how the descendants of Noah settled in the land of Shinar (now southern Iraq), learned how to build with bricks, and said to one another: ' "Come let us build a city, and a tower with its top in the heavens, and let us make a name for ourselves, lest we be scattered abroad upon the face of the whole earth." And the Lord came down to see the city and the tower, which the sons of men had built. And the Lord said, "Behold, they are one people, and they have all one language; and this is only the beginning of what they will do; and nothing that they propose to do will now be impossible for them. Come, let us go down, and there confuse their language, that they may not understand one another's speech." So the Lord scattered them abroad from there over the face of the earth, and they left off building the city.'

Actually, the Bible is just as capable of propaganda as any piece of written history, and the Genesis version of events glides over the fact that there were effectively two Babylons. Babylon I, the original, was succeeded over 1,000 years later by Babylon II, which in the true Hollywood tradition of sequels had to over-reach Babylon I with more action and better special effects. Archaeologists believe that the Tower of Babel, along with the Hanging Gardens, belonged to the later phase. This belief was endorsed by the first modern historian, Herodotus, who travelled to Babylon in 460 BC, when it was already a ruin. Herodotus measured the city's circumference as over fifty-five miles and described a largely intact tower, reaching up eight storeys and with a spiral way running around the outside as at Samarra. Nothing remains of it today.

The modern image we have of Babylon belongs to the more colourful Babylon II of Schwarzenegger-Nebuchadnezzar, which dates from around 600 BC. Very little has been found from Babylon I, which was probably founded around 3500–3000 BC, and was rather a different animal. With the Sumerian city of Ur as its uncle, Babylon I was the first recorded example of a sophisticated civilization, and it was here that writing, mathematics, schooling, agriculture, astrology, etc. were gradually developed. In that early manifestation the city was by no means a centre of iniquity. In fact one of its early kings, Hammurabi, was the first ruler to establish and publish a code of law which gave rights to people as well as to kings. Hammurabi provided for, among other things, compensation by the state for property lost in a robbery in which the robber has not been apprehended, and he ruled that a man who falsely accuses a married woman of adultery should be flogged. This is not quite as enlightened as it might sound, because if the case of adultery was unproven either way, then the onus was upon the accused woman to jump into the Euphrates, and it would be God's decision as to whether she was pure and could therefore survive. The rule of law only went so far.

Modern Babylon has been only partially reconstructed. It is fronted by a replica Ishtar Gate, glazed blue and decorated with animals; the original gate is in Berlin, but even that is only a poor imitation of what used to be, because a great quantity of gate stones were lost when a barge carrying them capsized in the Gulf. Inside, in an inner courtyard, are the trappings of tourism in the form of a souvenir shop, the first and last we saw in Iraq, and a small museum full of images of how artists have imagined the Tower of Babel to look over the years. A couple of them looked eerily prescient of New York's Twin Towers during their dying moments on September 11th.

We were assigned a guide, Muna, a well-spoken woman who ran us first of all through prehistory from Noah's descendants via the Sumerians to the first foundation of

Babylon, and then walked us through the city of Nebuchadnezzar, producing floor plans to demonstrate how 'very huge' the royal palaces used to be. Sadly, it was not as impressive as it should have been and it took a giant leap of imagination to visualize it as it once was. Saddam's rebuilding was like the construction phase of a Disney magic kingdom which had got as far as the stud walls and was now waiting for the scenery painters and the animators to move in. As we walked from one bare enclosed space to another we could have been exploring the vacant bays of an airport car park, for all the sense of history that remained.

Out the back, where the Lion of Babylon stands over its dying victim, Iraqi archaeologists were using earthmoving equipment (a major transgression in the modern world of archaeology) to try to find the library – every Mesopotamian city had one, but Babylon's had never been found – and sending up clouds of dust. As for the Hanging Gardens, created by Nebuchadnezzar for his beautiful but sad wife to stop her pining for the mountains and the wildflowers of her Armenian homeland, there was no sign even of a hanging creeper.

'I don't see why they couldn't re-create the Gardens, too,' said Torsten, petulantly.

'Quite. We've come all this way,' added Ms Lovebody.

'The archaeologists couldn't agree where they used to be,' explained Muna.

We spent that night in Nasiriyah, a town on the Euphrates within striking distance of Ur which not long afterwards was to become the scene of so much fighting. The hotel was little better than the previous night's, with holes in the wall and a carpet which had worn so thin that it felt like sticky floorboards, but this time there were no histrionics among the group. During the day the core of complainers had reached the conclusion that we'd over-stayed our welcome and the Iraqis didn't want us in their country any more. This was less an indication of the reality – the local hospitality was unwavering – and more a textbook transfer of their own mental state into their interpretation of their surroundings. However, the siege mentality brought the group together again, and dinner passed off without argument. Ms Lovebody was holding forth about how she hated wearing the same clothes twice on a trip and Yvette was running through the practicalities of life on the road in meticulous detail for whoever wanted to listen. 'I always unpack the soap first and put it under the mirror. I find it most useful there, don't you think?' Talking was just a way of filling the otherwise empty air.

I left the hotel late in the evening to walk along the riverside path, to look at the lights rippling in the inky river. Initially I turned left and walked towards where most of the people seemed to be hanging out, but there was no mistaking the aggression in the jeering young men strolling in groups or lounging on the riverside embankment.

'Look.'

'Look at his legs.'

'Look at his nose. Big nose.'

'Walks like a baboon.'

'Flabby white man.'

'Spy.'

Among them were several soldiers in uniform. A couple, who'd been sauntering in my direction, now turned and kept pace with me, but at a distance. This was the first time I'd been aware of being shadowed since arriving in Iraq. Glancing in at the windows of a large and busy riverside building, I could see more young men doing press-ups and sitting in their vests on the edge of bunk beds, polishing their boots. This was clearly an army garrison, but not for the usual soldiers who litter Iraqi life, the men who wear a uniform simply to get a pay packet; these were soldiers with a mission, for whom my presence was insulting. Probably the Republican Guard.

It was my first experience of open antagonism since arriving in Iraq, and it felt every bit as real as a blow to the solar plexus. To have continued along that path would have been truly provocative, so I swung on my heel and walked back the other way, away from the hostility and towards a much quieter stretch, heading towards a road bridge over the river. After a while my uniformed escort faded away and left me to walk alone, and my heart-rate began to slow. It had not been a pleasant feeling, being resented not for what I was but for what I represented, and I suspect it would only have taken one of them to have thrown a stone for the others to join in.

Accordingly I was about to give a wide berth to a further group of three young men sitting on the river wall, when one of them stood up, advanced towards me a couple of paces and murmured a soft 'hello'. There was something nervous and clandestine about this approach which set it apart from the others, so I stopped, and we talked. They were three friends, explained the first man, respectively a student, an accountant and a tax inspector. Our conversation started innocently enough – where was I from, what was I doing, where was I staying – and yet they seemed painfully anxious, and kept casting furtive glances up towards the light and the garrison. They were either drug dealers, seditious intellectuals or gay. And then, when I said I was British, they started to talk about how many deaths had been caused in the town by NATO bombing.

'The bridge,' said one, pointing downriver. 'Two years ago, a bomb, fifteen people killed.'

'Every day,' chimed in another, 'every day people are killed.'

'I'm very, very sorry,' I said, genuinely upset, and putting my fist to my chest in the traditional Arab gesture of something deeply felt. It is hard to describe how distressing it is to encounter death meted out on innocent people by some remote power whom they've never wronged.

Not knowing what else to say, I repeated how sorry I was, and they all nodded silently, accepting those apologies. The tax inspector, who so far had been quiet, took the opportunity to speak up.

'The bombing is not the problem,' he said. 'The problem' – and now he was whispering – 'is Saddam Hussein. He kills our people. And yet the people . . .' and here his language wasn't up to what he wanted to say, so he made a gesture as if to indicate someone confused or mad '. . . Saddam Hussein.' After a few more stumbling sentences I had the essence of what he – and they – wanted me to understand. It was the Iraqi paradox; the leader killed his own people, and yet they remained loyal, not daring to question, or even to contemplate rebellion, because that's how leadership was. And how it ever had been. It was as if the whole population had been mesmerized by some hypnotic, venomous snake, and could do nothing to help themselves.

We didn't talk long. To have been overheard making these sorts of statements about their country would have spelled the end for these three men, and I could see distant faces down the promenade turning in our direction, wondering what we might be talking about. I shook each hand solemnly and said farewell, and I could feel the emotion in those handshakes. They'd had something they'd wanted to entrust to me, and now that they'd shared it, it was as if they'd given me something precious to take away to my country, where I could keep it and ruminate over it, or try to pass it on to the rest of the world.

At the time I remember fervently hoping that the act of talking to me hadn't gone badly for them. And when Nasiriyah became the focus of war, a few short months later, I thought again of those three men, and the garrison of soldiers with whom they were sharing the river path. I hope they all survived.

The next day was a normal November Saturday for Nasiriyah, but for me it was the day when finally, 3,000 miles from London, after so many days of rumbling wheels first on iron, then on tarmac and now sometimes on sand, I was getting right back to the beginning of things. To where my storyline began. There was but one short push from here to Agatha's final destination, Ur, one of the earliest cities of mankind. In my mind it represented more than just the beginning of civilization; it was the setting for the crucial romantic encounter which had changed my heroine's life, and it was the end of a personal journey for me.

Aboard the Nemesis bus the social cement was being ground into dust by enduring each other's company through every inch of every day. Sean spent most of his time with Mohammed and Ahmed. The talkers had long since said what they had to say, although that didn't stop them saying it all again, and the listeners were so fed up with listening that they barely feigned interest any more. The back-of-the-bus people came and went through the rear door, grimly satisfied as long as the itinerary was adhered to, and murmuring unhappily when the pushy front-of-busers threatened to alter something or came up with some new plan. Geoff, his eyebrows in a permanent state of agonized rictus, tried to liaise between everyone to keep the whole show on the road. Myself, I sat somewhere between the camps, fantasizing about being a sort of authorial Deus ex Machina, fashioning Agatha-type plotlines which would have finally blown everyone apart. In the event, NATO nearly did it for me.

Outside the bus window the landscape had become raw, baked and scarred by earth-moving equipment and no more hospitable than the surface of the moon. It hadn't always been so, because we were now moving across the former territory of the Marsh Arabs, who had been so lovingly written about by Wilfred Thesiger and Gavin Young. But gone are all those miles of whispering reeds, waterways, floating islands, bitumen-covered canoes, fish, birds, insects and a 5,000-year-old spear-fishing, buffalo-herding culture that dated back to Sumerian times. Inside twenty years the habitat and the houses had been dried up by the sun and blasted away by the wind, just as every other civilization had been before it. Some 90 per cent of the marshland, which once covered 6,000 square miles in a triangle bordered by the Tigris on one side and the Euphrates on the other, had been drained by Saddam. Over those twenty years the number of Marsh Arabs had declined from 500,000 to just 40,000, most of whom had been resettled in designated areas elsewhere in the country.

The government justified this eviction by creating more land for agricultural development, but the fact was that the Marsh Arabs and their impenetrable waterlogged kingdom were too independent of central control and too much of a thorn in the side of the regime to be allowed to continue. During the Iran–Iraq war several Iranian raids were launched from here, and the waterways became a sanctuary for deserters and rebels. So in the early 1990s, after the Iranian war fizzled to a close, the army moved in, clearing the way for heavy drainage-digging equipment and moving the water-dwellers to resettlement zones. Once the water was diverted, the sun quickly turned any remaining vegetation to dust. Latterly it's as if the marshes never existed, and the only reminder is the occasional reed cathedral – the traditional hospitality house of the Marsh Arabs – by the side of the road. There are no waterways, no boats, no flittering birds or butterflies, no gurgling coots, nothing blue and nothing green. Only a sea of brown.

It was clear as we drove through that a strong military presence had been installed to ensure that the Marsh Arabs stayed where they were put, to protect the new embankments against sabotage, and to maintain the lines of defence against the hated neighbour, Kuwait, whose border was not far away. The most obvious sign of this presence was a little spaghetti-western fort every couple of miles, where a handful of soldiers would be squatting in the shade, playing cards, and waiting for their leave to come around again. These forts were a full-size version of the sort of thing an eight-year-old might have made out of sand or wooden bricks. Each had a square, waist-high wall with a little turret on every corner. The wall was broken by an arched gateway which gave on to a low, whitewashed guardhouse in the centre of the compound, inside which the soldiers ate, slept, prayed, and hoped they would never be attacked. These were not soldiers ready for war.

Occasionally, though, we'd pass something more significant. A tank, perhaps, or a built-up machine-gun emplacement, and on a couple of occasions a substantial missile resting on a leggy cradle out on the sand. Gradually the presence of this hardware intensified, with compounds walled at the top by razor wire, shanty-towns of repair workshops and accommodation blocks and then, finally, a barrier across the road with a checkpoint bristling with security. This was Ur, the jet fighter station and missile site that just happened to have a Ziggurat in the middle. It was like putting a boot camp in Egypt's Valley of the Kings. To go any further we needed a military escort.

Ahmed and Mohammed were sweating visibly as we waited for the paperwork to be completed at the Ur barrier, presumably from the tension of entering into such a high-security zone with an unpredictable cargo of Westerners. The two men may have started out as the enemy, but we'd grown to like them and believed that they liked us. And now they presumably had to tell missile station security that we were a biddable group of eccentrics who only had eyes for archaeology, not SAMs or satellite tracking systems, and we wouldn't be installing any mini-cameras or letting off any flares. If anything went wrong here, then they were the people who would get into serious trouble – the sort of trouble that might even threaten their lives, as it had done with some of those who'd escorted the UN weapons inspectors.

How different this was from the moment in 1928 when Agatha arrived at Ur Junction on a train which had rattled and shaken so much that she found it impossible to read. She'd arrived at five o'clock in the morning, and the Woolleys had sent a car to meet her and carry her the three kilometres to the dig house. And there, despite the unprepossessing surroundings and the debilitating heat, she'd fallen in love with Ur, 'with its beauty in the evenings, the Ziggurat standing up, faintly shadowed, and that wide sea of sand with its lovely pale colours of apricot, rose, blue and mauve changing every minute'. Her journey was complete, and she felt a new self-confidence as an independent being, not just a wife who wrote. At Ur she concluded that her life had been fundamentally frivolous up till that moment, and found herself wishing that she had become an archaeologist.

It may be a virtually unknown name today, but Ur of the Chaldees was big news in the 1920s. In the Thomas Cook guide *How to See Baghdad*, which was published the year Agatha arrived, the entry for Ur is the most comprehensive of all, talking of important discoveries recently made.

Ur has biblical significance as the birthplace of the prophet Abraham, but it was also the oldest of the great cities of Mesopotamia, with a population of up to half a million people and two harbours on the Euphrates. It was a civilized society which celebrated piety, not pillage, in its wall carvings, but it also had less civilized neighbours who eventually brought about its end. The city was sacked, the fickle river moved and the walls, gates and temples spent the next 4,000 years subsiding into sandy mounds, populated by wild animals. When Kennet Loftus came here in the mid-nineteenth century during his survey of India, his dogs were eaten by Ur's population of hungry lions.

Loftus's account aside, Ur survived only as a dim biblical reference until the 1920s, when it was put back in the headlines thanks to Leonard Woolley's dramatic discoveries in the gold-filled Royal Cemetery and his claim to have found evidence of Noah's Flood. Agatha would have read Woolley's vivid descriptions and seen the pictures of harps and helmets of gold in the *Illustrated London*

News. She would probably have been as shocked as anyone by his revelation that one tomb in particular, that of Queen Pu-Abi, contained sixty-four bodies of servants, soldiers, courtiers and even wagons with oxen arranged in formation, each with a little poison goblet by his or her side. There is no better way to make sure your staff are watchful and protective of you than by ruling that when you die, they die too. But what a waste of life.

For Agatha, the unexpected bonus was the living people she found at Ur. She was impressed by Leonard Woolley, whom she described as 'inspirational' in her autobiography. He had the ability, she wrote, to see Ur as it had once been in his mind's eye and he could communicate that vision to non-archaeologists. In fact the archaeologist may not have looked so kindly on his celebrity visitor were it not for the ministrations of his wife Katharine, who had just read *The Murder of Roger Ackroyd* and thought the book was so wonderful that she instructed everyone else on the dig to read it too.

Katharine was a siren, widely known as a difficult, self-centred person who could be very attractive to men, and who exploited her control over people quite ruthlessly. Agatha described her as an *allumeuse*, a woman who lit sexual bonfires. Max noted in his autobiography that 'she had the power of entrancing those who associated with her when she was in the mood, or on the contrary of creating a charged poisonous atmosphere'. She was so highly strung that existing under the same roof as her was like walking a tightrope, and although she preferred male company, sex was definitely not on the menu – or, as Max put it rather coyly, 'she was not intended for the physical side of matrimony'. She had been married before, to a Colonel Keeling who'd mysteriously committed suicide at the foot of the Pyramids. The suggestion was that he'd taken his own life when he realized that he would never have sex with his wife – a radical solution – and furthermore that Leonard Woolley had been forced to spend the first night of his own wedding to Katharine in an armchair in the bedroom. In the dig house at Ur, Woolley was relegated to the bedroom next door, and she was rumoured to have had a long string attached to his toe so that she could pull it to awaken him whenever she needed room service. Every morning he rose early to make her a bowl of hot soup, and considered it his privilege to do so.

As a quiet people-watcher and a completely undemanding house-guest, Agatha posed no threat to this volatile modern-day queen, who expected her retinue to die for her as they had for Pu-Abi. She was able to observe Katharine closely, and the result was the barely disguised pen portrait in the character of Louise Leidner, the victim in *Murder in Mesopotamia*. The book was dedicated to 'My many archaeological friends in Iraq and Syria', several of whom formed the basis for other characters too. It was a risky thing to do to portray Katharine in this rather unflattering light, because by then the Woolleys had become good, if not close, friends, but either Mrs Woolley did not recognize herself, or she didn't think the portrait particularly insulting.

She wasn't quite as phlegmatic, though, over the affections of a young man whom she listed in the ranks of her closest supporters, a certain Max Mallowan, Leonard Woolley's twenty-five-year-old dig assistant. Among Max's daily schedule of tasks was Katharine's massage and the brushing of her hair.

Today it is hard to imagine anything romantic happening in Ur. The Euphrates has long since departed in search of deserts new, but the Ziggurat still stands much as it did in 2250 BC, one of the most brutally impressive bits of ancient architecture in the Middle East. It can be seen from miles away across the flats, looking like a giant transplanted Mayan temple with a long proboscis of a staircase stretching down to the ground. These days it is flanked by a crescent of military bunkers which recede into the quivering distance, and we were warned severely and repeatedly to keep our eyes – and our cameras – averted when we reached the top.

There we were met by Raif, a wiry, rat-faced man who looked immaculate but uncomfortable in a shirt and trousers which had obviously been washed and ironed for the occasion. He was the grandson of a dig foreman who'd worked with Leonard Woolley, whom he diplomatically described as a 'very nice man'. After he'd filled us in on the detail of Woolley's discoveries and pointed out the salient features of the site – including the newly reconstructed Abraham's house – he led us down to the steep and difficult staircases which descended into the cool, musty darkness of those vaulted brick tombs where so many had died prematurely on Pu-Abi's orders. Empty, dark and forbidding, and the ideal setting for murder. It was here that the gemstone necklaces and daggers and headdresses of gold that now fill several cases in the British Museum were found, and here that Woolley had uncovered the carefully arranged bodies of all those servants and soldiers who had had to die.

When we were back up in the sunlight, I got Raif to point out where the Woolleys' dig house once stood, on a piece of waste land a couple of hundred yards from the Ziggurat. While the others walked back to the bus via Abraham's house, I made my own little pilgrimage out across a crust of baked mud to the actual place where Max and Agatha had first met. The rusty remains of a couple of light railway trucks marked the spot, but otherwise there was nothing, absolutely nothing, which indicated that anyone had ever even walked here before, let alone built a house, started a new life or had their toes tied up with string. The 6,000-year-old Ziggurat may have been still standing, but every last trace of a 100-year-old dig house had been wiped away.

It was at that moment that the air-raid siren sounded.

In fact there were two of them, one after the other, from different quarters, and they rose slowly, steadily, like a pair of keening widows getting into their stride. I looked up. On first impression it seemed that the blue, cloudless sky was unsullied by any imperfection; this was, after all, the heart of the no-fly zone. But then there was a speck of something that glittered like angel dust, very high up in the deep, deep blue. 'Smile,' I said to myself. 'You're on camera,' and I wondered whether my face was appearing on a TV screen in the Pentagon, where it would be compared by computer with several thousand files of known terrorists or Iraqi sympathizers. It was possible, I supposed, that I might look like one of them, but I thought I looked more like Harrison Ford.

There didn't seem undue cause for alarm. The few dig workers who were working for Raif had downed their tools and taken shelter in Abraham's house, where they were calmly unwrapping flaps of bread. I was thinking of strolling across to join them when whatever it was that happened, happened, and all the time-lines and story-lines of this book – the return to the genesis of modern civilization, the beginning of Agatha's romance, the final destination of my journey, and the present and future fate of the nation called Iraq – collided with a symbolic thump. Actually, it was more like a double thump, and it seemed as much inside my head as anywhere else.

The air juddered for a couple of seconds, followed by a strange silence where my ears felt as if they had filled with water. A pall of white smoke started to drift across the land of the Chaldees about 150 yards away, heading in the general direction of Nebuchadnezzar's Babylon. I watched this low cloud with detached interest as it twisted and drifted across a scene which had been busy with soldiers moments before, but now was completely devoid of people.

'I think we've just been bombed,' I said to myself, out loud, to see if I could still hear myself speak and was therefore still alive.

'Or perhaps not.'

If it'd been a bomb, surely the smoke would be rising from the point of impact? This smoke was completely rudderless and anchor-free, nonchalant even in the way it tried itself out in different shapes. Perhaps, I thought, something had been fired from the ground, and this was the percussion cloud. Or possibly it was some sort of gas, in which case Nebuchadnezzar could keep it.

And then I became aware of another noise, the urgent sound of distant shouting, accompanied by a dull pounding. There was something familiar about the voices, and it took only a moment to locate them. It was my group, back in the bus, hammering on the windows and mouthing at me through the glass like fish in a tank. And suddenly I could see what they meant. My head may have been full of the romance of a first meeting between a famous authoress and a young assistant archaeologist, but I was standing in the middle of a NATO target zone. My interest in Agatha and her crisp pieces of fiction had finally been overhauled by a far bigger story, a whodunit where the world may have been still unsure of the actual nature of the crime, but the punishment was already on its way.

EPILOGUE: THE GARDEN OF EDEN

I'll tell you everything I can
If you will listen well:
I met an erudite young man
A-sitting on a Tell.
'Who are you, sir?' to him I said,
'For what is it you look?'
His answer trickled through my head
Like bloodstains in a book.

He said: 'I look for aged pots
Of prehistoric days,
And then I measure them in lots
And lots of different ways.
And then (like you!) I start to write,
My words are twice as long
As yours, and far more erudite.
They prove my colleagues wrong!'

But I was thinking of a plan
To kill a millionaire
And hide the body in a van
Or some large Frigidaire.
So, having no reply to give,
And feeling rather shy,
I cried: 'Come, tell me how you live!
And when, and where, and why?'

He said: 'I hunt for objects made
By men where'er they roam,
I photograph and catalogue
And pack and send them home.
These things we do not sell for gold
(Nor yet, indeed, for copper!),
But place them on Museum shelves
As only right and proper.'

I heard him then, for I had just
Completed a design
To keep a body free from dust
By boiling it in brine.
I thanked him much for telling me
With so much erudition,
And said that I would go with him
Upon an Expedition . . .

And now, if e'er by chance I dip
My fingers into acid,
Or smash some pottery (with slip!)
Because I am not placid,
Or if I see a river flow
And hear a far-off yell,
I sigh, for it reminds me so
Of that young man I learned to know –

Whose look was mild, whose speech was slow
Whose thoughts were in the long ago,
Whose pockets sagged with potsherds so,
Who lectured learnedly and low,
Who used long words I didn't know,
Whose eyes, with fervour all a-glow,
Upon the ground looked to and fro
Who sought conclusively to show
That there were things I ought to know
And that with him I ought to go
And dig upon a Tell!

(From 'A-Sitting on a Tell', by Agatha Christie, with her apologies to Lewis Carroll)

When Agatha Christie met Max Mallowan at Ur she was a single mother and celebrated crime novelist. He was a serious-minded dig assistant who'd read Classics at Oxford and spent the last five years grubbing around among ancient civilizations in the Middle East. She was thirty-nine, he was twenty-six. Their mutual suitability was not obvious.

Max had been recommended to Leonard Woolley straight out of Oxford University. The Dean of Divinity at New College, which had also been Woolley's alma mater, had encountered the student one morning crossing the quad and asked, 'What are your plans, dear boy?'

In the true string-pulling tradition of the time an appropriately worded letter of recommendation secured Max a place in the Woolley team and at Ur he was proving a diligent assistant, learning a great deal about ancient civilizations. His experience of the rest of the world, however, was limited – particularly as far as women were concerned. His family life had been centred around his two brothers, his boarding-school had been single sex and his university college was all male. His only close experience of the opposite sex was his mother, an emotional, mercurial Frenchwoman, and the volatile Katharine Woolley. He was probably still a virgin.

Max and Agatha didn't actually meet on Agatha's very first visit to Ur, because Max was away on leave recovering from appendicitis at the time. But Agatha was exhilarated by the success of her lone journey across Europe and she'd resolved to return again the following season. In the meantime she'd kept in good contact with the Woolleys, encouraging them to use her London house over the summer. In response they had invited her back out to Ur in 1929, suggesting she travel back home with them at the end of the dig season. She wanted to widen her experience of the archaeological treasures of the area by travelling in their company. She certainly wasn't expecting to find a second husband.

It was by no means love at first sight. Max later wrote that he found her 'immediately a most agreeable person', but for her part Agatha felt slightly nervous of the thin, grave-looking young man. In fact it was Katharine who threw them together. She assumed Max to be safely loyal to her own cause, and instructed the young dig assistant to take Agatha on a tour of other sites in the vicinity while the Ur dig was being wound down and packed up. Agatha had deep misgivings at the thought of being sent off with a young man who was 'probably yearning for freedom and some fun in Baghdad after the strain of a three month season at Ur', but they soon started to enjoy each other's company in a way for which neither was quite prepared.

Their itinerary was never easy, but they made light of it. Out in the wilds by Al'Ukhaidir castle they went swimming – at Agatha's suggestion – in Lake Razzazeh, even though neither had appropriate swimming wear and she had to improvise with a silk vest and double knickers. In Kerbala, the Shia holy city which was supposedly full of dangerous dissidents, they spent the night on rolls of bedding on the floor of a cell in a police post, and she had to summon Max in the middle of the night to escort her to the evil-smelling hole in the ground that was the lavatory.

As they walked around the archaeological sites he talked earnestly of ancient civilizations, and as they bumped across the desert between stops she taught him songs which they then sang together to pass the time. They ate dinner under the moon, picked wildflowers and listened to an Arab policeman repeat part of the opening section of Shelley's 'Ode to a Skylark'.

'It was heaven. The world seemed perfect,' Agatha noted later in her autobiography. As for Max, he'd decided this woman was the right life-partner for him from the moment when the car they were travelling in got bogged down in the sand and she had made absolutely no fuss, but simply settled down in the shade to wait while a passing member of the camel corps went to get help in digging it out.

Although nothing romantic passed between them during those few days, Katharine Woolley sensed the altered chemistry when they returned. During the home-ward journey she tried to reassert her control of Max with a combination of tantrums, wilful demands and headaches that required his special massage. In Aleppo, where Max had run a hot bath for Agatha in the Baron Hotel, she marched in and took it instead – and Max had let her, without a murmur. The next day Katharine declared she wanted to be alone, and then was furious when Max and Agatha had taken her at her word and spent a whole, happy, day out in the Dead Cities without her.

From Syria the group had taken ship – presumably Lloyd Triestino – to Athens, where Agatha received an alarming telegram informing her that her daughter Rosalind had pneumonia. Straight away she'd altered her plans to catch the next train home, and when she sprained her ankle on an Athens pavement Max volunteered to accompany her, changing his travel plans too. Even this journey was eventful, with Max and Agatha alighting at Milan to buy oranges, unaware that the train's stop was to be only a brief one. They'd had to hire a taxi to catch the express up again at Domodossola, with all the passengers leaning out of the train windows and egging them on. By the time Agatha got back to England Rosalind was long out of danger and improving rapidly, and Max and she had well and truly bonded.

A couple of months later he proposed. Agatha didn't agree straight away. After the disaster with Archie she'd resolved never to marry again, and the difference in age was, she thought, a huge barrier. But she was eventually persuaded and the banns were published that summer on the Isle of Skye, whither she retreated for the duration to avoid any potential publicity; after the Harrogate experience she had no wish to appear on the front pages of any newspapers again. They were married in Edinburgh on 11 September 1930, with the minimum of ceremony and no guests. Thus began what Max eventually described as 'forty-five years of a loving and merry companionship. Few men know what it is to live in harmony beside an imaginative, creative mind which inspires life with zest.'

There was time for a short, happy honeymoon in Greece before Max had to return to Ur to prepare for the new dig season, having been warned by Leonard (aka Katharine) that wives were not welcome, even when they were famous ones. A year later he transferred to Campbell Thompson at Nineveh so that Agatha could join him, and their archaeological and crime-fiction partnership was truly launched. Henrietta McCall's biography of Max records how Agatha wrote to him in World War II, when he was an officer in the Air Ministry stationed in Cairo and she had remained behind in London, with the words, 'If I had been so faint-hearted as not to marry you, I should have missed the best and the happiest fifteen years of my life.' When the war was over, they were to return to Iraq and Syria for many happy years more.

I never found out whether the incident at Ur was a bomb, a missile or a gas attack, but it was undoubtedly part of the softening-up process prior to war and a stern message to non-combatants that it was time to get out of there.

It also inserted an emphatic full stop into my journey emulating Agatha's. Up until the moment of that double explosion our two itineraries had been neatly interwoven, but from then on they came apart at the seams. She'd travelled back with Max via Aleppo and the boat to Athens, still unaware of how pivotal this journey was to prove for the rest of her existence. I'd returned with my busload of strained relationships and mixed agendas to Damascus, where we'd all taken flights home and melted into the crowd, promising to meet again and knowing we never would.

Three months later, with a new chapter of modern warfare about to begin – deadly for some, and a video-game for others – Lieutenant-Colonel Tim Collins stood by the Kuwait/Iraq border and addressed his men of the Royal Irish with the following words: 'You will be shunned unless your conduct is of the highest, for your deeds will follow you down history. Iraq is steeped in history. It is the site of the Garden of Eden, of the Great Flood, and the birth of Abraham. Tread lightly there. You will have to go a long way to find a more decent, generous and upright people than the Iraqis.' His words were widely reported, and from my armchair in Chiswick I was hollering for his promotion to commander-in-chief, but nobody above him in the command structure seemed to be listening. Treading lightly didn't seem to be part of the plan.

The subsequent liberation of Iraq didn't take long, but whether victory will finally bring peace or enlightenment to that decent, generous and upright people is still a moot point. As I write this, Babylon is only open for visitors once a week, and Ur is not open at all. We have to hope that, just as Agatha found a new life in the Middle East out of the ashes of the old, so will Iraq.

There is but one parallel I can draw between the Mallowans' happily-ever-after story and ours, because on that fated morning, after our visit to Ur was so rudely interrupted, the bus hurried us away to the Garden of Eden, where Adam discovered Eve and all the vicissitudes of love had supposedly begun.

In theory the timing of this visit would have been very appropriate to my story of newly discovered love, but in practice there is little of purity or even innocence to the Garden today. How and when it came to be nominated as the original paradise nobody really knows, but its symbolic location may have been enough. It stands at the meeting point of the two fountains of life, the two rivers which made the whole Cradle of Civilization possible.

After loitering teasingly down through many hundreds of friable miles, the Tigris and the Euphrates finally come together at a small town called Al Qurnah, about seventy miles east of Ur. As a town, Qurnah has no architectural merit, and its narrow dusty streets are lined with poor-looking farmers trying to sell even poorer-looking meat and vegetables.

On that afternoon, word of our arrival riffled like a hot wind down this line of indolent traders, and children started to appear from dark back rooms while our bus was still bottoming out in all the potholes. They were all heading in the same direction, and by the time we stepped out by a low-walled compound next to the Garden of Eden Rest House ('closed for renovations'), a substantial crowd awaited us. As each group member stepped down from the bus we'd be greeted by a ragged chorus demanding pens and dollars, and as we tried to move away a cluster of children would move along too, hissing for attention, shoving and plucking at clothes and patting pockets. Until then our meetings with Iraqi children had generally been a delightful experience, but in Al Qurnah it was hard to pretend that any pleasure was being taken from the encounter by either side.

Ahmed and Mohammed summoned a task force of broom-wielding workmen from the Rest House, and together they managed to force a way through this difficult crowd and into the hot, humid compound which was all that remained of the supposed Garden. There, in a small enclosure of paving stones, we stood for a group photograph in front of the Tree of Life, which was definitely no apple tree and indeed seemed barely alive. It was a stark, unsympathetic setting for the world's first romance, and the near terminal state of the tree – more like a crucifix than a living thing – seemed portentous of what was to come.

As for the twin rivers which had been there to witness everything from Genesis to Nemesis, they couldn't have cared less about the affairs of man, now or then. They slipped past, sizzling gently with insect life, to merge just beyond the Rest House's garden wall. There they mingled their two voyages without ceremony, as they had done in the age of Abraham, of the Babylonians, of the Assyrians, of the Mallowans and of Saddam Hussein. From there onwards the conjoined waters progressed in a single, impassive band of mercury, on its last short journey to the sea.

ILLUSTRATION CREDITS

The map on pp. viii–ix is by Hardlines.

All the photos in the illustrations section are the author's copyright except for the following:

Orient Express Poster: © Photorail/Diaporama.

Agatha Christie; Archibald Christie: both Topfoto.co.uk; *Daily Mirror* front page, 7 December 1926: Mirrorpix; Cook's brochure, 1927: Thomas Cook Archives, Peterborough; dining car, Orient Express: © Photorail/Diaporama; *L'Illustration* front page, 23 February 1929: Ruhrlandmuseum, Essen.

Agatha Christie and Max Mallowan on a visit to Tell Halaf, 1935: photo Richard Barnett, courtesy of the Department of the Ancient Near East, British Museum, London.

INDEX